Foundations

Foundations

Contemporary Topics in Christian Education

Matthew Etherington

FOREWORD BY
Edwin Boyce

WIPF & STOCK · Eugene, Oregon

FOUNDATIONS
Contemporary Topics in Christian Education

Copyright © 2025 Wipf and Stock Publishers. All rights reserved. Except for brief quotations in critical publications or reviews, no part of this book may be reproduced in any manner without prior written permission from the publisher. Write: Permissions, Wipf and Stock Publishers, 199 W. 8th Ave., Suite 3, Eugene, OR 97401.

Wipf & Stock
An Imprint of Wipf and Stock Publishers
199 W. 8th Ave., Suite 3
Eugene, OR 97401

www.wipfandstock.com

PAPERBACK ISBN: 979-8-3852-0323-9
HARDCOVER ISBN: 979-8-3852-0324-6
EBOOK ISBN: 979-8-3852-0325-3

VERSION NUMBER 05/14/25

Where noted, Scripture quotations are from New American Standard Bible (NASB)®, Copyright © 1960, 1971, 1977, 1995, 2020 by The Lockman Foundation. All rights reserved.

Where noted, Scripture quotations are from The Holy Bible, English Standard Version. ESV® Text Edition: 2016. Copyright © 2001 by Crossway Bibles, a publishing ministry of Good News Publishers.

Where noted, Scripture quotations are taken from THE MESSAGE, copyright © 1993, 2002, 2018 by Eugene H. Peterson. Used by permission of NavPress. All rights reserved. Represented by Tyndale House Publishers, Inc.

Where noted, Scripture quotations are taken from the Holy Bible, New International Version®, NIV®. Copyright © 1973, 1978, 1984, 2011 by Biblica, Inc.™ Used by permission of Zondervan. All rights reserved worldwide.

Where noted, Scripture quotations are taken from the New Century Version®. Copyright © 2005 by Thomas Nelson. Used by permission. All rights reserved.

This book is dedicated to Dr. Edwin Boyce, a *scholar, lifelong learner, supportive friend and colleague, leader, mentor, and one of the faithful.*

Contents

Author Biographies | ix
Foreword by Edwin Boyce | xv
Introduction by Matthew Etherington | xix

Chapter 1: Topics in Christian Education | 1
—Matthew Etherington

Chapter 2: Flourishing in Christian Schools: Insights from Research | 28
—Lynn E. Swaner

Chapter 3: Food for Thought: Faith, Secularity, and Curriculum | 44
—David I. Smith

Chapter 4: Strangers in the Classroom | 61
—Stephen J. Fyson

Chapter 5: The Buffered Learner and Religious Conviction | 77
—Matthew Etherington

Chapter 6: The Promise of School Choice Policies for Cultivating an Educational Ecosystem | 89
—Albert Cheng

Chapter 7: How the Bible's Narrative Framework Is the Basis for a Holistic and Integrated Approach to Scripture | 114
—Alan Gilman

Chapter 8: Theological Foundations of Christian Education: Trinitarian Relationality and Friendship | 130
—Kevin A. Mirchandani

Chapter 9: Take Up Your Cross? Christian Asceticism and Teacher Well-Being | 149
—Anna Lise Gordon and Stephen G. Parker

Chapter 10: Teachers as Shepherds: A Renewed Mindset | 164
—June Hetzel and Nicholas Block

Chapter 11: The Major Threat to Christ-Animated Learning: Confusion About Hospitality to Non-Christians at Christian Educational Institutions | 181
—Perry L. Glanzer

Chapter 12: Let's Keep This Between Us: A Primer on AI in Education and a Theology of Knowledge | 195
—Sam Burrows

Chapter 13: Faith in Education: Elements of a Catholic Theological Theory of Education | 212
—Bert Roebben

Author Biographies

Nicholas Block, PhD, began his teaching career in Bogotá, Colombia, as a science teacher at both elementary and secondary levels. It was there that he had his first exposure to dual language education. Subsequently, he taught for twenty-seven years in the United States, mainly at the elementary school level. After completing his doctoral studies at Claremont Graduate University, he has been full-time faculty at the Biola School of Education for ten years, teaching a variety of courses and overseeing the program for the induction of new teachers. Research interests have been in the areas of dual language education, vocabulary development, and how teachers live out their faith. He especially enjoys helping teachers to think about integrating their faith with their careers.

Sam Burrows is the director of professional learning for Christian Education National, a network of Christian schools across Australia. He is also a lecturer in biblical studies and worldview studies for the National Institute of Christian Education. Before moving to Australia at the beginning of 2024, Sam worked as a lecturer at Laidlaw College in Auckland, teaching theology and education papers. Sam also completed a master of theology in 2022, with a thesis exploring current faith and spirituality trends. He is passionate about how theology can speak to pedagogy, epistemology, and culture.

Albert Cheng is an associate professor at the Department of Education Reform at the University of Arkansas, where he directs the Classical Education Research Lab and teaches courses in education policy and education philosophy. He conducts quantitative research about classical education, faith-based schooling, homeschooling, and school choice policy and is also a senior fellow for Cardus.

Matthew Etherington achieved his PhD in philosophy from Macquarie University in Sydney, Australia, while completing doctoral research at the Ontario Institute for Studies in Education (OISE). He is a tenured professor at the School of Education at Trinity Western University, British Columbia, Canada. Matthew is the director of the Institute of Indigenous Issues and Perspectives (IIIP). His primary interests are in the philosophy of education, environmental and outdoor learning, Indigenous sovereignty, Elderhood, and sociocultural worldview analysis. Matthew is an interdisciplinary researcher and has published several books and articles in education, philosophy, and spirituality.

Stephen J. Fyson is a Christian psychologist by trade and a Christian teacher at heart, meaning he has taken the opportunity to study psychology, education, and theology, culminating in a PhD where he had the freedom to explore all three. Dr. Fyson has worked as a youth pastor, addictions counselor, community health manager, planner, and a "schoolie." This last calling has been for over thirty-five years, in many diverse roles in Christian schools—counseling psychologist, teacher, developer, and principal. Stephen continues to work as a Christian educational consultant in this field while also teaching in the Christian tertiary ministry.

Alan Gilman is a freelance Bible teacher, writer, and podcaster. He and his wife, Robin, both graduates of Ontario Bible College (now Tyndale University) in Toronto, are Jewish believers in Jesus. They homeschooled all ten of their children, the majority through high school. Alan's passion is helping people connect with the grand narrative of Scripture. He is the Bible teacher at St. Timothy's Classical Academy in Ottawa, Ontario. For more information visit https://alangilman.ca.

Perry L. Glanzer is a professor of educational foundations at Baylor University and a resident scholar with the Baylor Institute for Studies of Religion. He has coauthored, authored, or edited a dozen books, including *Christian Higher Education: An Empirical Guide*, *Stewarding Our Bodies: A Vision for Christian Student Affairs*, *Identity Excellence: A Theory of Moral Expertise for Higher Education*, *Identity in Action: Christian Excellence in All of Life*, *Christ-Enlivened Student Affairs: A Guide to Christian*

Thinking and Practice in the Field. He is currently editor-in-chief of *Christian Scholar's Review* and edits the *Christ Animating Learning* blog.

Anna Lise Gordon is professor of education and co-director of the Centre for Wellbeing in Education at St. Mary's University, London, UK. Previously, she was head of the School of Education at the university, with a particular focus on initial teacher education and professional development for teachers. Anna Lise has experience teaching in different school settings. She is keen to explore recruitment and retention issues in the profession, particularly where well-being related issues are a key factor. She is particularly interested in research and practice on teacher well-being and bereavement in education.

June Hetzel, PhD, completed doctoral studies in education at Claremont Graduate University. She has served in the roles of teacher, principal, curriculum specialist, writer, editor, professor, chair, and dean. She serves as dean of education at Biola University, La Mirada, California. She is a professor as well, teaching Introduction to Spiritual Formation for Christian Educators, Textbook Development, Curriculum Practicum, and Grant Writing in the School of Education. She also supervises doctoral students in the PhD and EdD programs at Talbot School of Theology. Her primary interests are spiritual formation, literacy, curriculum development, and the spiritual lives of teachers. She most recently published *Biblical Integration Models for Education* (Hetzel, Coddington, Block, Eastman, Stranske, Cid, and Canillas, 2023) with Kendall Hunt Publishers. She has a heart for global outreach and has served in various capacities in Thailand, North Africa, Indonesia, Malta, and England.

Kevin A. Mirchandani is a PhD candidate in educational studies at Biola University. He has served in various K–12 educational leadership roles and is the K–12 director of instruction and Christian formation at Langley Christian School in British Columbia. He is also an adjunct professor in the Education and Leadership Departments at Trinity Western University. Kevin researches, writes, and coaches leaders on educational leadership issues and faith integration in organizational practice. He has consulted with several local and international Christian curriculum development initiatives to support the lifespan development of Christian educational leaders and their learning communities.

Stephen G. Parker is director of the Centre for Catholic Education, Research and Religious Literacy and professor of education and religious history at St. Mary's University, London, UK. He has published widely on religious education in different settings, policy, curriculum and pedagogy. He is editor-in-chief of the *Journal of Beliefs and Values: Studies in Religion and Education*. Stephen has taught across age ranges in schools in different settings and is fascinated to understand teachers' philosophies and values and how these shape and interact with their personal goals, identity, and well-being.

Bert Roebben holds the chair of religious education at the Faculty for Catholic Theology at the University of Bonn. Before then, he taught at the universities of Leuven (Belgium), Tilburg (Netherlands), and Dortmund (Germany). He was a student of—among others—theology and educational studies at Leuven, and starting from these two areas, Bert developed an interest in learning processes at schools, in congregations, and in the public area, especially in processes that do not only receive and impart theological content but produce new content themselves. His core business as a professor of religious education is theologizing with students and exploring empirically and hermeneutically how the issue of God inspires and/or irritates our society today. This academic endeavor must always be embedded into a broader European and global context. Currently Bert is the president of the European Forum for Teachers of Religious Education.

David I. Smith is professor of education, director of the Kuyers Institute for Christian Teaching and Learning, and coordinator of the de Vries Institute for Global Faculty Development at Calvin University. He serves as senior editor of the *International Journal of Christianity and Education*. His book *On Christian Teaching* was awarded the 2021 Lilly Fellows Program Book Award, a biennial award for work focused on teaching and scholarship in the Christian intellectual tradition.

Lynn E. Swaner is the president, US, at Cardus, a non-partisan think tank dedicated to clarifying and strengthening the ways in which society's institutions can work together for the common good. She is the editor or lead author of numerous scholarly articles and books, including *Flourishing Together: A Christian Vision for Students, Educators, and Schools* (Eerdmans, 2021). She holds a doctorate in organizational leadership from Teachers College, Columbia University, and a diploma in strategy and innovation from University of Oxford's Saïd Business School. Dr. Swaner previously served as a professor of education and a Christian school leader in New York.

Foreword

AS WE CONSIDER THE foundations of Christian education, we are confronted with classical understandings of those foundations and, also, we are confronted by contemporary ways of understanding and practicing those understandings in formal and informal Christian education. This is important in research studies as well as in teacher preparation for the implementation of best practice.

The ways in which Dr. Matthew Etherington has brought together the various elements available to him shows a clear structure of allowing the Bible to be the foundation of thinking and acting in Christian education. We are struck by the concepts of renewal of mind and of changes in environmentally determined constructs. The great strength of the way in which this book is put together is that it connects classical Christian education theory and practices with our modern day through contemporary topics as per the title of the book. The essential contention that God's truth is all truth is not only contemplated but admired and protected in the form of a celebration of the presuppositions and basic assumptions underpinning the collective mindset of the writers.

Dr. Matthew Etherington has brought to us in this book a fascinating complexity and a thematic unity under the concept of examining, analyzing, and interpreting foundations of Christian education in our contemporary world. The topics covered are widespread, diverse, and exciting. In chapter 1 by the editor himself, we see the scene set for the whole of the book with regard to a critical theoretical understanding of the interpretation from different persons, with different backgrounds and with different experiences to bringing out a deeply sensitive and rich vein of knowledge, leading to wisdom. In this introduction to the thoughts in this book, the place of faith and science, including facts and scepticism, means that the mind of the reader will be full of self-examination and challenges to what is written. It is through this analysis and examination that we can truly flourish in the understanding and practice of authentic Christian education. The diversity of content from various perspectives encompasses areas of thoughts such as flourishing and then more particularly using the concept of food in thinking about faith secularity and curriculum.

Central to the theme of the book is acceptance of the place of the Bible from teaching truth. Therefore, as many of the chapters address the theme, we are drawn to not just the Bible but the author of the Bible that is God himself. Much is made of relationships for effective teaching and learning including the renewed mindset that views teachers as shepherds.

Implicit in the writings is the understanding of the Bible as narrative and this is connected seriously to the concept of flourishing. The biblical concept of pruning of vines is included in these chapters as is also the place of hospitality both from the point of view of the giver and the recipient.

However, flourishing cannot occur unless the presuppositional bases of the writer acknowledge the One who is behind the flourishing. Coming out of this understanding there are interesting thoughts on teacher well-being and a definite mindset toward relationality as central to growth in understanding and knowledge and a clear outworking of biblical truth in the context of a continually changing world of thought and activities.

Somewhat striking is the strong appreciation for the dignity of humanity in that Christian education is for every human being. The understanding of our humanism encompasses intentionality through the created minds that we as humans have been given. Relationships are paramount as we live in a domain of a changing world. Within that framework the German concept of *gemeinschaft* comes through of living in fellowship and community, after allowing the individuality and differences between persons.

A surprising element in the book is the admixture of past and present in different environments and in different phases of history and in different cultural context. All in all, the book relates to its promise to understand the foundations of Christian education from our time going backward and of being the basis of future understanding and developments within the exciting precinct of Christian education.

I expect that this excellent treatise of an accumulative company of articles has been brought together with a high degree of unity. This unity is based on the foundations underpinning the general thesis of the book. I trust that this book will be a great benefit to academics as to practicing Christian education and will be a challenge to general educators around the world. The word that comes to mind is from the German language: *gemeinschaft*, which holds together the concepts of fellowship and community. Therefore, the wholeness of this book is its great strength.

Edwin Boyce

Introduction

THIS BOOK IS FOR undergraduate and graduate students, in-service teachers, school administrators, organizational leaders, theologians, researchers, and education practitioners. It uncovers topics exclusive to education in general, particularly Christian education, while highlighting the experiences and perspectives of individual scholars in various contexts.

This tenth-anniversary volume of *Foundations of Education: A Christian Vision* (2014) focuses on current topics for today, such as AI, hospitality, language, community, agency, and identity topics. Each chapter ends with discussion questions that offer the reader freedom of thought and expression and an opportunity to engage with others, preferably in smaller groups.

The Sabbatical

It is a humbling experience to organize the moving parts of a book, especially one that confronts topics related to faith and learning. However, no one does it alone. I am indebted to the theological and philosophical minds of those more significant than mine for discoveries and insights.

I write this during a six-month sabbatical in the Great South Land, specifically Australia. I am reminded that a sabbatical is deeply biblical. The term "sabbatical" refers to the practice of observing a Sabbath or a period of rest and renewal. According to Leviticus, every seventh year was appointed as a sabbatical year, during which the land was to rest from cultivation, debts were to be forgiven, and slaves were to be set free. This practice was intended to promote social justice, environmental sustainability, and a reliance on God's provision.

Unsurprisingly, sabbaticals offer rest, reconnection, and renewal. In our fast-paced world, slowing down is not sensible. We convince ourselves that slowing down and resting means falling behind or laziness. So, the sabbatical reminds us that we do not have to work to earn rest, but God gave us rest as a gift. It is wise for Christian organizations to offer sabbaticals to their employees. A discussion could involve asking employees how long God wants them to take a sabbatical and how they will prepare their hearts for what God will do during that time of rest and renewal.

House-Sitting and Writing

Since I no longer live in Australia, I am preparing this book while my family and I house-sit in various homes in Queensland, caring for the owners' homes and their beloved pets. House-sitting is part of a growing range of practices identified as the sharing economy, where people create spaces for sharing access to a home, goods, and services.[1] The required care reminds me of the biblical practice of hospitality, which assumes trust and humility since you own nothing but must care for everything as if it were yours. As we house-sit, I think of the caring needs of house owners and sitters. I also think of the early church and its members' practice of sharing their possessions, which exemplified the spirit of generosity and community. Finally, I think of how this could translate to a classroom and school community if there is a "home-sitting" practice of trust, hospitality, humility, generosity, and sharing goods and services with the neighboring community and those in need.

Christian education recognizes the insufficiency of merely receiving, retaining, and relaying knowledge; instead, knowledge is generously shared with others as a gift in a trusting and humble act of service. In this way, the purpose of Christian education is recognized not primarily as integrating faith perspectives but as a unique relational and restorative approach to life guided by a community of people committed to truth, integrity, wisdom, and purpose. Unfortunately, these virtues are often absent in modern culture, so Christian education offers a unique counter-cultural

---

1. J. Hamari, M. Sjöklint, and A. Ukkonen, "The Sharing Economy: Why People Participate in Collaborative Consumption," *Journal of the Association for Information Science and Technology* 67:9 (2016) 2047–59 https://doi.org/10.1002/asi.23552.

experience to all. We invite everyone to "taste and see that the LORD is good; Oh, the joys of those who take refuge in him!" (Ps 34:8).

How We Imagine Ourselves

I am a citizen of both Australia and Canada. While visiting and living in both countries for extended periods, my thoughts often go to where I *really* belong, where my home *really* is, and where I find my identity. Psychological research describes this as gaining an acculturated sense of self.[2] Of course, identity is not found instantly; it occurs through the moments of challenge, serendipity, triumph, and the people we meet.

While on sabbatical during this reflective process, I have observed many similarities and differences between Australia and Canada, which I find to be fascinating *and* frustrating.[3] I authored an article a few years ago titled "Australia Is More Rational, Canada Is More Just."[4] I will not describe the article's contents here, but I think that, in retrospect, I should have used the word "individualistic" rather than "rational." Of course, Western culture is diverse in terms of how people perceive themselves and communicate with each other, including a range of political, economic, and religious differences. However, in Australia, people prefer to function as individuals instead of the extent of sharing, in some measure, a common culture—which would entail sharing common traditions that profit the group, community, or collective *above* the individual. Ties between individuals are loose, individual rights are paramount, and everyone is expected to look after him/herself. There is a low tolerance for uncertainty and ambiguity (especially when driving on the roads).

Dutch social psychologist Geert Hofstede's sociological research on individualist cultures provides a framework for understanding cultural differences and explains these subtle cultural differences in ways that I would have initially overlooked.[5] What maintains these standard

---

2. See Brent Crane, "For a More Creative Brain, Travel," *Atlantic*, Mar. 31, 2015, https://www.theatlantic.com/health/archive/2015/03/for-a-more-creative-brain-travel/388135/.

3. See Matthew Etherington, "Australia Is More Rational While Canada Is More Just: Personal Reflections About the Canadian and Australian Experience," *Australasian Canadian Studies* 33:1/2 (2016) 73–99, https://search.informit.org/doi/10.3316/informit.048078770662742.

4. Etherington, "Australia Is More Rational While Canada Is More Just."

5. From 1967 to 1973, while working at IBM as a psychologist, Geert Hofstede collected and analyzed data from over one hundred thousand individuals from fifty

practices is a widely shared sense of legitimacy, a type of collective understanding.[6] Recognizing these standard cultural practices is often difficult until we step away from our assumed ways of living and experience other ways of living together. As we become more individualistic, we increasingly isolate people outside of our bubble, which makes empathy and understanding other mindsets more difficult.

During my sabbatical in Australia, I heard glimpses of the *collective understanding* via the speeches of politicians and various leaders. We can gain a sense of this when representatives declare in a speech, "That is not the way we do things in this country" or "That is un-Australian, un-American, or un-Canadian." As I learned recently, one can even make "un-Australian" remarks: "Swimming Australia terminates Michael Palfrey's contract after Paris Olympics incident, citing 'un-Australian' comments."[7] A collective practice of the "way we do things around here" is a genuine and confirmed central feature of culture, even individualistic cultures.

This all leads me to the question of the *collective understanding* of Christian education. How *have* we, how *do* we, and how *should* we "imagine" ourselves? As the American educational philosopher Maxine Greene said, "to think of things as if they could be otherwise in our schools."[8] How we think of ourselves is important to discuss regularly, especially when we invite children and adults to learn together in a Christian community.

The Primary Topics in Education Today

What are the main topics in education today? The answer might depend on who is asking. For example, a veteran teacher and a beginning teacher have unique interests, needs, and concerns.

---

countries and three regions. See Geert Hofstede, "Dimension Maps of the World: Individualism," https://geerthofstede.com/culture-geert-hofstede-gert-jan-hofstede/6d-model-of-national-culture/.

6. Charles Taylor, *Modern Social Imaginaries* (Durham, NC: Duke University Press, 2004), 23.

7. Karen Hardy, "'Un-Australian' Coach Sacked After 'Go Korea' Olympic Comments," *Canberra Times*, Sept. 6, 2024, https://www.canberratimes.com.au/story/8754936/un-australian-coach-michael-palfrey-sacked-by-swimming-australia/.

8. See Maxine Greene, *Releasing the Imagination: Essays on Education, the Arts, and Social Change* (San Francisco: Jossey-Bass), 197–98.

When I first began teaching, one of my biggest hopes was to make the students like me so much that they would regard me as a good friend and not necessarily a teacher. Indeed, I thought that having a teacher who was more like a friend in contrast to *just* a teacher was what students wanted. It took one veteran teacher to inform me that this was unnecessary. "Be friendly," he said, "but do not strive to be friends," because children need a wise, compassionate, and knowledgeable teacher more than a teacher-friend. A good and wise teacher is like an elder who can point the *Way* and show the *Way*. Being an "elder" is not about being older but a role one has in life, based on the ability to encourage others with wisdom. In his book *Come of Age: The Case for Elderhood in a Time of Trouble*, author Stephen Jenkinson argues that elderhood is a *function* rather than an identity—it is not a position earned simply by the number of years on the planet or the title parent or grandparent. It is a role sought after by those who seek it, not seek to be it. In other words, elder wisdom is achieved according to which you engage the problems of your particular time and place. Elders provide nourishment, guidance, and wisdom in times of crisis.

The wisdom of those who have come before us strengthens our lives and communities. Consequently, we have the opportunity to create the conditions necessary for elderhood to flourish.

Faith Integration

Faith integration is a prevalent focus in Christian education. Discussions involve how to practice faith integration authentically and biblically. There are different ways to practice faith integration. Some are personal, some denominational, but faith integration is always situated in a "cultural setting and always dependent on the utilization of cultural resources."[9] Consequently, different methods are applied to faith integration. Educators may perceive this as a strength since people can practice Christian education in diverse ways, such as daily devotions and prayer requests, adhering to biblical principles such as loving your neighbor, relating scripture to lessons, or practicing Christian virtues. However, the heart of the debate is often over the best means to advance the vision and mission of the school on which most agree and the best

---

9. J. Bruner, *The Culture of Education* (Cambridge, MA: Harvard University Press, 1996).

means to ensure that Christian education *is* authentically Christian. I am not convinced that Christian integration is the best or wisest way to make education "Christian."

Dualisms

Although Christian institutions of education, including Christian universities and colleges, are not the church, they serve as an *academic* arm of the church. As such, they promote a life of faith and community togetherness, intellectual rigor, knowledge production, and evaluation. As an academic arm of the church, they also assess dualisms in whatever form they take. For example, some of the dualisms that can occur in Christian education and the church community include the following:

a. Four metaphysical dualisms (sacred/secular, eternal/temporal, spirit/matter, heaven/earth),

b. Two anthropological dualisms (soul/body, spirit/flesh),

c. Four epistemic dualisms (faith/reason, fact/value, head/heart, freedom/authority),

d. Five ethical-political dualisms (private/public, belief/behavior, individual community, church/state, Christ/culture).[10]

The problem with dualisms is not that they are necessarily right or wrong. I would agree, in principle, with many of the examples above. The challenge is assuming these are entirely independent of each other; they stand alone in isolation. Dualisms are helpful for analysis since they offer a definite point of comparison and contrast; however, the problem lies in their frequent association. Faith is not blind but grounded in evidence, while evidence comes in many forms (scientific, experiential, etc.) and influences how we reason and what we count as *convincing*.

We use our "heads" *and* "hearts" to make decisions and behave. Think of those who experience a "change of mind" after hearing a story that "spoke to my heart." In terms of the soul in contrast to the body, Christians should study the thoughts of seventeenth-century French philosopher and mathematician René Descartes, who gave this dualism

---

10. David Naugle, "Renewing Integrity: A Christian Worldview and Educational Practice," cited in Octavio Javier Esqueda, "Biblical Worldview: The Christian Higher Education Foundation for Learning," *Christian Higher Education* 13:2 (2014) 91–100, DOI:10.1080/15363759.2014.872495, 92.

its classical formulation, beginning with his famous dictum *cogito, ergo sum* (Latin): "I think, therefore I am." Although this is a foundation of Western epistemology, who I am depends on many influences such as family, culture, friends, faith, peers and colleagues.

Anxiety and Depression

There is also the topic of childhood anxiety and depression. Research reveals that one in four youth globally experience clinically elevated depression symptoms.[11] A measurable surge began in 2010 and spiked during SARS-CoV-2. This has led to increasingly complicated experiences for teachers and parents with student learning, teaching, behavior, and classroom management. Furthermore, in terms of anxiety and depression, there is no clear connection between religiosity and the likelihood that people will describe themselves as being in "very good" overall mental health. According to a Pew Research Center report that examined survey data from the United States and another two dozen countries, only three out of the twenty-six countries studied showed the actively religious as likely to report better mental health than everyone else.[12] This is not the result we hope for because we also know by experience that faith in God does make a difference to the highs and lows of life.

Artificial Intelligence: Blessing or Curse?

There is the topic of artificial intelligence (AI) and concerns about plagiarism and heightened academic cheating. Granted, students have been employing others to author their scholarly work for a long time, so this is not a new problem. However, AI is currently a topic of discussion in the media and academia and is often portrayed as either a blessing or a curse.

However, must AI be perceived as either a blessing or curse, and should AI-generated writing and research worry Christian universities

---

11. Nicole Racine, et al. "Global Prevalence of Depressive and Anxiety Symptoms in Children and Adolescents During COVID-19: A Meta-Analysis," *JAMA Pediatrics* 175:11 (2021) 1142–50.

12. Pew Research Center, *Religion's Relationship to Happiness, Civic Engagement and Health Around the World*, Jan. 31, 2019, https://www.pewresearch.org/religion/2019/01/31/religions-relationship-to-happiness-civic-engagement-and-health-around-the-world/.

and schools, or does AI's arrival expose something in education that needs to be resolved?

The first question is to inquire if the threat of AI is proportionate to how we have come by default to define and deliver education. If education is about transmitting information, then yes, we have a significant problem to face. However, is transmitting information the best and proper way to characterize and practice education? As Kevin Brown notes, "What about the formative development of students—their intellect, character, morality, wisdom, judgment, prudence, service, capacity, and unitive understanding of the world they inhabit and how they act within it?"[13] Suppose Christian education is about encouraging the whole person, a three-dimensional mind, body, and spirit person, within a community of mutual love and care. In that case, Christian institutions will always have significant relevance for individuals and society, even in a society increasingly occupied by AI. Ultimately, AI can never empathize, care for, and love us like our fellow humans can.

However, AI is a wake-up call for the Christian community who believe that good teaching is more than information transmission. If education concerns the individual's intellectual, emotional, spiritual, and physical well-being, then AI is not the problem that it potentially could be.

The Role of Passion in Education

There is the topic of the "passionate" educator. Educators are encouraged to be "passionate" about teaching and learning, but what does it mean to be a passionate educator? The Christian academic Nicholas Wolterstorff had three questions for future teachers: Do you love it [teaching]? Are you good at it? Finally, is it worthwhile?[14] The first needs an emotional response, the second requires a skills-based reaction, and the third concerns the teaching profession. In other words, there are various factors to consider for becoming a teacher, and *passion* may only occupy one-third of the equation.

---

13. Kevin Brown, "Why Educators Shouldn't Be Worried About AI," *Christianity Today*, Dec. 23, 2022, https://www.christianitytoday.com/2022/12/ai-chatgpt-artificial-intelligence-education-university/.

14. Nicholas Wolterstorff, *Educating for Life: Reflections on Christian Teaching and Learning* (Grand Rapids, MI: Baker Academic, 2002).

There are always best-teaching practices to discuss, curriculum policies to negotiate, and theories to evaluate. Many of these have permanence, while others have lost popularity. Educators live and breathe pedagogy, curriculum, and learner needs. For Christian educators, faith-informed teaching is at the heart of learning. A characteristic of Christian education is forming and supporting a faith-based community in a culture of individualism and consumerism. I think of the popular Temu infomercials that pop up regularly on my television and computer. The "Shop Like a Billionaire" lyrics is a worldview to consider:

> I like it (Yup), it's mine
> The prices blow my mind (Cha-ching)
> I feel so rich (Oh yeah)
> I feel like a billionaire

These lyrics are typical of a consumerist worldview that we are encouraged to endorse. This worldview centers on me, is predominant in popular culture and classrooms, and occasionally can even affect the church. It promises fulfillment and joy through the continual acquisition of goods. Students need to be able to distinguish between community needs and the communally destructive process of materialism. These are just some of the topics that influence education and the Christian education community at large.

The Format of the Book

This book brings together international scholars and practitioners. Scholars can experience the joy of investigating culture's current philosophies and ideas, testing everything, and holding fast to the good while helping to restore and advance healthy learning communities. This book can begin productive and healthy dissent—an ancient and scholarly tradition that has been a fundamental tenet of the academy for centuries.

Each chapter is written from the author's perspective and experience. The authors consider these topics essential for educators to discuss. Each chapter concludes with questions for deeper discussion, and readers are encouraged to work through each question in small groups. The authors are curious to know how their topic affects educators now and potentially in the future.

If you are like me, you enjoy reading for many different reasons. Therefore, consider this advice before reading this book:

> I find [smartphones] and [computers] very educational. Every time someone turns one on, I go into the other room and read a book.—Groucho Marx[15]

Matthew Etherington

---

15. Wanda Lincoln and Suid Murray, *The Teachers Quotation Book* (California: Dale Seymour Publication, 1986).

CHAPTER ONE

Topics in Christian Education

Matthew Etherington

If educators witness cues of approaching shifts in the weather, they can accurately predict the coming of a storm or hot spell.

The Signs and the Times

IN THE NEW TESTAMENT, Luke the physician instructs believers to be aware and alert,

> And there will be signs in the sun, in the moon, and in the stars; and on the earth distress of nations, with perplexity, the sea and the waves roaring.... Now when these things begin to happen, look up and lift up your heads, because your redemption draws near. (Luke 21:25, 28)[1]

Looking for signs should come naturally to the Christian educator. Believers are called to "be watchful" (1 Cor 16:13–14), to "be awake" (Mark 13:37), and to "be alert" (Acts 20:31). To read the signs in education, Christian educators perform thoughtful observation and analysis. As a Christian teacher-scholar, an opportunity to contribute to developing

---

1. Scripture quotations in this essay are from ESV.

public intellectualism and share thoughtful analytic skills with students is a necessary and worthy goal.

Christian educators comprise Roman Catholics, mainline Protestants, evangelicals (including non-denominational), and Orthodox Christians.[2] So, how can Christian educators learn to read the "signs of the times," and what are these so-called "signs"?

I am a member of a solo online kayaking group. Members consistently post pictures of themselves kayaking alone. The posts often include commentary about the experience, stimulating discussion about their kayaking equipment, and other members noting similar kayaking experiences. The group is advertised as an online kayaking community. Last week, the group moderator asked the 240+ kayaking members: "How does kayaking make you feel?" An open-ended question gives members the freedom to respond diversely.

However, by the end of the day, the moderator had closed the post and prevented members from responding to the question. The explanation was that a member had posted a comment that the moderator identified as "the G-word." What word starting with *g* caused the moderator to abruptly close the discussion?

While reading through the group responses, it was apparent that the "G-word" references God. One of the kayaking members responded to the moderator's open-ended question: "Kayaking makes me feel closer to God." Discounting those two-thirds of the online community who replied to the post with vitriolic comments, not to mention the group administrator describing the reflection as using the "G-word," many of the members supported a reference to God. The response from the moderator confirmed that some people perceive the inclusion of God in an online community discussion as inappropriate. The absurdity reveals itself when a group publicly honors diversity and nature but does not include a diversity of people who associate God with nature.

---

2. A *Christian* educator is someone who personally and corporately associates with the Christian tradition and can be Roman Catholic, mainline Protestant, evangelical (including non-denominational), or Orthodox and is a formally educated degree holding individual, teaching full time or part time in a traditional faith-based private school or public school, also including homeschooling. A homeschooling educator may also be a parent or caregiver who does not hold a formal teaching degree.

Epistemological Diversity

The compartmentalization of religion from mainstream culture has an extensive history, so it is *not* a new challenge.[3] While others may agree with the example given, the moderator's actions, and whatever side of the discussion we find ourselves on, the emphasis is on the challenge raised by epistemological diversity. What types of knowledge should be included in mainstream culture? Is sharing religious beliefs in the public domain alongside an age of diversity and inclusion unreasonable?

Living in a pluralistic culture, we respect, appreciate, and learn from our non-religious neighbors, including those with diverse spiritual traditions. However, in practice, we all tend to simplify, reduce, essentialize, generalize, stereotype, abstract, and make forms of fiction toward people and their ideas that "create collective identities ('us' versus 'them'), to claim the superiority and exclusion of the 'us' (and emphasize the inferiority of the 'them')."[4]

Although epistemological diversity should be uncontroversial, Western culture still exhibits "ongoing unresolved struggles for dominance between neo-liberal, social-democratic, and authoritarian conceptions of the purposes and necessary forms of organization and administration of education."[5] Consequently, the academy has not yet undertaken a wholesale epistemological plan to overhaul, broaden, and fundamentally reorient knowledge production toward an authentic practice of epistemological diversity and inclusion.[6]

Holy Spirit epistemology is just one example of epistemological diversity. The idea is that there are beliefs that we all hold, are rational in having, and know to be true but that are not grounded in inference from other beliefs, arguments, and evidence. The Holy Spirit produces in us a conviction of the truth without needing the confirmation of other types of evidence. Epistemological diversity is one topic the Christian community can discuss, practice, and model for generations.

---

3. If you have the patience and time to read an eight hundred-page book, I highly recommend Charles Taylor's *A Secular Age*. Challenge yourself to read it. You will not be disappointed.

4. Roeland, "Why We Need to Complicate Things," 145.

5. O'Neill, "Social Imaginaries," 4.

6. Gaudry and Lorenz, "Indigenization as Inclusion, Reconciliation, and Decolonization," 218–27.

Skepticism and Critical Thinking

As a doctoral student, I was taught, rightly or wrongly, that skepticism is a virtue, and an integral part of critical thinking, a goal of a good education. Critical thinking requires being in a state of doubt. Perspective-taking was essential to bring about a position of doubt and minimize bias. This is one reason I loved being in higher education.

During my four-and-a-half-year research thesis, I met monthly with my doctoral supervisor to share the ongoing analysis and results I had collected from mature-age schoolteachers in Canada and Australia. As I sat in my supervisor's office, handing over my latest version, my supervisor would review my findings and analysis. He never looked thrilled with what he was reading, and one day, with his eyebrows raised, he looked up and questioned:

> Matthew, how do you know they [interviewees] are telling the truth, and how do I know *you* are not fudging these results?

My first reaction was, why would these mature-age individuals not tell the truth, at least as they experienced it? Worse still, why would I fudge the results? Not too long after these thoughts, when my research methods classes were restored to memory, I recalled that his skepticism was an example of critical thinking—he asked me to supply reasons to support what he was reading and offer some background evidence. Of course, there are various types of knowledge production, i.e., epistemology, which count as evidence, including experiential, historical, scientific, and mathematical, and each knowledge type has its supporters, so what counts as *evidence* is not universally recognized. Also, in my experience, one of the tasks of the doctoral supervisor is to be skeptical from the beginning, assuming what is before them has been changed in some form to mirror the researcher's bias, political persuasion, or personal agenda.

Since these academic encounters with my supervisor and with my doctoral experiences now far behind me, I approach data and information claims with a healthy skepticism. This should not concern Christian educators since believers should evaluate everything and hold on to the good—i.e., the truth, no matter how authoritative the claims. We are expected to be critical, skeptical, and thoughtful (Acts 17:10–11, 1 Thess 5:19–21, 1 John 4:1). Skepticism means to inquire or to "look around" for evidence before accepting claims of truth. Moreover, extraordinary claims to truth do not require extraordinary evidence—all that is needed is evidence.

Consequently, thoughtful skepticism is a goal for Christian education; therefore, we should never hear statements such as, "We don't ask those types of questions around here!" Critical thinking and investigation are needed to advance truth. Therefore, Christian education honors the questions students raise as much as the answers. This is important as Christian education has been criticized for "invariably adopting authoritarian pedagogies that are hard on free thinking."[7] Christian education ought to empower teachers and students to avoid simple and trite responses to topics that are due much respect and thoughtfulness.[8]

Critical thinking involves examining everything to hold firmly to what is good (1 Thess 5:21). If we model this to students, we can hesitate to make a final judgment, display open-mindedness, and discuss ideas and claims to truth, no matter how authoritative. We consult with others raised in environments and worldviews that contrast ours. To do this confidently, wisely, and humbly, we pursue what we believe and know *why* we believe it, for when we know *why*, other truth claims do not pose a problem.

While there is much to complain about in academia today, there is one thing that I appreciate and keep valuing: the fact that knowledge transfer (education) and knowledge construction (research and critical thinking) can occur together in one place.[9]

The Topics for Consideration

The school and university uphold a particular learning culture, one that is guided by a vision and a mission, and educators are encouraged to create and support this with guidelines, responsibilities, and expectations. Humphries and Burns distinguish a school culture as "unwritten cultural norms, developed and reinforced by managers, teachers, and students, which impact teaching practice."[10]

However, school cultures do not exist independently of more significant ideological constructions. They are local instantiations of

---

7. Symes and Gulson, "Crucifying Education," 22.
8. Biemers, "Case for Christian Schools."
9. Roeland, "Why We Need to Complicate Things," 149.
10. Humphries and Burns, "'In Reality It's Almost Impossible,'" 241.

broader beliefs and norms that shape how knowledge is organized and valued within and outside the education system.[11] Political and ethical ideas influence schools, colleges, and universities. The curriculum is a form of socialization that transmits the values and norms of the broader society through the values the school promotes.[12] These ideological constructions are sometimes benevolent, although not always. Therefore, the practice of looking, seeing, and exploring what is before us applies to followers of Christ—test, analyze, and hold fast to the good (1 Thess 5:21). So, what signs are to be analyzed and discussed?

The choice of topics is mine; therefore, this chapter reflects my experiences. Like any story or personal reflection, it applies to current topics necessary for ongoing discussion. The topics include education and schooling, passion and education, faith integration, individualism, and community.

Topic 1: We Don't Need No Education?

The word *education* is derived from the Latin terms *educere*, *educare*, and *educatum*, which mean "to learn," "to know," and to "lead out." Education leads out a child, adult, or learner's internal hidden talent, regardless of age.

In 1979, Pink Floyd sang a song about education, which became a mega-hit to this day:

a. We don't need no education,

b. We don't need no thought control

c. No dark sarcasm in the classroom

d. Teachers leave them kids alone,

e. Hey! Teacher, leave them kids alone,

f. All in all it's just another brick in the wall.[13]

Although the character-narrator's perspective is limited in time and space, the song's central theme is the feeling of abandonment and isolation, which has no limits in time or space.

11. Liddicoat, Scarino, and Kohler, "Impact of School Structures and Cultures," 4.

12. Ho, "Music Education Curriculum and Social Change," 270; Jukić and Kakuk, "Socialization Role of School," 3407.

13. "Another Brick in the Wall, Part 2," Pink Floyd, EMI Records: UK, 1979.

Whenever I hear this song in a café or car radio, I think about my teaching career. Was I too authoritative? Did I ever abandon or isolate children? What would people say about the education I delivered to students? As teachers, we have ambitious standards; as believers, we are encouraged and aspire to a pedagogy of compassion, fairness, slowness to anger, and wisdom, and we are to display and live out the "fruits of the Spirit."

In that famous line, there is much to meditate upon. Pink Floyd says: "We *don't* need *no* education." Using the double negative of *don't* and *no*, and employing the word "ed-u-cation," the line had the suitable meter and timing to sound rhythmical and powerful. However, the catchphrase "We don't need no education" may persuade listeners to overlook what the character-narrator is *not* saying: "We don't need *any* education."

A closer examination would reveal that education is essential for humanity to counter abandonment and isolation.[14] To experience abandonment and isolation is to be deprived of learning. Finding someone alive who does not want to learn and be educated would be hard—even Pink Floyd would agree. *How* one is educated and taught makes all the difference.

However, we know that education is possible *without* formal schooling; education can be *informal*. One of the defining characteristics of informal learning is that it tends to defy organization and location,[15] as education occurs anywhere. Informal learning can be homeschooling, outdoor learning, or any learning in everyday life.

Although a conventional institution of learning is not necessary for education, it could be sufficient and has been for many people, including myself. However, attendance at a formal education institute is not necessarily needed for education to transpire. Education is a lifelong and organic process that begins at birth and continues till the end of life, a process that can occur anywhere. To name just a few famous people who experienced learning outside a traditional educational institution, Dietrich Bonhoeffer was homeschooled by his mother, Paula. Helen Keller, deaf and blind from a fight with an illness, was tutored at home alongside institutional learning. C. S. Lewis was taught at home with the help of a governess and "an endless stack of books." Beatrix Potter was homeschooled for most

---

14. Agha-Golzadeh and Ghorbanpour, "We Don't Need No Education," 12–13.
15. Johnson and Majewska, "Formal, Non-Formal, and Informal Learning."

of her schooling years. American tennis stars the Williams sisters were homeschooled from elementary to high school.

Unlike informal learning, formal schooling encompasses a prescribed curriculum operated within a fixed location, with an organized setting, time, and specific rules and protocols. Some view education and schooling, like love and marriage, as the same phenomenon necessary for living a whole and happy life. The British philosopher and educator Richard Stanley Peters expounds:

> There is a general concept of "education," which covers almost any process of learning, rearing, or growing up. Nowadays, when we speak of education in this general way, we usually mean going to school, to an institution devoted to learning.[16]

To be schooled is to be educated, or so it seems. And yet, education, like breathing, continues throughout life and will occur in multiple contexts, formal and informal. In earlier times, the family, the church, apprenticeship, neighborhood, local community, and other social agencies played an important and meaningful role in educating its young. And it did so with the firm belief that it does take a "village" to raise a child. Unsurprisingly, when teachers, parents, or students (including Pink Floyd) express a lack of confidence in education, it is not in education but in *how* they were taught.

We see the consequence of parents choosing alternate schooling for their children. In Canada, trends in education and educational changes in 2023 show evident fluctuations in educational choice.[17] For comparison purposes, Statistics Canada, which supplies sixteen years of data from 2006 to 2022, confirms that formal public schooling had the smallest total enrollment increase, at 4.5 percent, while independent school enrollments grew by about 23.8 percent. Homeschooling enrollments almost tripled at 264 percent.[18] In Canada, the K–12 school-age population dropped below five million students, while the number of Canadians aged five to seventeen attending formal schooling declined by 6.6 percent from 2000 to 2015.

Parents and students increasingly pursue education in non-formal settings. Across the United Kingdom, online learning at home and homeschooling have risen by about 40 percent over three years since 2016.

---

16. Peters, "Justification of Education," 238.
17. Van Pelt, "Charting New Horizons for Independent Education."
18. See Van Pelt, "Charting New Horizons for Independent Education."

Many personal stories from parents and children explain why this is occurring, and it would be wise for all school leadership to listen and consider how education and pedagogy can be conducted more virtuously. As Pink Floyd reminded generations of learners, no one, teachers nor students, desire to be *just another brick in the wall*.

Topic 2: The "Passionate" Educator

> The only way to do great work is to love what you do.
> —Steve Jobs

One thing is evident when looking over job postings: a passion for passion is growing. Jobs for educators often include *passion*: "We are seeking a *passionate* educator for this role." Consequently, it would not be mistaken to believe that a great teacher is a passionate teacher, and the best educators teach with passion.

Job postings are rampant, with promotions about teacher practitioners being *passionate*. There are published readings on *passion*, to name just a few: *The Power of Passion*, *Five Ways to Reignite Your Passion*, *Cultivating Your Passion*, *How to Restore Your Passion*, and *The Passionate Educator*.[19] These are based on an assumption that exceptional teaching and *passion* are synonymous. I have increasingly heard education instructors in K–12 and higher education often repeat to their students to "just be *passionate*" and that people become teachers because they are *passionate*. Unsurprisingly, *passion* and education occupy a prominent position in the psychology of teachers and soon-to-be teachers.

These catchy expressions seem upbeat and reasonable: what parent or child would not want their teacher to be *passionate* about their calling? The image is of a teacher excited about their subject, energized, moving energetically about the room, fully present, and regularly engaging with their students. Teaching is a labor of love that aligns with one's beliefs and values. We admire an educator when they exhibit *passion* instead of aloofness or disengagement with students.

However, the phrase is vague and loaded with images that, I contend, cannot be sustained. If *passion* means to be enthusiastic, then this is a worthwhile goal. However, the word means something more than enthusiasm.

---

19. See Fried, *Passionate Teacher*.

In my experience with K–12 and higher education, I have collaborated with skilled and knowledgeable educators who do not "love" their work. They do not despise their work either; they value and respect teaching but do not *love* it. Should they express love for their work, and what does it mean to "love" your work? Suppose we had a choice between two educators, for instance, Teacher A, an excellent communicator who is knowledgeable and skilled, and Teacher B, who does not have the skills of Teacher A but expresses their *love* and *passion* about their career. On what *educational* grounds would we choose Teacher A or Teacher B? What reasons would we have, or should have, for wanting one teacher over the other? Should *passion* be a factor for making the decision, and how much *passion* should one express? Moreover, who should ultimately decide if it is enough? These are questions I am thinking about and testing, and I believe all educators could consider thinking about too.

It is likely the *passion* principle is a type of "eduspeak," a buzzword, sometimes referred to as educational jargon, above all, murky and overused. Alfie Kohn proposes that it is unfair to tar the whole field with allegations of "eduspeak," however, the real culprits pushing these slogans tend to be those working in higher education.[20] One reason words like *passion* are embraced so quickly is that it saves people time, helps people bond with one another, and makes us feel part of a particular club. There is nothing wrong with timesaving, bonding, and being a team member, but is the *passion* team the most valuable "team" to be a member of?

Most of us—I assume—would agree that an educator who is "passionate" about education is advantageous for motivating students to learn and is a worthy ambition to strive for and hopefully achieve. I will set aside the fact that *passion* is an emotion and, like any emotion, has a limited duration, particularly when conditions in the classroom become chaotic. Erin Cech, the author of *The Trouble with Passion*, suggests that *passion* feeds into a culture of individualism and overwork. Moreover, having to be "passionate" encourages people to tolerate precarious employment who will gladly sacrifice their time, money, and leisure for the work they are supposedly "passionate" about.[21]

Rather than recommending teachers be "passionate," I would suggest that the focus is on developing the craft of teaching and/or improving pedagogical content knowledge. As my colleague would often say, if

20. Kohn, "'Eduspeak' Reconsidered."
21. Cech, *Trouble with Passion*.

my surgeon is preparing for open heart surgery and it is on me, I want the surgeon to be the best and most skillful with their craft.[22] Expressing "passion" is inconsequential, especially if complications occur during the operation because a skilled and knowledgeable surgeon pulls us through tough times—knowledge and skill are sufficient.

New York writer Dana Goldstein, author of *The Teacher Wars: A History of America's Most Embattled Profession*, outlines the problem of telling teachers to do things that are not helpful for teachers nor the profession. According to Goldstein, great teachers are said to be "miracle workers" who can "walk on water" and "change the world" while also "helping to reduce poverty," which, as Goldstein suggests, is "magical thinking and not reality."[23] No wonder there is teacher burnout.

So what if educators are exceptionally good at their craft but not necessarily "passionate" about what they do? Should they try to acquire some *passion*? Is *passion* so significant that it should be vital for becoming an outstanding teacher? What if we turned the *passion* principle to parents and proposed that the "best" parents are "passionate" parents—would that be reasonable?

In many work types, one cannot always be an individual or express one's desires. The work expectations for many careers require a calm and methodical approach such as the paramedic, emergency nurse, doctor, clinical psychologist, airline pilot, copilot, or flight engineer.

The *passion* expression is romantic language that clinical psychologist Randi Gunther suggests favors female needs more than a man's needs and does not allow for what captures a man's heart.[24] However, what could be more important is the *expression* of *passion* is culturally biased. A few years ago, I spoke with teachers from the Middle East. I asked them if they were *passionate* about their work, particularly their work as teachers. They smiled, and some laughed as they explained that work *passion* was irrelevant. The critical consideration was work skills and whether someone was willing to learn. The importance rests in being skilled and dependable at your work.

If the *passion* principle is culturally inspired, it does not enjoy universal importance. As life experience shows, *passion* is an emotion that comes with a time stamp, yet being skilled at your craft is permanent. Implying that educators should be *passionate* can make anybody doubt

22. Recognition to professor emeritus Dr. Kenneth Pudlas.
23. See Posner, "As If Teachers' Jobs."
24. Gunther, "Romantic Phrases That Melt Hearts."

their chosen work. However, if *passion* language is simply an expression of enthusiasm, then this has merit; however, a teacher can be invested in their career for many other reasons besides *passion*. If educators are prepared for a profession loaded with inspiration, successes, challenges, and disappointments, they will need the ongoing knowledge and skills necessary for their craft. Shulman describes craft knowledge as the "accumulated wisdom gained through teachers' experience and understanding and their research on teaching practice and the meanings attached to the numerous dilemmas inherent in education."[25] What usually distinguishes a craft specialist from an educator is pedagogical content knowledge (PCK).[26] PCK equips the educator with the skills to represent, illustrate, and explain ideas in a way students can grasp.[27]

We should not promote *passion* as an essential motivator for all educators. There are distinct reasons why people want to become educators, and *passion* might be one of many motivators. People have pragmatic reasons for teaching, and who is to say this is not a superior or more and meaningful motive?

Topic 3: Faith Integration and the Sacred-Secular Divide

> There is no inch of creation where Christ does not rule and consequently no dimension of our lives in which he is not present.
> —Abraham Kuyper

In recent decades, the term *integration* has been commonly used to describe the relationship between faith and learning. The American evangelical educator Frank Gaebelein coined the phrase in the 1950s. Gaebelein was committed to integrating the Bible with every subject. He even proposed to remove the Bible department as an independent entity at Stony Brook School in New York.

However, faith integration is a complex concept with no standard conceptual integration model.[28] Educators are encouraged to integrate faith across the arts, sciences, and humanities and could consist of a devotional, a theological concept, knowledge, or applying Christian ethics. Although integration and the English word *integrity* point to

---

25. Shulman, "Knowledge and Teaching," 327.
26. Shulman, "Knowledge and Teaching," 327.
27. Guzmán, "Developing Craft Knowledge," 327.
28. Cosgrove, "Variations on a Theme," 230.

a similar range of ideas such as wholeness, completeness, perfection, soundness, and corruption,[29] that is not how the expression is always understood.

One school, which will remain anonymous, describes their faith-integration:

> One of the primary goals of a Christian school is to provide an environment where faith can be integrated into every aspect of daily life. This school exemplifies a faith-based institution that effectively blends spirituality with academic excellence. Several distinct characteristics set it apart from secular schools and contribute to its appeal to families seeking faith-integrated education.

The concern with "faith integration" coincides with educational institutions building departments to pursue the integration of faith and learning. Teachers are encouraged to "integrate" faith into their pedagogy, subjects, and curriculum. The assumption is that God's knowledge, virtues, values, identity, and his creation are neither present nor knowable until "integration" has occurred. Although the faith integration movement can be an important area of scholarship and practice, reviewers like myself continue to experience difficulties with the concept and practice.

The first concern is that the very assumption of faith integration, as Glanzer notes, gives the impression that knowledge is being produced or performed by the secular academy while the Christian community is sustaining faith. Thus, as Glanzer writes, "When scholars integrate faith and learning," they have already admitted that the original learning created failed to demonstrate faith, and therefore, faith must now be "integrated."[30] "The Christian community must interweave faith into what the secular folks have produced."[31]

My experience is that faith integration inadvertently fosters dualistic thinking, ensuing in an artificial distinction between the sacred and the secular.[32] All of life, the land, the sky, the water, that is, the whole of creation, is a reflection of God's knowledge (epistemology), His values (axiology), and His identity (ontology) articulated by a story

---

29. Dockery, "Educational Integrity," 1.
30. Glanzer, "Why We Should Discard," 44.
31. Glanzer, "Why We Should Discard," 47.
32. I am using "secular" in relation to Charles Taylor's definition. The secular is understood as the ordinary, with no relation to a transcendent.

that accompanies all of creation (cosmology), which includes the fingerprints of God in all subject matter transmitted to students:

> The earth is the Lord's, and all it contains. (Ps 24:1)
> The heavens declare the glory of God; the skies proclaim the work of his hands. (Ps 19:1)

If God is sovereign over His creation of all things, visible or invisible, He must be all-knowing. Consequently, how does faith integration align with an all-knowing God, the creator of all, when integration implies that God is not present?

I remember attending a talk by an Indigenous Elder a few years ago. The Elder spoke of his ancient stories and the passing down of the stories through the generations, which were now buried underneath layers of reinforced cement that covered the modern city where he now lived. These places were where his grandparents and great-grandparents raised him and taught the next generation. Although the cement slabs now obscured the ancient stories, the fact that he could stand there looking over the city and visualize the land in its original state meant he could nonetheless "lift the land (the teachings) out from the city" (his exact words). Although entombed below the cement, the family stories were still alive; just like a seed lays dormant in the ground waiting to burst forth, his family stories were also waiting to be uncovered for teaching the next generation. Therefore, no integration was necessary; the stories were already there; they just needed someone to unearth them.

Similarly, the analogy of "lifting the land out of the city" is intended to explain how faith integration assumes that biblical truths are not present in the curriculum until someone introduces the integration process. Glanzer suggests Christian educators should practice *scholarship redemption* rather than faith integration. Everything in a fallen world, including all the academic subjects, needs rehabilitation. Therefore, the Christian community performs the biblical "operation" of redeeming the subjects, the curriculum and the academy.

Mathematics and Music

Researchers have discovered that music can be a powerful source of awe, inspiring to experience people and communicate positive and healthy ideas and feelings. However, music can also adopt degrading lyrics and make us feel emotions, some of which are negative. One example is the sexualization of women, which dramatically increased in the lyrics of songs during the nineties and 2000s. Released on April 19, 2024, Taylor Swift's album *The Tortured Poets Department* includes eleven of her thirty-one songs with an "E" under the album's description listing, which stands for "explicit," and several songs with the F-word in the lyrics.

What about mathematics and faith? Mathematical methods and techniques are typically used in engineering. Mathematics serves as the foundation upon which engineers invoke to apply their knowledge to solve real-world problems. For example, mathematics can restore or catalyze efficient sanitation and water treatment, successful transportation systems, reduce commuter congestion, and improve infrastructure. These are examples of how mathematics can restore "fallen" infrastructure or cities. Without mathematics, engineers would be severely limited in designing safe, efficient, innovative solutions to complex problems.

The Fall has created many opportunities for the Christian community to serve, rebuild, and restore, not necessarily *integrate*. Mathematics and music are examples of how the redemption of scholarship and infrastructure can exemplify restoration.

Topic 4: Christian Pedagogy

A Christian pedagogy aims to meet the theological needs of students, however, what is a *Christian pedagogy*?[33] To begin a discussion, I give my students the following scenario:

> When I use pedagogy, I refer to a general definition—*the science of teaching children*. Suppose pedagogy is the science of teaching children, and there was a video in your classroom, and you were to demonstrate a Christian pedagogy. How would those watching the video recognize your pedagogy as distinctively Christian?

Stop reading this now and discuss the question above with your peers. Explain what a Christian pedagogy could or *should* resemble.

---

33. Although there are various definitions of Christian pedagogy, service learning, which offers local community service, would come close to being a fundamental prerequisite to a Christian teaching practice. The question here is not about Christian teaching, which can have several applications, but more specifically, whether a Christian "method" leads to teaching Christianly.

With any pedagogy, educators seek specific teaching methods that use deconstruction *and* reconstruction strategies together with active learning exercises. Expanding teaching methods sets a path for learning preferences, cultural differences, and worldview development. As an example, teachers welcomed the pedagogical insights and results of the *Third International Mathematics and Science Study* (TIMMS), which recorded the classroom interactions of eighth-grade mathematics lessons. The research was conducted in 231 classrooms across the United States, Germany, and Japan. One goal was to observe the pedagogical and cultural practices of teachers in three countries.[34]

The study demonstrated that pedagogy has cultural power meaning that the pedagogies disclosed by each teacher were apparent within a specific cultural context. Some teachers exercised student-centered teaching practices while others displayed subject-centered instruction, representing the norms of their surrounding culture. Some of the teachers gave optimal time for reflection, contemplation, and discussion of profound and essential ideas in mathematics, while others supplied students with immediate answers to their questions. Each teacher displayed typical cultural teaching styles, for instance, student-centered (American), subject-centered, and teacher-centered classrooms (Japanese and German). It was clear that cultural expectations played significant sway in the pedagogical choices of each teacher leading to a vastly different student learning experience.

How does this relate to a Christian pedagogy? Teachers and learners vary in how they think about themselves and relate to others, employing a variety of cultural rules, expectations, and taboos. Christian centers of learning can offer students not necessarily a cultural pedagogy but a pedagogy that is distinct from the surrounding culture, taking the best and wisest cultural rules from what is available however restoring what has been lost or neglected by the culture—I call this a restorative pedagogy. A restorative pedagogy is not necessarily dependent on any one teaching *method* but rather *how* people learn together, serving together in peace, a patient and humble pedagogy. A restorative pedagogy places emphasis on community at the center of teaching and learning.

The TIMMS classroom also offers various pedagogical examples for the Christian educator to consider. Some of these include alternating teacher wait times after asking a question, collaborative and

---

34. National Research Council, *International Comparative Studies*.

independent tasks, cooperative assignments, diversifying lesson duration, modifying the physical settings to improve instruction and learning, and diversifying learning resources.

Pedagogical modifications that Christian educators can utilize could also include reviewing old and current material, practical activities, seatwork, the role of homework, gathering and analyzing data through independent practical activity to develop ideas in an inquiry mode, and finally, making connections between ideas and real-life experiences and issues. There are many different pedagogies that can enhance, or even, replace the dominant information transmission pedagogy. However, do any of these examples represent a Christian pedagogy? I would suggest that all the strategies exhibit a Christian pedagogy. The more important variable is the method/s the educator employs for each strategy. A Socratic pedagogy could involve a dialogue between the teacher and students, instigated by continual probing from the instructor. There could be a determined effort by the teacher to reveal the fundamental theories or beliefs that shape a student's epistemology (knowledge), bringing them to a particular truth or revelation. This could be justified pedagogically since Jesus regularly exercised a question/answer methodology to reveal truths with the people he was in contact.

If we label a pedagogy as "Christian" then, in my understanding, it would be a pedagogy that undoubtedly includes any one of these examples given above. However, a Christian pedagogy might be better understood as a pedagogy of service with students and educators serving their local community. Christian and non-Christian schools already service learning projects and mission trips to help students develop a heart for others. Serving others is distinctly Christian because Christ called his followers to serve others. This has involved students visiting and singing with local elders at the care home down the road, handing out food at the local shelter, serving in a soup kitchen, or thinking of ways to serve their classmates. I find the allegory of the long spoons helpful as an example of serving others. After reading the allegory in the next section discuss how your classroom resembles the rooms and how it could be restored to a place where acts of service are the distinctive pedagogy for which the school is known by others.

The Allegory of the Long Spoons

> In the middle of the room was a large round table. A large pot of stew rested in the middle of the table, which smelled delicious and made the man's mouth water. The people sitting around the table were thin and sickly. They appeared to be famished. They were holding spoons with very long handles strapped to their arms. Each found it possible to reach into the pot of stew and take a spoonful, but they could not get the spoons back into their mouths because the handle was longer than their arms.
>
> The man shuddered at the sight of their misery and suffering. The wise man said, "You have seen hell." They went to the next room and opened the door. It was exactly the same as the first one. The large round table with a large pot of stew made the man's mouth water. The people were equipped with the same long-handled spoons strapped to their arms, but the people were well-nourished and plump, laughing and talking. The man said, "I don't understand!" "It is simple," said his venerable guide. "It requires but one skill. You see, they have learned to feed each other, while the greedy think only of themselves."[35]

Jesus sets a similar example for us to follow and encourages us to follow his lead to serve each other. He washed the disciples' feet; he spent time with those no one cared to spend time with. I will never forget one of my teacher education students who, as an act of service and reconciliation, at the beginning of his oral examination, carried into the exam room a bucket of warm, soapy water and dry cloth and gently washed and dried the feet of the three First Nation Elders who were there to attend to his exam. Acts of service must be the dominant pedagogy that naturally flows out of and powerfully emphasizes—a biblical pedagogy.[36]

Topic 5: Experiencing the Bible in the Plural: Individuality and the *Me* Culture

> *Y'all* consider it all joy, brothers, and sisters, when *y'all* fall into diversified testing. (Jas 1:2)

---

35. See Spirit Science, "Parable of Long-Handled Spoons."

36. I use the term *worldview* social-culturally. A worldview is a story or cosmology that informs what is vital about personhood, their value, their identity, and how they should be treated while working toward restoration, i.e., how things *ought* to be.

After pursuing a master of theology, there was one class discussion that I will never forget—which was the importance of reading the Bible in the plural. Southerners from the Deep South in the United States understand this very well since life is often spoken about and lived in the plural.

Have you ever heard a Southerner say, "Y'all"? The English Bible also uses the word *you* for both, whether the author addresses a single person or a group of people. This can open the New Testament reader to misunderstanding. Here is one example to consider, taken from Paul in Phil 1:6 speaking to the Philippians: "He who began a good work in *you* [singular] will be faithful to complete it," and in the plural, "He who began a good work in *you guys* or *y'all*, will be faithful to complete it." The plural/singular distinction is obvious. There are many other examples, but the main point to consider is Paul tells the Philippian Christians they *collectively* make up the temple where the Holy Spirit lives. Consequently, if the Bible is understood and lived in the plural, we must also act on that plurality as Christian educators.

However, the values of Western culture encourage us to lead individualist lives. The sociologist Geert Hofstede refers to this as a cultural characteristic and contrasts "individualism" with "collectivism." Hofstede found that cultures which displayed individualism had loose ties between people and exhibited an *I* identity, as people would emphasize their individualism in conversation with a constant use of *I* and *me*. In contrast, people from collectivist cultures exhibited an identity of *we*. Moreover, in collectivist cultures, the tasks people perform come second to the community's relationship with each other, as harmony, rather than competition, is promoted in the group. In contrast, the opposite is experienced within individualist cultures. As an interesting side note, Hofstede discovered that the United States of America and Australia have the most elevated individualist societies.

Since Christians live within individualist cultures, what does the Bible say about these types of cultures? God creates people as communal beings, not just individuals. We are to be one body, to be in unity with that body (see Eph 4:2–6). Similarly, faith-based education refuses a learning culture of individualism. There is less emphasis on the individual self and more emphasis and encouragement on an evolving *personal* relationship with God, our neighbors, and the peer group. Faith and life in Christ are plural—*y'all*, with God in the center. Faith is always personal, but a *personal* relationship with God does not neglect our communal responsibilities to each other.

When we emphasize individualized learning experiences, student-centered learning, independent learning, or individual needs and talents, students employ the same beliefs to their "personal" relationship and walk with God. I do not deny for one second that it is essential for every believer to have a personal relationship with Jesus Christ; however, that "personal" emphasis regarding faith and living that faith has been so exaggerated that it is ruining the community life of the church.[37] Taylor refers to this as "religious individualism" with an insistence on personal devotion and discipline, which increases the hostility between older forms of collective ritual of togetherness and belonging.[38]

Western societies emphasize individualism as a core value, with an outcome and tendency to reduce religion to a personal, private, and individual experience. In such cultural contexts, Christianity can be perceived as a faith without a direct relationship to learning or education in general.[39] Individualism is evident in the Protestant practice of "individual church membership," which contrasts with the centrality of family and community.

One school rationalizes an individual approach to education on its frequently asked questions school webpage, clarifying why a family should consider their school:

> This school provides an excellent, *individualized* education for its students, always meeting the child where *they* are at. One of the key advantages of individualized learning is the ability to tailor instruction to each student's unique needs and learning style.

The focus on individuality and individualized education is a predominant trend not only in Christian education but also in Christian countries.[40] The sociologist Hofstede defined Christian countries as having over 50 percent of the population practicing some form of Christianity.[41] Hofstede noted that Christian countries strongly believe in individuality, with individual rights paramount.

When schools emphasize their commitment to individualized education, the opportunity to live together decreases since faith formation is always strengthened in a community. Moreover, a community of

---

37. Dawn and Peterson, *Unnecessary Pastor*, 215.
38. Taylor, *Secular Age*, 154–55.
39. Esqueda, "Biblical Worldview."
40. A Christian country recognizes a form of Christianity as its official religion.
41. See Hofstede, "Dimension Maps of the World."

the faithful is not only biblical but also makes life more bearable when suffering and crises occur. Living life together can occur more organically in smaller local communities, where people are motivated to invest in relationships and repair rifts when they happen.[42]

How does the church sometimes over-accentuate the individual? If we refer to popular Christian worship songs, there are indications. Here are three well-known devotional compositions, although there are many others, sung in churches today and assuming an individualistic faith journey. Due to copyright protections that safeguard musical works such as song lyrics, sound recordings, and music compositions in their material form, the following songs cannot be reproduced in writing, so readers are encouraged to use the links provided in the footnotes:

> **No Longer Slaves //** *Bethel Music* **(2015)**[43]
>
> **Good Good Father //***Chris Tomlin* **(2015)**[44]
>
> **Who You Say I Am //** *Hillsong Church* **(2018)**[45]

These captivating songs, which I have sung many times, reveal sacred and eternal truths. However, when we reflect on the corporate nature of the church, the lyrics are problematic. For those who might argue that these are just words, I refer to my linguistic and Indigenous colleagues, who have taught me that words form a language, and a language is a worldview composed of context, values, knowledge, and reality which directs one's behavior. A worldview begins with a story, and the story here is largely about *me*.

The songs express the theme of identity, and the identity is of an individualized nature within a self-referential worldview. They lack the communal reality of being a body in Christ. Words are not simply vocabulary but are full of values and imagery. The imagery is *me* and God and not *us* and God. Paul reminds the believers, "So, in Christ we, though many, form one body, and each member belongs to all the others" (Rom 12:5). The church is a community of people, a spiritual house, a body (1 Pet 2:5), a bride, a family, a corporate group (or corporate groups) of people. We should not lead purely solitary lives. Moreover, Paul is not writing to individuals; he is writing to multiple

---

42. Haidt, *Anxious Generation*, 9.
43. https://bethelmusic.com/resources/peace/no-longer-slaves.
44. https://genius.com/Chris-tomlin-good-good-father-lyrics.
45. https://hillsong.com/lyrics/who-you-say-i-am/.

congregations. One image that communicates a corporate faith life in Christ is a military parade with disciplined soldiers lined up in rows, marching in lockstep with each other.[46]

Aware of this problem, the differences between an *I* and *we* faith are raised by theologian Marva Dawn, who explains that we must remember the corporate significance of living the Christian life. We have forgotten to become Southerners when we read the Bible because to inhabit its world is to speak about our lives in the plural as *y'all*, instead of me or I (singular). Dawn notes that most of the descriptions and commissions in the Bible are plural, not including Timothy, Titus, and Philemon, which are personal letters with individualized instructions. Although pulling back against and replacing the Western individualized vocabulary that often infiltrates the church and faith-based education would be challenging, we must always try to live counter-cultural lives that are less about us as individuals and more about the corporate body. The following songs are enduring examples of the congregational nature of worship and life together:

> **All Creatures of Our God and King //** *St. Francis of Assisi, Italy* **(1225)**
> All creatures of *our* God and King
> Life up your voice, and with *us*, sing
> O praise Him, Alleluia
>
> **A Mighty Fortress Is Our God //** *Martin Luther, Germany* **(1529)**
> A mighty fortress is *our* God,
> A bulwark never failing:
> Our helper He, amid the flood
> Of mortal ills prevailing.
>
> **Holy, Holy, Holy //** *Reginald Heber* **(1826)**
> Holy, holy, holy! Lord God almighty!
> Early in the morning, *our* song shall rise to thee.
> Holy, holy, holy! Merciful and mighty!
> God in three persons, blessed trinity!

---

46. Medley, "Holy Spirit and the Corporate Church."

Although many other classical worship songs also express the closeness of God with individuals, e.g., "How Great Thou Art," many of the contemporary songs today reinforce the individualistic values of the surrounding culture. If language can play a significant role in how we and others perceive the world, how one perceives and experiences the life of a believer is central because it appears that at many levels of society, from the church house to the schoolhouse, we are vulnerable to a language that encourages us to think of ourselves as individuals. The consequence is to relate to others and God as individuals—*me* and God.

Yet, Christianity encourages believers to live *contrary* to the culture. Moreover, when we read the Bible correctly, as biblical scholar Marva Dawn notes, we would read it like a Southerner because to inhabit its world is to speak about and live as a community of believers, not as individuals, but as a collective, in the plural—*y'all* (you all).[47] Observing and living together within a collective body of believers is not to accept everything that the collective endorses, such as corruption for the sake of a faithful, but to live a virtuous life together. We all have a "log in our eye" with individual weaknesses and failures and are all responsible before God; however, an expressive individualist outlook is intended to aid me, and not my community, in pursuing self-exaltation and self-fulfillment. Any external constraints become less and less "rational" to accept.[48]

The fixation of the individual in the Western world has been associated with Jean-Jacques Rousseau, the father of the eighteenth-century Romantic movement. Rousseau's 1762 *Emile, or Treatise on Education*, translated the core themes of Romanticism into education principles. Rousseau believed that people were inherently good and, when left alone as individuals, would flourish as they should. This encouraged a movement that emphasized individuality and subjective experience. Human flourishing was impossible when society, teachers, parents, and authorities corrupted the young with false expectations and forced ideas, unnatural teaching, and irrelevant learning. Although Rousseau also believed that children should be taught community and working for the common good, the assumption was always in the innate goodness of the individual, and this, he believed, must always be protected and encouraged.

---

47. Medley, "Holy Spirit and the Corporate Church," 214.
48. Smith, *How (Not) to Be Secular*.

Individualistic cultures tend to privilege individual interests and individual priorities over those of the group since the individual is at the center of decision-making. In contrast, collectivist cultures perceive the individual as less essential within groups, expecting "individuals to conform to in-group norms, role definitions, and values at the expense of their individuality."[49]

As Western culture becomes increasingly *secular*, meaning a life absorbed exclusively by the ordinary events and happenings of the world (see Charles Taylor), one could ask how Christian education discourages individualism. One answer is that Christian education offers a learning experience that concentrates *less* on the individual and one's identity, by upholding an anthropomorphic shift from oneself to a community of believers. These people learn together in a unique way, collectively, with a transcendent being at the center.

Conclusion

This chapter has considered five topics in education that can be applied to K–12 and Christian education in colleges and universities. One must be a critical observer to read the signs of the times. My former colleague Harro Van Brummelen often said about critical observation, "The question for Christian educators is, what should we accept and what should we reject." We don't accept everything, and we don't reject everything. We keep the best and wisest, and we leave the worst. To engage in that question, we need regular critical reflection and dialogue.[50]

While faith integration does not endorse an exact understanding or practice, it is the primary approach for Christian education. I suggest rather than requiring teachers to integrate faith into subjects such as mathematics, science, and music, one could be encouraged to probe how mathematics, music, or science have fallen and how each can be restored for God's glory. If the world has fallen, then so have all the subjects of learning, including how they are taught. Redemption of the subjects is a more biblical approach to Christian education and, might I say, a more creative and critical thinking approach that produces generous dialogue and discussion.

49. Triandis, "Self and Social Behavior," 510.

50. As a suggestion, Edward DeBono's Six Thinking Hats offers a productive method for critical engagement with topics and can accommodate experienced and novice critical thinkers in small learner groups.

Questions for Discussion

1. In summary, what were your motives for becoming a teacher, and can you think of good reasons for becoming a teacher other than *passion*?
2. How does *faith integration* or *redemption of scholarship* help you in your journey as a Christian educator?
3. Have you considered the pros and cons of the individual and corporate wording of worship songs? Why or why not?
4. List some ways your class could examine the fallen nature of psychology, history, biology, literature, business, sociology, music, and mathematics "through the eyes of faith."
5. How does education use language to shape public opinion? How does it influence what teachers think about, remember, or forget through their choice of words?

References

Agha-Golzadeh, Ferdows, and Amir Ghorbanpour. "We Don't Need No Education: A Stylistic Analysis of Pink Floyd's 'Another Brick in the Wall.'" *Journal of Art and Language* 5:19 (2015) 1–16.

Biemers, Matthew. "A Case for Christian Schools." *The Banner*, Aug. 29, 2014. https://www.thebanner.org/features/2014/08/a-case-for-christian-schools.

Cech, Erin. *The Trouble with Passion: How Searching for Fulfilment at Work Fosters Inequality.* Oakland, CA: University of California Press, 2021.

Cooper, James M., and Amy Alvarado. "Preparation, Recruitment, and Retention of Teachers. Education Policy Series." The International Institute for Educational Planning and The International Academy of Education, 2006. http://staging.iaoed.org/downloads/5_Cooper_web_151206.pdf.

Cosgrove, P. B. "Variations on a Theme: Convergent Thinking and the Integration of Faith and Learning." *Christian Higher Education* 14:4 (2015) 229–43.

Dawn, Marva, and Eugene Peterson. *The Unnecessary Pastor: Rediscovering the Call.* Vancouver: Regent College, 2000.

Dockery, David S. "Educational Integrity: The Integration of Faith and Learning." International Alliance for Christian Education, Feb. 5, 2024. https://iace.education/journal-blog/educational-integrity-the-integration-of-faith-and-learning.

Esqueda, Octavio Javier. "Biblical Worldview: The Christian Higher Education Foundation for Learning." *Christian Higher Education* 13:2 (2014) 91–100. DOI: 10.1080/15363759.2014.872495.

Fried, Robert L. *The Passionate Teacher: A Practical Guide.* Boston: Beacon, 1995.

Gaudry, Adam, and Danielle Lorenz. "Indigenization as Inclusion, Reconciliation, and Decolonization: Navigating the Different Visions for Indigenizing the Canadian Academy." *AlterNative* 14:3 (2018) 218–27. DOI: 10.1177/1177180118785382.

Glanzer, Perry L. "Why We Should Discard 'the Integration of Faith and Learning': Rearticulating the Mission of the Christian Scholar." *Journal of Education and Christian Belief* 12:1 (2008) 41–51. https://doi.org/10.1177/205699710801200105.

Gunther, Randi. "Romantic Phrases That Melt Hearts: Men and Women Respond Very Differently to Expressions of Love." *Psychology Today*, Apr. 22, 2014. https://www.psychologytoday.com/intl/blog/rediscovering-love/201404/romantic-phrases-melt-hearts.

Guzmán, V. Carolina. "Developing Craft Knowledge in Teaching at University: How Do Beginning Teachers Learn to Teach?" *European Educational Research Journal* 8:2 (2009) 326–35. https://doi.org/10.2304/eerj.2009.8.2.326.

Haidt, Jonathan. *The Anxious Generation*. Dublin: Allen Lane, 2024.

Ho, Wai-Chung. "Music Education Curriculum and Social Change: A Study of Popular Music in Secondary Schools in Beijing, China." *Music Education Research* 16:3 (2014) 267–89. https://doi.org/10.1080/14613808.2014.910182.

Hofstede, Geert. "Dimension Maps of the World: Individualism." https://geerthofstede.com/culture-geert-hofstede-gert-jan-hofstede/6d-model-of-national-culture/.

Humphries, Simon, and Anne Burns. "'In Reality, It's Almost Impossible': CLT-Oriented Curriculum Change." *ELT Journal* (2015) 239–48. https://doi.org/10.1093/elt/ccu081.

Ingersoll, Richard M. "Is There Really a Teacher Shortage? A Research Report Co-Sponsored by Center for the Study of Teaching and Policy and The Consortium for Policy Research in Education." 2003. https://www.education.uw.edu/ctp/sites/default/files/ctpmail/PDFs/Shortage-RI-09-2003.pdf.

Johnson, M., and D. Majewska. "Formal, Non-Formal, and Informal Learning: What Are They, and How Can We Research Them?" Cambridge University Press and Assessment Research Report, 2022.

Jukić, R., and S. Kakuk. "Socialization Role of School and Hidden Curriculum." *EDULEARN19 Proceedings* (2019) 3404–12. https://doi.org/10.21125/edulearn.2019.0910.

Kohn, Alfie. "'Eduspeak' Reconsidered: When, Why, and to Whom Is Educational Jargon Annoying?" *Alfie Kohn* (blog), Nov. 3, 2022. https://www.alfiekohn.org/blogs/eduspeak/.

Liddicoat, Anthony, Angela Scarino, and Michelle Kohler. "The Impact of School Structures and Cultures on Change in Teaching and Learning: The Case of Languages." *Curriculum Perspectives* 38 (2017) 3–13. DOI: 10.1007/s41297-017-0021-y.

Luekens, Michael T., Deanna M. Lyter, and Erin E. Fox. "Teacher Attrition and Mobility: Results from the Teacher Follow Up Survey 2000–01." National Center for Education Statistics, Aug. 2004. https://nces.ed.gov/pubs2004/2004301.pdf.

Medley, Mark. "The Holy Spirit and the Corporate Church." Nov. 5, 2024. https://markmedley.org/wp-content/uploads/2019/12/The-Holy-Spirit-and-the-Corporate-Church.pdf.

National Research Council. *International Comparative Studies in Education: Descriptions of Selected Large-Scale Assessments and Case Studies*. Washington, DC: The National Academies Press, 1995.

O'Neill, John. "Social Imaginaries: An Overview." In *Encyclopedia of Educational Philosophy and Theory*, edited by Michael A. Peters, 1–6. Singapore: Springer, 2016. https://doi.org/10.1007/978-981-287-532-7_379-1.

Peters, R. S. "The Justification of Education." In *The Philosophy of Education*, edited by R. S. Peters, 28–38. Oxford: Oxford University Press, 1973.

Posner, Joe. "As If Teachers' Jobs Aren't Hard Enough, They're Asked to Fix Poverty, Too." *Vox*, Sept. 6, 2014. https://www.vox.com/2014/9/6/6111953/teachers-magical-thinking-dana-goldstein.

Racine, Nicole, et al. "Global Prevalence of Depressive and Anxiety Symptoms in Children and Adolescents During COVID-19: A Meta-Analysis." *JAMA Pediatrics* 175:11 (2021) 1142–50. DOI: 10.1001/jamapediatrics2021.2482.

Rah, Soong-Chan. *The Next Evangelicalism: Freeing the Church from Western Cultural Captivity*. Downers Grove, IL: IVP Academic, 2010.

Roeland, Johan. "Why We Need to Complicate Things: The Teaching and Learning of Religion Beyond Simplification." *Teaching Theology and Religion* 26:4 (2023) 144–50. https://doi.org/10.1111/teth.12654.

Shulman, L. "Knowledge and Teaching: Foundations of the New Reform." *Harvard Educational Review* 57:1 (1987) 1–22. https://doi.org/10.17763/haer.57.1.j463w79r56455411.

Smith, James K. A. *How (Not) to Be Secular: Reading Charles Taylor*. Grand Rapids, MI: Eerdmans, 2014.

Spirit Science. "Parable of Long-Handled Spoons." YouTube video, Oct. 17, 2020. https://www.youtube.com/watch?v=IG_AELnZqEQ.

Symes, Colin, and Kalervo Gulson. "Crucifying Education: The Rise and Rise of New Christian Schooling in Australia." *Social Alternatives* 24:4 (2005) 19–24.

Taylor, Charles. *A Secular Age*. Cambridge, MA: Belknap, 2007.

Triandis, H. C. "The Self and Social Behavior in Differing Cultural Contexts." *Psychological Review* (1989) 506–52.

Van Pelt, Deani. "Charting New Horizons for Independent Education in Canada." Cardus: Centre for Cultural Renewal, 2023. https://www.cardus.ca/research/education/perspectives-paper/charting-new-horizons-for-independent-education-in-canada/.

CHAPTER TWO
Flourishing in Christian Schools
Insights from Research

Lynn E. Swaner

MUCH EDUCATIONAL RESEARCH OVER the past few decades has given attention to measuring and improving academic achievement in schools. While cognitive learning is certainly a paramount outcome of schooling, it is a poor proxy for everything that educators, students, and families might hope would result from formal education. This is true regardless of school sector, but particularly so for Christian schools, which ground instruction in a biblical worldview and are animated by Jesus' mission to bring "life in all its fullness."[1] In this regard, a qualitative review of portrait of a graduate statements at over sixty leading Christian schools identified multiple categories of expected student outcomes beyond academics, including spiritual development, community engagement, excellence, impact, and servanthood.[2]

Across all educational sectors, calls for an expanded view of educational success are trending in the wake of the global COVID-19 pandemic. This is evidenced by a growing emphasis on areas like social and

---

1. John 10:10b (NCV).
2. Swaner, Marshall, and Tesar, *Flourishing Schools*.

emotional learning, student mental health, and wellness.³ As researchers and practitioners alike have searched for adequate language to describe a more holistic view of educational outcomes, many are settling on the term *flourishing*. Typically, they view the concept of flourishing as originating in Aristotelian virtue ethics, as an anchor for modern character education, or as rooted in positive psychology.⁴

Christian school educators will also recognize the biblical roots of the term, with "flourishing" appearing thirty-three times across twelve translations of the Bible. Harkening back to a time when agricultural seasons and rhythms were more normative than they are today, these biblical uses of the term often denote actions like growth, blooming, and budding. And in contrast to the deterministic and individualistic nature of most modern educational systems, the Bible frequently depicts flourishing as divinely originated and communally experienced. This is seen clearly in the psalmist's blessing, "May the LORD cause you to flourish, both you and your children."⁵ As communities of faith with an explicit intergenerational purpose, Christian schools will find that flourishing is not only a more capacious term to describe the aims of education, but also one that is deeply aligned with biblical principles.

The Flourishing Schools Research

With this in mind, and with a desire to bridge gaps in research on both holistic outcomes and the Christian school sector, the Association of Christian Schools International (ACSI) undertook a long-term, quantitative study of flourishing in Christian schools beginning in 2017. ACSI is the largest Protestant school association, with over two thousand member schools in the United States and three thousand around the globe.⁶ The resulting, empirically validated survey tool, the Flourishing School Culture Instrument (FSCI), has since been administered to over 150,000 school leaders, teachers, board members, staff, students, parents, and alumni across North America, as well as in international Christian schools in over twelve countries. Analysis of the components of

---

3. Hess, "After COVID-19"; Gray and Lewis, "Use of Educational Technology."
4. Kristjánsson, *Flourishing as the Aim of Education*; Keyes, "Mental Health Continuum."
5. Ps 115:14 (NIV).
6. Association of Christian Schools International, Fact Sheet.

flourishing from this study resulted in the development of the Flourishing Schools Culture Model (FSCM), below.[7]

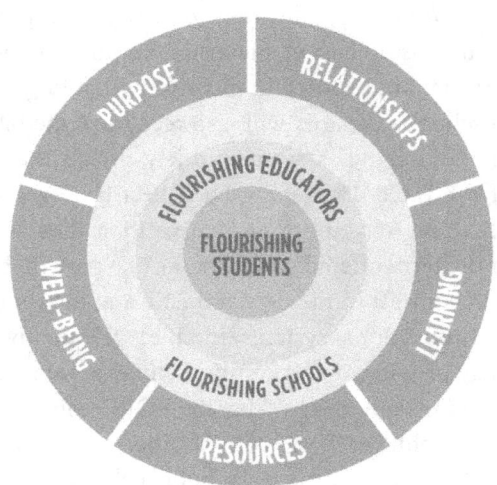

The model identifies five domains of flourishing: *Purpose, Relationships, Learning, Resources,* and *Well-being*. A total of thirty-five validated constructs are distributed across these domains, each of which correlates with flourishing outcomes for students, educators, and the larger school community, as depicted in the three concentric circles at the model's center. This chapter will describe each domain and highlight key constructs from the Flourishing Schools research, while foregrounding throughout the interdependence of all school constituents—students, teachers, leaders, families, and the school community—for flourishing together.

The Purpose Domain

A clear understanding of a school's collective purpose guides schools toward flourishing. Put simply, both agreement and clarity are needed on the reasons that leaders, teachers, and students come together at school. A shared purpose unites school constituents around specific goals and motivates them to strive collectively toward them. The Flourishing Schools research found that a commitment on the part of all school constituencies

---

7. Swaner, Marshall, and Tesar, *Flourishing Schools*.

to the central purposes of Christian education—for example, evidenced by shared responsibility, family-school partnerships, and holistic teaching—is strongly linked with flourishing outcomes.

First, the research found that positive outcomes are associated with all constituencies in the school community holding a shared sense of *responsibility*.[8] This responsibility goes beyond mere agreement or buy-in, but rather is nurtured through collective dialogue and reflection. It also goes beyond posting the school's mission statement on a wall or having staff memorize the school's core values, as important as that may be. Instead, a shared sense of responsibility involves leaders and teachers integrating their collective purpose into their daily lives and work. The research also found that a school's purpose must extend beyond its walls to include forming a genuine school-family *partnership*, as greater flourishing outcomes are linked with families' feeling included in the school's mission and knowing their involvement is valued.

For students, the research identified *holistic teaching* as important for flourishing. This means that the academic program incorporates teaching the heart and soul, as well as the mind. Students are multifaceted individuals who think, feel, act, and relate with others; a holistic education addresses all these aspects by incorporating not only the arts and athletics but also character development, morality and ethics, and spiritual growth, depending on the school's unique mission. In terms of faith development, flourishing is also linked to students viewing themselves as part of *God's story*. This means they see their lives as part of a bigger design and believe God can involve them in his redemptive work. At the same time, a school needs to be receptive to students *questioning* their faith. At schools where caring adults normalize and engage students' questions and doubts—rather than minimizing or dismissing them—flourishing faith is more likely to result.[9]

Taken together, constructs within this domain point to the importance of defining a community's "why," or its collective motivation that in turn shapes educational practices and guides its pursuit of outcomes. A view toward shared purpose can help schools affirm the holistic aims of education, move beyond narrow reform efforts that focus exclusively

---

8. Italicization is used here, and through the remainder of the chapter, to indicate that an FSCM validated construct is being referenced.

9. Swaner, Marshall, and Tesar, *Flourishing Schools*; Lee, Price, and Swaner, "Flourishing Faith Index."

on academic outcomes, and reimagine their purpose as educational ecosystems designed for flourishing.

The Relationships Domain

Education is inherently a "people business," centered on human connection and the ability to understand, support, and inspire people. The Christian faith prioritizes loving and serving others, following Jesus' example of compassion, humility, and selflessness. Thus, for schools that bear the name of Christ, their most important work happens in and through relationships. Not surprisingly, the Flourishing Schools research found that trust-filled, supportive, and authentic relationships between all school constituencies, as well as with the surrounding community, are key to flourishing outcomes. This includes relationships between leaders and teachers, leaders and the board, families and teachers, teachers and students, and school leadership and the community. Prior research also identified positive outcomes—like higher levels of student achievement and overall school improvement—as linked to school engagement with parents, community agencies, and organizations.[10]

Unsurprisingly, the Flourishing Schools research shows that teacher-student relationships matter deeply in schools. The research identified the importance of *mentoring* to student flourishing, when educators point out talent in each student, are aware of students' struggles at school or home, and truly come to know students on a personal level. Additionally, a *caring environment*—in which students feel safe and are protected from bullying—is positively linked with flourishing outcomes. This aligns with prior research that found that where healthy relational systems and processes are in place at a school, bullying levels are lower and student well-being levels are higher.[11]

The Flourishing Schools research also found that teachers need to cultivate effective *family relationships*, by engaging well with parents, guardians, or other key adults in students' lives. This includes regular and effective two-way communication between home and school. Likewise, school leaders need to prioritize *community engagement*, by regularly tapping into community resources, networking with community

---

10. Murphy, *Leading School Improvement*; Reynolds et al., "Educational Effectiveness Research"; Shannon and Bylsma, *Nine Characteristics of High Performing Schools*.
11. Loe, *Relational Teacher*.

stakeholders, and resource-sharing with other schools, churches, businesses, and community agencies. Interestingly, at schools where this is the case, alumni are more than twice as likely to report that they have an active faith, as compared with schools that do not engage the surrounding community well.[12]

When it comes to relationships between leaders, the Flourishing Schools research identified the importance of *leadership interdependence*. This entails all leaders—including the board of trustees—having diverse backgrounds and skillsets, being transparent about their weaknesses, and relying on other leaders to offset those weaknesses. When it comes to how leaders engage with staff, *supportive leadership* is key: flourishing outcomes are more likely at schools where teachers agree that leaders are trusted, "have their backs," and empower staff to make decisions.

In terms of teachers' relationships with their peers, the Flourishing Schools research found that *collaboration* between teachers is linked to flourishing in schools. The research defined this collaboration in terms of teachers' affirming that when they learn from other teachers, they grow and become better in their craft. Prior research similarly found that teacher collaboration around unpacking standards, mapping curriculum designing lessons, and constructing assessments was correlated with academic improvement.[13] This suggests a symbiotic relationship between the degree to which teachers learn together and the quality of their students' learning. This is likely because collaboration provides space for practitioners to "continually expand their capacity to create the results they truly desire, where new and expansive patterns of thinking are nurtured, where collective aspiration is set free, and where people are continually learning how to learn together."[14]

Schools are not composed of discrete programs and classrooms populated by isolated individuals. Rather, they involve webs of relationships between leaders, teachers, staff, students, families, and others—and the quality of these relationships clearly matters deeply. Christian school educators can recall the apostle Paul's teaching that members of the church are "all a part of the body" who are dependent on one another.[15] The same holds true for flourishing in Christian schools, as research shows that school constituents are interdependent when it comes

12. Swaner, Marshall, and Tesar, *Flourishing Schools*.
13. Chenoweth, *It's Being Done*; Chenoweth, "How Do We Get There from Here?"
14. Senge, *Fifth Discipline*, 3.
15. 1 Cor 12:25–26 (ESV).

to flourishing—from leaders to teachers, to students and families, to schools and the larger community.

The Learning Domain

Ostensibly, learning is what students are supposed to do at school—and the quality and depth of that learning is paramount. At the same time, the Flourishing Schools research found that student learning is inextricably linked to the learning of educators. In other words, where there are few flourishing adults, there can be few flourishing students. Many of the validated constructs in this domain suggest the importance of educators engaging together as a "community of practice," or a group of people who "share a concern or passion for something they do and learn how to do it better as they interact regularly."[16]

For students, the Flourishing Schools research found that *engaged learning* is linked to flourishing—particularly when students participate in activities that promote critical thinking, evaluating information, and problem-solving. Other researchers and practitioners have used various terms—such as "deeper" or "transformational"—to describe this type of learning, which is active (versus passive), collaborative (versus solitary), and holistic (versus reductionist) in nature. Some go as far as to assert that learning is not truly possible without student engagement.[17] As mentioned earlier, student flourishing is linked to that of educators, inclusive of this domain; the Flourishing Schools research found that at schools where student engagement levels are high, teacher turnover rates are lower than at schools that do not engage students well in learning.[18]

The research also found that a strengths-based or *individualized instruction* approach, which includes helping students discover how they learn best, is positively linked to flourishing. This includes providing students with the opportunity to reflect on their own learning; previous research indicates that journaling, discussions, learning portfolios, and similar reflection methods can lead to improvements in students' knowledge retention and stronger connections across subjects.[19] Additionally, the Flourishing Schools research found that *responsiveness*

---

16. Wenger and Wenger-Trayner, "Communities of Practice," 1.
17. Senge et al., *Schools That Learn*, 69.
18. Swaner, Marshall, and Tesar, *Flourishing Schools*.
19. D'Erizans and Bibbo, "Time to Reflect."

to special needs, or schools having effective processes and resources to serve students with disabilities, is linked with greater flourishing for all students—not just students with special needs. For example, at schools that practice inclusion well, alumni of all abilities are more than twice as likely to report that having an active faith.[20]

Of course, learning that is engaged, individualized, and supportive of students with disabilities does not happen by accident. Indeed, the Flourishing Schools research points to the importance of developing a *culture of improvement* that is future-focused and growth oriented. Several constructs within the model are related to creating this kind of culture among instructional staff. First, educators need to embrace an *outcomes focus*, by consistently prioritizing learning activities that benefit students. This is easier said than done, with today's classrooms busier than ever and a myriad of demands competing for teachers' attention. Leaders can play a pivotal role in cutting down the number of non-essential tasks, meetings, and other distractions from the high-quality teaching that is necessary for high-quality learning.

Along these lines, the Flourishing Schools research found that leaders need to employ *systems thinking* when making decisions. This entails using an analytical approach that considers the interconnectedness of constituents' perspectives and experiences within the school environment, in order to anticipate impacts and create effective solutions. *Data-driven improvement* is a key focus of this way of thinking, and includes broadening the outcomes examined within the school as well as data collection methods used (e.g., both qualitative and quantitative activities like formative assessments, teacher evaluations, and involving students in designing their own assessments).

Schools can also support student learning by investing in teachers' ongoing growth and development. In addition to high-quality, on-site *professional development*, the Flourishing Schools research found that real-time *feedback* on teaching significantly enhances flourishing outcomes. While this might bring to mind formal observations by administrators seeking to evaluate teachers, the research indicates that peer observation—where other teachers give immediate, constructive, and non-evaluative feedback to their peers—is often more effective for

---

20. Swaner, Marshall, and Tesar, *Flourishing Schools*.

teacher learning.[21] Likewise, feedback from instructional coaches and peer mentors can also help teachers to flourish in their craft.

Developing a community of practice where student learning and teacher growth go hand-in-hand requires relentless intentionality on the part of leaders and teachers. The Flourishing Schools research shows that a school culture marked by growth and improvement, for students *and* educators alike, is correlated with flourishing outcomes for both. In short, the research shows that reciprocity—or an ongoing exchange that provides mutual benefit—is key when it comes to impactful teaching and learning in Christian schools.

The Resources Domain

Schools are influenced by their access to physical, technological, and human resources, which in turn affects the flourishing of students, educators, and families. Not surprisingly, having sufficient *resources*—such as classroom materials, technology, and well-maintained school buildings—is positively linked to flourishing in schools. The Flourishing Schools research also found that having *qualified staff*—those who are credentialed and have ample professional experience—is associated with better flourishing outcomes, as is a board of trustees that has *resource planning* as a strength.

Beyond tangible resources, the Flourishing Schools research also found that leaders' beliefs about resources can hinder school flourishing—specifically, when leaders focus on *resource constraints*, or believe the school could be more effective if not for financial limitations and a lack of resources to make changes. While resource shortages are a common problem in schools, it turns out that leaders' focusing on what their schools lack (instead of what they already have and how they can steward it effectively) is a difference maker in terms of flourishing. This echoes Carol Dweck's research on "fixed" versus "growth" mindsets.[22] When leaders focus on limitations only, they often fail to consider creative solutions they can create using available resources. Conversely, a growth mindset can lead to innovative ideas such as repurposing spaces in creative ways,

---

21. Reeves, *Reframing Teacher Leadership*; Reeves, *Transforming Professional Development*.

22. Dweck, *Mindset*.

phasing out outdated programs for new ones, and reassigning staff based on strengths and growth opportunities rather than seniority.

Any discussion of resources must acknowledge disparities that exist between schools in different communities and settings worldwide, which often result from inequitable educational funding systems or lack of economic opportunity. The way educational systems are organized and funded across the world point to the real value (or lack thereof) societies place on nurturing the potential of children and young people, who are arguably their most valuable resource. At a macro level, policy makers need to ask whose potential is maximized through access to resources like good schools, enrichment programs, safe housing, quality healthcare, and technology—and whose potential is hindered by a lack of these resources. While structural inequalities in school funding models may feel insurmountable at the local level, educators are not powerless. They can work collaboratively with community members, agencies, and businesses to develop creative solutions to resourcing issues. Many Christian schools across North America are doing exactly this, whether through entrepreneurship programs that involve their students in small business collaborations (e.g., coffee shops, greenhouses, teaching kitchens) or third-source income streams (e.g., facilities leasing, on-campus thrift shops or stores).[23]

The Flourishing Schools research highlights the importance of excellence in educational and school management practices. At the same time, it points to the importance of beliefs, attitudes, and mindsets that shape the use of resources in schools. This suggests that "simply 'having' enough is not really 'enough.' Instead, practicing good stewardship and generosity when it comes to resources contributes to flourishing, whereas competition and scarcity-mindedness inhibits it."[24] The benefit of collaborative partnerships birthed from an abundance mindset are not only additional resources to support the school's mission, but also innovative learning experiences for students and deeper relationships with the surrounding community.

---

23. Swaner et al., *Future Ready*.
24. Swaner and Wolfe, *Flourishing Together*, 8.

The Well-Being Domain

Issues around student well-being in schools have become particularly challenging in recent years. A sharp decline in adolescent well-being in the past decade has been marked by significant increases in persistent feelings of sadness or hopelessness, as well as in rates of suicidal ideation.[25] Educators are not faring much better: data reveals that nearly half of teachers experience high levels of professional stress, similar to nurses and higher than physicians, with four-fifths of teachers reporting feeling physically and emotionally drained daily.[26] Nancy Lever and colleagues at the University of Maryland highlight the interconnectedness of educator and student well-being, noting that teacher burnout predicts lower student academic performance and motivation and can also impact students' stress levels.[27] Similarly, the Flourishing Schools research found that the well-being of educators and students is not a secondary concern—but rather is significantly linked—to flourishing outcomes.

First, the Flourishing Schools research has highlighted *resilience* as a crucial factor specifically tied to student well-being. Resilience can be defined as "the existence of assets and protective factors in the social context, the ability to adapt to combat adversity, or the developmental outcomes that result from coping positively with adversity."[28] Students with higher levels of resilience tend to perform better academically and exhibit greater critical thinking along with various non-cognitive skills, which in turn lead to more life opportunities.[29] In recent years, schools have increasingly focused on resilience by integrating social and emotional learning objectives and providing faculty and staff with training to foster resilience through evidence-based practices.[30]

The Flourishing Schools research also found a positive connection between flourishing outcomes and *healthy living*, which involves sufficient rest, nutrition, and physical activity. Sporadic programs aren't enough to create a school environment that fosters well-being; instead, a cohesive and deliberate approach is necessary. This could begin with a well-being assessment, where a team of stakeholders discusses concerns about the

---

25. Centers for Disease Control, "Youth Risk Behavior Survey."
26. Lever, Mathis, and Mayworm, "School Mental Health."
27. Lever, Mathis, and Mayworm, "School Mental Health."
28. Briggs et al., "Assessing and Promoting Spiritual Wellness."
29. Blackburn, "Five Ways to Strengthen Student Resilience."
30. Tomlinson, "One to Grow On."

school environment (including the physical buildings, daily schedule, academic calendar, etc.) and identifies areas for improvement. Including students in this team not only offers valuable perspectives but also helps them develop problem-solving skills and achieve learning goals in health, science, psychology, and other subjects. The key question guiding these efforts should shift the focus from addressing well-being "only if time allows" to making it a priority, as well-being provides the foundation for learning, growth, and overall flourishing. Schools may need to tap into community resources, such as qualified mental health professionals, to foster ongoing conversations about well-being.

In addition to students, educator well-being is also crucially important in schools. The Flourishing Schools research revealed that *stress* among both teachers and leaders—characterized by constant feelings of being overwhelmed and a lack of time for preparation or self-care—is negatively associated with school flourishing. Put simply, educators can only serve their students, colleagues, and schools from a place of personal and professional well-being. Otherwise, educator burnout—and poorly educated students—are more likely to result.

Strategies to alleviate leaders' stress can include implementing collective leadership, reassessing workloads, empowering leaders with more decision-making authority, and prioritizing mental health.[31] Rest also plays an important role in staff well-being. One quantitative study involving thirteen hundred teachers from Christian schools in the USA, Canada, Indonesia, and Paraguay found that teachers who engaged in Sabbath practices experienced lower levels of burnout. This raises the question of how schools can promote Sabbath-keeping through their policies, schedules, and other practices (e.g., like ensuring school events are not scheduled on Sundays, prohibiting tests from being administered on Mondays, limiting email communication over the weekend, etc.).[32] Taken together, these kinds of efforts can help improve educator and student well-being at the same time—reflecting the reality that the well-being of one person within a given school community affects the well-being of others.

---

31. DeWitt, "We Should Be Concerned."
32. Cheng, Lee, and Djita, "Cross-Sectional Analysis."

Implications for School Change

Since the launch of the Flourishing Schools research, qualitative data has been gathered on the ways in which it is impacting practice in Christian schools. School leaders have reported that insights from the research have helped them "to telescope out to the level of culture, to identify what 'matters' the most for improvement, and to make mission-aligned change."[33] This includes using the research to inform or direct strategic planning, accreditation efforts, and professional development. These formal or routinized school change mechanisms are powerful pathways for refocusing a school community on flourishing.

At the same time, educators are using the Flourishing Schools research in more informal ways—for example, as a reflective tool for examining their everyday work. One specific practice, "Walks in the Garden,"[34] is based on the research and has been used by school teams to cultivate a new way of gauging flourishing within their contexts. This practice is anchored in Jesus' proclamation, found in the Gospel of John, that "I am the true vine, and my Father is the gardener . . . every branch that does bear fruit he prunes so that it will be even more fruitful."[35] It involves a team taking "learning walks" through the school to identify places or ways the school is abiding in the "vine" of Jesus, by living out a Christian vision for education; bearing fruit and flourishing well; not yet bearing fruit or showing signs of dormancy; or in need of "pruning" to help the school be more fruitful, by enabling both educators and students to flourish even more.

Like exploring a garden, team members should spend about an hour walking through the school once or twice a month. During these walks, they should look for evidence of flourishing not only in public displays (e.g., chapel sermons) but also in more common places, like student interactions during group work, the layout and flow of the lunchroom, and the engagement of teachers and custodial staff. These walks are not formal observations but rather an invitation to see the school environment from a new perspective—much like a gardener looking slowly, carefully, and purposefully, whether for new shoots of growth, for places to trim or cut back, or for potential threats to the garden's flourishing. Once a rhythm for these learning walks is established, new team members should be invited

---

33. Swaner, Dodds, and Lee, *Leadership for Flourishing Schools*, 31.
34. Swaner and Wolfe, *Flourishing Together*, 256–57.
35. John 15:1–2 (NIV).

to join to provide diverse perspectives. This should include students, who can provide valuable insights that are not always noticeable to adults in schools. After each walk, the team should gather to share observations, identify common themes, and plan how to best cultivate growth in the school both now and in the future.

Although insights from the Flourishing Schools research are being used in both formal and informal ways in Christian schools, it would be a mistake to think of flourishing as just "one more thing" that educators and students need to do. Rather, the five domains of flourishing—*Purpose, Relationships, Learning, Resources,* and *Well-being*—provide a more capacious way of thinking about what it means for students, educators, and schools to thrive together. By engaging reflectively and purposefully with the research, Christian educators can find fresh energy to re-imagine their schools as places where God can enable all to flourish—together.

Questions for Discussion

1. If schools were designed around educational flourishing, what student outcomes might they prioritize? What might that also mean for educators? For school families? For the school community as a whole?
2. How do current educational realities limit holistic learning and growth for students—as well as for educators?
3. When looking at the five domains of flourishing (*Purpose, Relationships, Learning, Resources,* and *Well-being*), which ones are the most challenging for schools today?
4. How might a holistic model of educational flourishing, like the one identified in the Flourishing Schools research, be used in practical ways in schools?
5. What might schools and educators have to stop (versus start) doing, in order to engage with a broader vision for flourishing?

References

Association of Christian Schools International. "Fact Sheet." https://www.acsi.org/docs/default-source/website-publishing/communications/brand/acsi-fact-sheet.pdf?sfvrsn=510cc3c3_6.

Blackburn, Barbara R. "Five Ways to Strengthen Student Resilience." *The Education Digest* 83 (2018) 47–50.

Briggs, Michelle Kielty, et al. "Assessing and Promoting Spiritual Wellness as a Protective Factor in Secondary Schools." *Counseling and Values* 55 (2011) 171–84.

Centers for Disease Control. "Youth Risk Behavior Survey: Data Summary and Trends Report." https://www.cdc.gov/healthyyouth/data/yrbs/pdf/YRBS_Data-Summary-Trends_Report2023_508.pdf.

Cheng, Albert, Matthew H. Lee, and Rian Djita. "A Cross-Sectional Analysis of the Relationship Between Sabbath Practices and US, Canadian, Indonesian, and Paraguayan Teachers' Burnout." *Journal of Religious Health* 62 (2022) 1090–113.

Chenoweth, Karen. "How Do We Get There from Here?" *Educational Leadership* 75 (2015) 16–20.

———. *It's Being Done: Academic Success in Unexpected Schools*. Cambridge, MA: Harvard Educational Publishing Group, 2007.

D'Erizans, Roberto, and Tamatha Bibbo. "Time to Reflect: E-Portfolios and the Development of Growth Mindsets." *Independent School* 74 (2015) 78–85.

DeWitt, Peter. "We Should Be Concerned About the Mental Health of Principals." *Education Week*, Aug. 22, 2020. https://www.edweek.org/leadership/opinion-we-should-be-concerned-about-the-mental-health-of-principals/2020/08.

Dweck, Carol. *Mindset: The New Psychology of Success*. New York: Ballantine, 2007.

Gray, Lucinda, and Laurie Lewis. "Use of Educational Technology for Instruction in Public Schools: 2019–20." National Center for Education Statistics at Institute of Education Sciences, 2021. https://nces.ed.gov/pubs2021/2021017.pdf.

Hess, Frederick. "After COVID-19, Schools Are Spending Big on Social and Emotional Learning. Is That a Problem?" *Forbes*, Sept. 26, 2022. https://www.forbes.com/sites/frederickhess/2022/09/26/after-covid-19-schools-are-spending-big-on-social-and-emotional-learning-is-that-a-problem/?sh=5bc36af6472b.

Keyes, Corey L. M. "The Mental Health Continuum: From Languishing to Flourishing in Life." *Journal of Health and Social Behavior* 43 (2002) 207–22.

Kristjánsson, Kristján. *Flourishing as the Aim of Education: A Neo-Aristotelian View*. London: Routledge, 2020.

Lee, Matthew H., Eric W. Price, and Lynn E. Swaner. "The Flourishing Faith Index: Measuring Biblical Worldview and Spiritual Formation in Christian Schools." *ACSI Blog*, Feb. 12, 2024. https://blog.acsi.org/the-flourishing-faith-index.

Lever, Nancy, Erin Mathis, and Ashley Mayworm. "School Mental Health Is Not Just for Students: Why Teacher and School Staff Wellness Matter." *Report on Emotional and Behavioral Disorders in Youth* 17 (2019) 6–12.

Loe, Rob. *The Relational Teacher*. 2nd ed. Cambridge: The Relational Schools Foundation, 2016.

Murphy, Joseph. *Leading School Improvement: A Framework for Action*. West Palm Beach, FL: Learning Sciences International, 2016.

Reeves, Douglas B. *Reframing Teacher Leadership to Improve Your School*. Alexandria, VA: ASCD, 2008.

———. *Transforming Professional Development into Student Results*. Alexandria, VA: ASCD, 2010.

Reynolds, David, et al. "Educational Effectiveness Research (EER): A State-of-the-Art Review." *School Effectiveness and School Improvement* 25 (2014) 197–230.

Seligman, Martin E. P. *Flourish: A Visionary New Understanding of Happiness and Well-Being.* New York: Free Press, 2011.

Senge, Peter. *The Fifth Discipline: The Art and Practice of the Learning Organization.* New York: Doubleday, 1990.

Senge, Peter, et al. *Schools That Learn: A Fifth Discipline Fieldbook for Educators, Parents, and Everyone Who Cares About Education.* New York: Crown Business, 2012.

Shannon, G. Sue, and Pete Bylsma. *Nine Characteristics of High-Performing Schools.* Olympia, WA: Office of Superintendent of Public Instruction, 2007.

Swaner, Lynn E., Cindy Dodds, and Matthew H. Lee. *Leadership for Flourishing Schools: From Research to Practice.* Colorado Springs: Association of Christian Schools International, 2021.

Swaner, Lynn E., Charlotte A. Marshall, and Sheri A. Tesar. *Flourishing Schools: Research on Christian School Culture and Community.* Colorado Springs: Association of Christian Schools International, 2019.

Swaner, Lynn E., and Andy Wolfe. *Flourishing Together: A Christian Vision for Students, Educators, and Schools.* Grand Rapids, MI: Eerdmans, 2021.

Swaner, Lynn E., et al. *Future Ready: Innovative Missions and Models in Christian Education.* Colorado Springs: Association of Christian Schools International, 2022.

Tomlinson, Carol Ann. "One to Grow On: Growing Capable Kids." *Educational Leadership* 71 (2013) 86–87.

Wenger, Etienne, and Beverly Wenger-Trayner. "Introduction to Communities of Practice." June 2015. https://www.wenger-trayner.com/introduction-to-communities-of-practice/.

CHAPTER THREE
Food for Thought
Faith, Secularity, and Curriculum

D*AVID* I. S*MITH*

I*T IS COMMON FOR* modern societal debates about Christianity and education to focus on the incidence or absence of explicitly religious language, claims, or practices in the context of schooling. Energies cluster around the presence or absence of elements such as prayer, religious instruction, or inculcation of faith-grounded moral stances, and there is a recurring temptation among both detractors and endorsers to treat such elements as somewhat conceptually detached from the remainder of educational practice. Raftery notes the existence of scholarly resistance to finding "anything noteworthy in Church interference in learning."[1] The language of "interference" implies that education is a normatively autonomous and secular sphere within which any detected religious influence will be an improper and alien intrusion, extrinsic to the concerns of education proper. Identifying the interfering agent as the "Church" further suggests intrusion by a rival institution (rather than, say, a matter involving the beliefs of teachers, learners, and curriculum designers

---

1. Raftery, "Religions and the History of Education," 43.

in their function as educators), reinforcing the sense of an incursion of external interests. Where a faith-informed education is advocated, it is common for energies to be focused on whether there is space for prayer in schools, for the Bible in the curriculum, for doctrines of creation in science classes, and so on. Where such emphases become focal, they can function as the flip side of the "interference" picture, implying that the key concern is whether certain Christian beliefs and practices should be admitted into the arena of schooling, an arena that is otherwise mundane unless controversial religious practices are in play. Behind such societal debates lurk implicit or explicit assumptions about what it means for education to be secular, and about how we should think about the mechanisms and outcomes of secularization. If we assume that secularization basically means the subtraction of God-talk and devotional practice from the educational environment, that assumption is likely to reinforce the feeling that, for those who value faith, the key focus should be on whether such talk can be re-added.

In this chapter, I will revisit and extend a subset of some material presented in a previous paper with the goal of illustrating some of the complexity of a Christian interest in curriculum.[2] The earlier paper drew from Charles Taylor's account of secularization to examine some significant changes in language textbooks from two centuries, suggesting that the process of secularization in those texts was about more than whether or how religious language or topics were included. Here I propose to look more closely at how the topic of food is handled in three different language textbooks. With that concrete example in hand, I will then return to the question of what Christian belief might have to do with curriculum and its secularity.

Food and Its Contexts: The *Orbis Pictus*

One useful way of probing at the limits of our own assumptions about how things should work is to visit other times and places with attentiveness not just to differences from our own setting, but to how those differences are motivated. I propose two such visits and then a return to the present. Our first visit will be to the *Orbis Sensualium Pictus* (*World of Sensory Things in Pictures*) by John Amos Comenius, an enormously successful

---

2. Smith, "Language Textbooks and Social Imaginaries."

and influential language textbook first published in 1658.³ Comenius's innovative text, with its array of striking images and wide-ranging bilingual narrative, famously pioneered a shift in school curriculum toward a broad, realistic, and visually enticing exploration of the world.⁴ The book includes significant explicit attention to religion,⁵ but I focus here on another topic, the focus on everyday sustenance contained in a series of thirteen chapters on food and drink.

At the start of this sequence, chapter 45 transitions from the theme of human nature to matters of sustenance and related professions. The opening lines of this new section tell us (in the English/Latin edition) that "the first and most ancient sustenance, were the Fruits of the Earth. Hereupon the first labor of Adam, was the dressing of a garden [*Horti cultura*]."⁶ After description of the protection, nurturing, and beautification of a garden, we shift in the next chapter to farming (*Agricultura*). Amid an enumeration of farming implements, roles, and techniques, the text notes that "Tillage of ground, and keeping cattle, was in old time the care of Kings and Noble-men; at this day only of the meanest sort of people [*infirmae Plebis*]"—the epithet here denotes less unpleasantness than lowliness, weakness, or powerlessness.⁷ Food cultivation is thus introduced in the context of biblical narrative, with Adam as the first harvester, and in its social context, with commentary on decline in the social status of farm laborers.

The next ten chapters interleave two main themes. Some detail more specific sources of basic food and drink: beekeeping and honey production, fishing, fowling, hunting, and viticulture. Other chapters focus on food preparation: grinding corn into flour, baking bread, butchery, cooking, wine making, and beer brewing. In each case, the work of those involved is concretely and concisely described and the workers are depicted in the accompanying images going about their work.

The sequence culminates in a chapter on "a feast" (*convivium*) that focuses on the duties and processes of hospitality during shared meals.⁸ Guided by the accompanying text, our eye travels around the

---

3. Comenius, *Orbis Sensualium Pictus*.
4. Turner, "Visual Realism of Comenius."
5. Spicer, "Religious Representation."
6. Comenius, *Orbis Sensualium Pictus, Facsimile*, 92. All textual quotations here are from the parallel English and Latin text in this edition.
7. Comenius, *Orbis Sensualium Pictus, Facsimile*, 96.
8. Comenius, *Orbis Sensualium Pictus, Facsimile*, 118.

accompanying image in a spiral (figure 1):⁹ a guest is greeted at the door by the host (top right), water is provided for the guest to wash their hands (far right and bottom right), food is presented and served (bottom left), and a toast is drunk to the guests (center). The act of eating comes at the end of the chapter, the final thing mentioned in the text. The ability to enjoy food comes as the culmination of an exploration of the work of those who grew and prepared it and the norms of community and hospitality that frame its sharing. After the feast the next chapter returns us to the wider world to survey other forms of work.

Figure 1. *Convivium*, from *Orbis Sensualium Pictus*

The chapters dealing specifically with food sit within a larger narrative sequence. The book begins with an invitation to wisdom and a chapter about God, then surveys the main kinds of creatures in the world, examines human nature, details a wide range of human callings, and places these in the context of virtue ethics, social relationships, fields of learning, and varieties of religion. This sequence includes attention to moral and natural calamities (warfare, shipwreck, storms, despair), and ends with accountability at the day of judgment and an exhortation to continue seeking wisdom. As the food sequence places food in the context

9. The image used here is from https://commons.wikimedia.org/wiki/File:Orbis Pictus_118.jpg, reproduced from Comenius, *Orbis Sensualium Pictus*.

of work, community, hospitality, and biblical narrative, the overarching sequence in turn places all of these facets of food in the context of a vulnerable, holistic, and accountable quest for a wise life within the social context of seventeenth-century Europe.

Since Comenius wrote extensively on the goals and processes of learning, we can access clear accounts of the concepts and commitments framing this design for learning. Though the *Orbis Pictus* has been celebrated as a significant turn toward realism and the world of things in schooling, its realism is not simply empiricism.[10] Comenius urged that "real things should be looked at individually and in their own context as arranged with divine skill in the fabric of the world, the structure of the human Mind, and the eloquence of the word of God."[11] Each creature is part of a fabric, not an object but a thread woven into relationships to other creatures, to human vocation, and to biblical narrative as a representation of ultimate purpose. In his *Didactica Magna* (*Great Didactic*), Comenius argued that education must address three basic human needs and potentials: our capacity for reason and understanding, our need to cultivate virtues that can properly channel the power we have over the world and over other people, and our need for a proper orienting center, expressed as our need to find delight in the God whose delight we are. These three capacities, he emphasized, are "so intimately joined that no separation among them can be admitted."[12] Human nature is an interwoven whole that becomes chaotic if we try to separate the intellectual, the moral, and the spiritual or if we seek to center ourselves in ourselves or in some other creature.[13] Specific topics in the *Orbis Pictus* are therefore to be understood within an ethical and spiritual as well as a social and empirical context.[14]

Human worth, and therefore eligibility for a human(e) education, is grounded in divine affirmation. Since being worthy of an education and of the full development of one's capacities is grounded in God's dignifying of human nature at the incarnation, worthiness for education is not determined by gender, social class, ethnicity, or ability. Human education is for

---

10. Smith, "It Would Be Good"; Kully, "Order and Things."

11. Comenius, *Panorthosia or Universal Reform*, 49.

12. Comenius, *Didactica Magna*, 4.2. Translations in this article from the *Didactica Magna* are my own, drawn from the Latin edition in Comenius, *Opera Didactica Omnia*.

13. Comenius, *Centrum Securitatis*; Hábl, *On Being Human(e)*.

14. Szórádová, "Contexts and Functions of Music."

every human.[15] The relationship of humans to the world calls for understanding, responsibility, and delight. The things in the world about which we learn and over which we have power are parts of a whole created to be an enticement to love.[16] Education, then, as Comenius warns in the preface to the *Orbis Pictus*, cannot be a simple stocking of the mind or honing of skills, but must be a formation toward wise living: "This will be that *grace* of one's life, *to be wise, to act, to speak.*"[17] Wise living entails actively serving and delighting in God, our neighbor, and other creatures.[18] This, in barest outline, is the story about learning within which the details of agriculture, food preparation, and shared meals are embedded.

Changing Contexts: *The London Vocabulary* and *Kontakte*

For purposes of comparison and contrast I will now more briefly consider two other treatments of food in language textbooks. *The London Vocabulary*, first published in 1711, is a successful Latin textbook from the next century that shows both influence and significant differences from the *Orbis Pictus*.[19] *Kontakte* is a widely used current German textbook that reflects a modern, Western, secularized social imaginary and is closer to what many language teachers today might assume to be normal practice.[20] Placing these two texts alongside the *Orbis Pictus* allows us to see both the effects of shorter-term cultural change on a text of somewhat similar design and the striking differences between then and now.

The London Vocabulary has only one chapter on food, titled "Of Meats and Drinks."[21] Its illustration depicting a feast underway is slightly reminiscent of the feast chapter in the *Orbis Pictus*. More notable, however, are the differences. We no longer find the text narrating the occupations, processes, and social contexts of food. Instead, we see parallel lists in English and Latin of food terms for memorization, mostly nouns. The

---

15. Comenius, *Pampaedia*, 15–16; Dobbie, *Comenius's Pampaedia*, 19–20.
16. Comenius, *Didactica Magna*, 3.3; Smith, "Test of Character."
17. Comenius, *Orbis Sensualium Pictus, Facsimile*, np.
18. Comenius, *Didactica Magna*, 10.8.
19. Greenwood, *London Vocabulary*; Starnes, "London Vocabulary and Its Antecedents."
20. Terrell, Tschirner, and Nikolai, *Kontakte*.
21. Greenwood, *London Vocabulary*, 52.

lists lean toward the eating practices of the wealthy. The accompanying image (figure 2) skips the practices of hospitality and zooms in on the eating and drinking.[22] Judging by their fine clothing, the participants seem wealthier than those at the earlier feast. A servant, with whom no one is making eye contact, offers an extravagant supply of ale. Any reference to farming or farmers, to bees or birds, to the preparation of flour, bread, or meals, to Adam or the duties connected to hospitality is now absent, part of the null curriculum. It seems that food first appears at the end of the servant's arm, and all we need is the ability to name it. Ethical and spiritual contexts of food are not referenced.

XV. Of MEATS and DRINKS.

Figure 2. "Of Meats and Drinks," from *The London Vocabulary*

If we step back to consider the book as a whole, certain aspects of the overall narrative structure echo the *Orbis Pictus*. God is still mentioned, as is church. An array of creatures is followed by attention to human nature, human professions, and society. But the sections on ethics and religion are gone, there is less attention to human vulnerability, and instead of an arc from wisdom and God to the day of judgment, the overall sequence now travels from "Of Things" and "Of the Elements" to closing chapters focused on grammatical categories.

22. This image was captured from hard copy of Greenwood, *London Vocabulary*.

The author of this text, James Greenwood, tells us in his preface that he does not see why learners should learn language items that are not relevant for "immediate use."[23] By this he means not use in the life context of the learner, but use for reading classical texts. He assures us that "care has been taken to let no Word come in here, but what is purely Roman, and has the Authority of some one or more of the Classic Authors."[24] Alongside this classical focus, there are aspects of the book's presentation that seem reflective of its eighteenth-century context. Reality is subjected to taxonomy and objectification as the reader of the text is presented with a great array of "things" to be surveyed and catalogued in a rather distanced, dispassionate manner. The goal is to tidily stock the mind.

Jumping forward to the present, we find that the fifth edition of *Kontakte*, a widely used first-year German textbook, also has a single chapter on food, though much longer than in the previous texts.[25] The food chapter is now titled "Eating and Shopping." The chapter moves through sections on what is eaten at different mealtimes through the day, favorite and healthy foods, regional specialties and changes in typical German foods, kitchen appliances, a short story about an apparent murder in a cafe, food shopping, cooking, and eating at restaurants. Students write recipes and shopping lists, rank kitchen appliances based on price, practice restaurant dialogues, and express a range of preferences. The predominant focus appears to be on the individual buying, cooking, and eating food. Many of the questions provided as prompts for student utterances relate the topic back to individual preferences ("Do you like burgers?") and possessions ("Which appliances do you have?"). A video interlude expands the focus by addressing the trend toward choosing organic food because of health concerns and discussing why organic food is more expensive than regular food. This activity provides the only moment where food is traced back to contexts before its arrival in stores and eateries, though it is anchored in the concerns of the consumer (healthy choices, concerns about price). While the video and literary material expand the scope somewhat beyond immediate practical concerns to touch on ethics, the learner is most frequently

---

23. Greenwood, *London Vocabulary*, iii.

24. Greenwood, *London Vocabulary*, iv–v.

25. Terrell, Tschirner, and Nikolai, *Kontakte*, 270–310. The fifth edition is not the most recent edition but is the edition that I have used in class and with which I am most familiar. My intent here is not to offer an evaluation of the most recent version of *Kontakte*, but simply to outline the emphases apparent in a sample language textbook from recent years.

addressed and invited to participate as a consumer focused on personal choices and ease of access to desired foods. There is no sign that spiritual concerns are taken to be a relevant context for considering food.

How does this treatment of eating and shopping sit within the larger scope of *Kontakte*? The preface announces the intention to provide "natural contexts within which students can acquire and practice language" in a way that should "reflect real world language use."[26] Like both the *Orbis Pictus* and *The London Vocabulary*, then, *Kontakte* claims that its choice and arrangement of material is driven by relevance, by what students need for the most pertinent demands of real life. What is conceived of as real life here is marked by an emphasis on a range of self-expressive and transactional uses of language that might enable learners to share basic personal information and preferences, access various services, and gain awareness of some orienting cultural context. The consumerist bent of the materials is at times quite explicit. In the second full chapter, headed "Besitz und Vergnügen" ("Possessions and Pleasures"), the instructor is informed that the focus will be on "the [students'] immediate environment outside the class: things they have, things they would like to have, and what they like to do."[27] The natural world and the social world outside of immediate transactions and close personal relationships are notable for their near absence. The student's environment is configured around the individual self and imagined largely in terms of the potential for consumption and amusement.

Relevance, Selection, and Subtraction

None of these texts are aimed directly at religious education, Bible curriculum, or devotional practice; they are designed for second language learning. Beyond this basic shared purpose, care should be taken in drawing too close an equivalence between them. The significance of Latin in the school curriculum has already changed between the *Orbis Pictus* and *The London Vocabulary*, reflecting its gradually shifting status away from being an active mode of communication in Europe. The *Orbis Pictus* is not only teaching languages but also serving as a general elementary text on a range of topics, providing a content-based approach to language learning. *The London Vocabulary* is more

---

26. Terrell, Tschirner, and Nikolai, *Kontakte*, xi–xii.
27. Terrell, Tschirner, and Nikolai, *Kontakte*, 79.

specialized. *Kontakte* is written for undergraduate students with a great deal of schooling already behind them. Each of the three texts reflects details of its historical, social, and cultural context. It will be apparent that the cursory summaries provided above do not amount to systematic evaluations of any of these three texts, and I am not claiming that they are precise equivalents to each other. All that I have sought to do here is to draw attention to some significant emphases and differences. I have selected features for discussion based on their relevance to my initial question about what Christian belief might have to do with curriculum and its secularity. It is time to turn back to that framing question.

It is striking that all three of these texts claim that their design has been driven by attention to real-world relevance and the most pressing needs of students. Yet comparing them soon raises further questions: Which real world? Which aspects of reality are selected and omitted? What narrative frame, social imaginary, and developmental vision are in view? The need to develop a practical wisdom infused by ethics and oriented around a proper spiritual center, the need to meet the learning demands of a classical curriculum, and the need for pragmatic transactional skills and basic cultural referents to aid navigation of a foreign context during travel are all part of the "real world." Reality offers too many possible foci of attention to fit into a single text. Appeals to reality and relevance tend to rhetorically veil the act of selection. The claim to real-world relevance, in these cases as in others (such as the common present-day move of suggesting that economic reality is the "real world" for which students most need preparation), is really a proposal that we prioritize certain aspects of human experience as the most deserving of our attention. Such claims and proposals are grounded in implicit visions of what is good and how we should grow through learning. This opens the possibility that the differences between the three texts are not reducible simply to differences in historical and social context, but also intersect with more enduring questions of meaning.

If we are interested in how Christianity intersects with curriculum and construe this in terms of mention of religion, the most obvious point of contrast seems to be how each textbook directly intersects with religious discourse and practices. The *Orbis Pictus* follows an introductory invitation to wisdom with a chapter on God and mirrors this with a closing chapter on divine judgment. There are other chapters that address Christian theology and virtues. Within the food chapters, the sequence begins by drawing us back to Adam's responsibility for the garden in

Genesis. *The London Vocabulary* still mentions and depicts God in the opening chapter and has a chapter on church matters later in the book. Yet the opening chapter is titled "Of Things," and God is included partway through a long list of nouns naming the basic "things" in the world, a configuration that is in significant tension with the Christian theological assertion that God is not a thing or item among other things in the world but transcends created reality.[28] At the end of the book, the chapter on final judgment has been replaced by grammar. In *Kontakte*, religion is barely mentioned. Reference to God occurs only in stock phrases such as "thank God!" The narrative sequence begins with the self and its possessions and ends with "Modern Society." If we are so inclined, we can trace a version of secularization based on the gradual sidelining and eventual removal of direct treatment of God and biblical narrative in these language texts. Resting there, however, would be premature.

Here it is helpful to turn to Charles Taylor's account of the gradual changes in the social and cosmic imaginary that guided the secularization of Western culture during the course of modern European history.[29] An important framing idea in Taylor's account of secularization is his resistance to what he calls "subtraction stories." He explains:

> I mean by this stories of modernity in general, and secularity in particular, which explain them by human beings having lost, or sloughed off, or liberated themselves from certain earlier, confining horizons, or illusions, or limitations of knowledge. What emerges from this process—modernity or secularity—is to be understood in terms of underlying features of human nature which were there all along, but had been impeded by what is now set aside.[30]

A subtraction story about secularization, then, is one that imagines religious practices as a distinct, superimposed layer resting upon a more basic empirical substrate. Strip that layer away—stop talking about God, say, or stop appealing to a "supernatural" reality—and what is left over is the real world beneath the stories, "natural" reality. If we approach educational history as a subtraction story, we will look primarily for when and how educational materials stopped mentioning God, prayer, or Scripture, with the underlying assumption that the processes of

---

28. Greenwood, *London Vocabulary*, 3; Begbie, *Abundantly More*, 126–31.
29. Taylor, *Secular Age*.
30. Taylor, *Secular Age*, 22.

learning languages, history, or math are a separate layer that progresses independently. When talk of God fades away, curriculum content remains, and we still need to learn food vocabulary.

Taylor argues persuasively that subtraction stories about Western secularization are inadequate to account for what happened. Indeed, they illegitimately privilege modern, naturalistic accounts by structuring into the story the idea that such accounts are simply what is left over once illusions have been stripped away. Modern secularism is offered as simply what the world looks like once the trappings have been removed. Taylor continues:

> Against this kind of story, I will steadily be arguing that Western modernity, including its secularity, is the fruit of new inventions, newly constructed self-understandings and related practices, and can't be explained in terms of perennial features of human life.[31]

What actually happened, Taylor argues, was a gradual reframing of how we imagine humans, their place in the world, the nature of reality, society, and a host of other things. The new self-understandings are also constructed ways of seeing. Rather than a simple subtraction, there was a gradual change in the social and cosmic imaginary that involved constructing new accounts of reality that made it possible to imagine the world without God and to imagine that as the world's natural state.

If we imagine secularization in education as a subtraction story and entertain the desire, perhaps from Christian motives, to resist secularization in the name of the continued relevance of faith, then we are likely to imagine resistance as an addition story. We need to add prayer back into schools, Bible verses to curriculum, religious examples to teaching materials, and so on. Those might or might not be good things to do, considered on their own terms. The point here is not to dismiss such practices, but to note what they miss. They miss the ways in which our way of teaching about (for instance) food has not sat inert while religious language has been subtracted. Our self-understanding in relationship to food has shifted, and that is reflected in (for instance) language curriculum.

---

31. Taylor, *Secular Age*, 22.

Curriculum and Meaning

Each curricular text described above projects a particular way of imagining the needs and context of the learner and invites the learner to inhabit that projected self-image. The *Orbis Pictus* imagines a self that is living within an ordered, created cosmos that has an ethical trajectory. Provision of food is tied to a range of human callings that are varied responses to a divine call to responsible human action in the world. Our ability to eat depends on the skills and labor of a wide range of people, people who may at various times be ennobled or demeaned by society's construal of their work, and there is an immediate experiential link between the circumstances of production and consumption. The purpose of food preparation is not merely individual consumption, but hospitality and service. *The London Vocabulary* imagines a more detached self, a dispassionate observer surrounded by an array of things and concerned to know their names but not invited into any relationship of direct responsibility for them. This self has little need to attend to the lifeworld of those who labor to grow and prepare food, or to norms of hospitality and ways of enacting them. This self seeks to gain vocabulary for academic advancement and assumes a life of plentiful provision. The self as imagined by *Kontakte* is strongly interested in talking about itself, expressing and exercising preferences, and obtaining goods and services. Food production happens largely off-stage unless it impacts consumer choices. Language is a means to individual self-expression and consumption, and food collocates most naturally with eating and shopping.[32]

We can bring these choices into focus by both expanding and narrowing the lens. Moving in the direction of expansion, we might ask ourselves what range of possible connections could in principle frame the topic of food in a learning context. With what is food connected? An exhaustive list is hardly feasible, but our list could include, for instance, shared family time, nutrition, labor practices, immigration, deforestation, farming, festivals, prayer, consumerism, gender, symbolism, marketing, enjoyment, aesthetics, health, eating disorders, weddings, funerals, fasting, time (fast and slow food), food deserts, protest, treatment of animals, poverty, inequality, gardening, community gardens, profit motives, fair trade, pollution, gluttony, self-control, ethnicity, art, status symbols, the Eucharist, food waste, careers, sustainability, food banks, charity, and much more. It is very far from obvious that invoking real-world relevance

---

32. Cf. Sandlin and McLaren, *Critical Pedagogies of Consumption*.

means that food naturally goes with supermarkets and recipes, unless we have decided ahead of time that our experience as individual consumers is the most real and relevant part of our environment.

Narrowing the focus, we might ask ourselves what ways of imagining food might nest fittingly within a Christian account of the world and our place in it. What if we live in a richly diverse creation, with "God fully present in love to each and every particular,"[33] in which we are called to responsible action and grateful delight but also driven by fallen appetites, fears, and hostilities, and in which our trajectory should be framed by love of God and neighbor and modeled on Christ's hospitality? How might we then want to frame an educational conversation about food that also responds to the complexity of our own social environment? Without suggesting that any of the textbooks briefly considered here is the perfect text, or that we can simply retrieve texts from past contexts and paste them into our own, it is still meaningful to ask which of the texts surveyed seem closer to or further from key Christian hopes, and this question does not reduce to whether there was a chapter about God. Once we ask the question this way it quickly becomes apparent that if we were to add Bible verses and references to prayer into *Kontakte*'s narrative of individual preference and consumption, that might not render it Christian or reverse its secularization. If we extend such questions to each other aspect of reality dealt with in the school curriculum, the field of potential interplay between Christian convictions and curriculum becomes much broader than the question of whether religion is given a spot or whether the church is interfering in school.

Yet this field of interplay does not place Christians outside the cultural fray as a kind of external force seeking intrusion into education proper. Christians are implicated in historical shifts in our relationship to food and its production and consumption. Christianity as an intellectual, ethical, and practical tradition also contains resources for thinking about the meaning and place of food in ways that reach beyond the immediate context and quest for ways of relating to food that resonate with God's action in the world.[34] Yet the individualist, consumerist world invoked by *Kontakte* is the normal, accepted world for many if not most Christians in the North American social context that it addresses and may not seem alien or objectionable to Christian learners. The social

---

33. Begbie, *Abundantly More*, 176.
34. Volf, "Theology for a Way of Life."

worlds evoked by the other two texts no doubt also made intuitive sense to Christians living in those historical contexts. Thinking about food differently and rooting that thought in responsible, shalom-fostering practices requires a contextually sensitive effort of imagination and inquiry, not simply the application of pre-existing, ahistorical Christian worldview categories. Such an effort requires a sufficiently broad-based literacy in Christian sources of reflection to suggest the possibility of alternatives to default cultural assumptions. It also requires attentiveness to critiques of our present relationship to food that emerge from non-Christian sources. Christians do not think, speak, or eat in a place outside history. The practice of education is likewise embedded in a changing social imaginary, so that what looks like a normal, sensible way to teach about food in the language classroom shifts over time as both the social experience of food and societal values and self-narratives change. These changes are not merely technological; they are also ideological. Christians, educators, and those in both categories must reflect on the hoped-for meanings of curriculum from within these shifts while making articulate the meaning frameworks guiding their choices. Questions of faith are thus implicit in the act of designing curriculum and addressing teaching to an implied learning self.

Faith does not poke its head in from outside the educational building, nor does it manifest solely in religious moments, nor does it provide a single acceptable way to do curriculum. It does, however, create a basis from which to enter into discussion about the meanings projected by how we teach and reinforced by curricular inclusions, omissions, and narrative biases. Discussions of the place of prayer or religious education remain, of course, important, but too much is conceded if these discussions are thought of as ways of avoiding the subtraction of faith from an otherwise empirical curriculum. The secularization of the curriculum is a process of transformed narrative and self-understanding, not a subtraction story. Christian engagement with the curriculum, therefore, requires more than addition.

Questions for Discussion

1. Do you typically think of mundane topics such as those related to food as part of the relationship between faith and teaching? Why or why not?

2. Comenius argued that human nature is violated if we try to separate the intellectual, the moral, and the spiritual. In what ways are these separated or held together in your classroom or your school?

3. Which of the three learning resources discussed most closely reflects your own unconscious, everyday assumptions about how food fits into the world? Which of the three is closest to your conscious theological beliefs?

4. When you talk about the "real world," what aspects of reality do you tend to have in mind? What aspects are you missing?

5. Why is it not enough to look for whether God is mentioned in curriculum if we want to understand the secularization of education or what faith might contribute?

References

Begbie, Jeremy S. *Abundantly More: The Theological Promise of the Arts in a Reductionist World*. Grand Rapids, MI: Baker Academic, 2023.
Comenius, John Amos. *Centrum Securitatis*. Heidelberg: Quelle & Meyer, 1964.
———. *Opera Didactica Omnia*. 1657. Prague: Academia Scientiarum Bohemoslovenica, 1957.
———. *Orbis Sensualium Pictus*. Nuremberg: Michael Endter, 1658.
———. *Orbis Sensualium Pictus. Facsimile of the Third London Edition 1672*. Sydney: Sydney University Press, 1967.
———. *Pampaedia: Lateinischer Text und deutsche Übersetzung*. Edited by Dmitrij Tschižewskij, Heinrich Geissler, and Klaus Schaller. Heidelberg: Quelle & Meyer, 1960.
———. *Panorthosia or Universal Reform, Chapters 19–26*. Translated by A. M. O. Dobbie. Sheffield: Sheffield Academic Press, 1993.
Dobbie, A. M. O., trans. *Comenius's Pampaedia*. Dover: Buckland, 1986.
Greenwood, James. *The London Vocabulary, English and Latin*. 21st ed. London: A. Bettesworth, 1797.
Hábl, Jan. *On Being Human(e): Comenius' Pedagogical Humanization as an Anthropological Problem*. Eugene, OR: Pickwick, 2017.
Kully, Deborah. "Order and Things: Comenius's '*Orbis Pictus*' and Baroque Representation." *Thresholds* (2005) 87–99. http://www.jstor.org/stable/43876209.
Raftery, Deirdre. "Religions and the History of Education: A Historiography." *History of Education* 41 (2012) 41–56. https://doi.org/10.1080/0046760X.2011.640355.
Sandlin, Jennifer A., and Peter McLaren, eds. *Critical Pedagogies of Consumption: Living and Learning in the Shadow of the "Shopocalypse."* New York: Routledge, 2010.
Smith, David I. "It Would Be Good to Have a Paradise: Comenius on Learners Past and Present." In *The Restoration of Human Affairs: Utopianism or Realism?*, edited by Jan Hábl, 29–44. Eugene, OR: Wipf & Stock, 2022.

———. "Language Textbooks and Social Imaginaries: Secularization in the *Orbis Pictus* and *The London Vocabulary*." *Journal of Christianity and World Languages* 21 (2020) 73–95.

———. "A Test of Character and an Enticement to Love: Comenius on Educating for Human Responsibility Toward Other Creatures." In *Environmental Education: An Interdisciplinary Approach to Nature*, edited by Matthew Etherington, 28–40. Eugene, OR: Wipf & Stock, 2023.

Spicer, Andrew. "Religious Representation in Comenius's *Orbis Sensualium Pictus* (1658)." *Reformation and Renaissance Review* 21 (2019) 64–88. https://doi.org/10.1080/14622459.2019.1568373.

Starnes, DeWitt Talmage. "*The London Vocabulary* and Its Antecedents." *Studies in English* [19] (1939) 114–38. http://www.jstor.org/stable/20779512.

Szórádová, Eva. "Contexts and Functions of Music in the *Orbis Sensualium Pictus* Textbook by John Amos Comenius." *Paedagogica Historica* 51 (2015) 535–59. http://dx.doi.org/10.1080/00309230.2015.1051551.

Taylor, Charles. *A Secular Age*. Cambridge, MA: Belknap, 2007.

Terrell, Tracy D., Erwin Tschirner, and Brigitte Nikolai. *Kontakte: A Communicative Approach, Instructor's Edition*. 5th ed. New York: McGraw Hill, 2004.

Turner, James. "The Visual Realism of Comenius." *History of Education* 1 (1972) 113–38. https://doi.org/10.1080/0046760720010201.

Volf, Miroslav. "Theology for a Way of Life." In *Practicing Theology: Beliefs and Practices in Christian Life*, edited by Miroslav Volf and Dorothy C. Bass, 245–63. Grand Rapids, MI: Eerdmans, 2002.

CHAPTER FOUR
Strangers in the Classroom

Stephen J. Fyson

A FEW TEACHERS WERE sitting in the faculty room, taking time to debrief about the different lessons from which they had just returned. One teacher lamented: "I don't think I am too old to teach. But after lessons like that, I do wonder." His friend seemed to understand the thought: "I know what you mean. I don't recognize who they are anymore."

"What? They are the same kinds of kids we've always had, aren't they?"

"No, they are not—well, in some ways yes, but in other ways, something significant has changed."

"What? What has changed that much to make them strangers to you?"

"What is important for these students seems so far away from what I think—what I know—that counts. I try to bridge the gap, but it seems like I am from another planet...."

The friend considered this, and again offered to find a way through the uncertainty: "But isn't that what happens in each generation? The young believe they have all the answers, and the older ones—that is us now—think that the young are simply dreamers. It's just life."

"No, it's more than that. I can't quite put it into words. But is seems the current young generation simply understand life in so many different ways. It's just so confusing."

They sipped on their coffee quietly, thinking about what to do for the next class.

What Has Shifted?

The patterns of everyday life can be described in many ways. These patterns are built on what we believe to be good and true to do. A key aspect of these basic assumptions about life is how we understand our basic nature—that is, "who are we as human beings?"

For example, if we believe that we are but animals with bigger and more clever brains, then is our good simply like the rest of the animal kingdom? What would that look like in how we lived? It would be the equivalent to the biblical saying, "Let us eat and drink, for tomorrow we die" (1 Cor 15:32).[1]

The apostle Paul described this view of life in contrast to the hope that is based in the resurrection of Jesus Christ. He was honestly admitting that if this is not true—that if Christ did not rise from the dead—then we have no *Christian* basis for hope. Instead, our best lot would be to enjoy what we can while we can, now.

This contrast is perhaps an apt example for understanding what Christian teachers might consider as the "strange" views of life that they can see in their classrooms in their Christian schools. The "strangeness" comes from recognizing that their Christian habits of mind may be different from what is now commonly expressed in the patterns of thinking evident in their students—particularly with reference to who we are as humans and what is good for us.

In the rest of this chapter, we will examine some theorists who have given us some hints on how to understand these "strangers in our classrooms."

Among the Pagans

How much do our current social norms coincide with ancient patterns? An author who helps us to understand this relationship between the past

1. Scripture quotations in this essay are from ESV.

and now is Steven D. Smith, who is the distinguished professor of law at the University of San Diego. In his 2018 work,[2] Smith explains that the times in which Jesus of Nazareth found himself, outside of his Jewish community, were of a particular sort of paganism. There were many sociocultural religious practices, but these traditions revolved around what he termed an *immanent* heart. In this worldview, the search for meaning, which was ultimately religious, was focused on this physical world and making the most of our time here (like "eat and drink and be merry"). This contrasted with the *transcendent* heart of the Christianity that emerged from the first to fourth centuries. This worldview was focused on the one true Creator God, and the reconciliation in Jesus Christ, that made a difference now because it was focused on eternity with him.

Smith explores whether this contrast is again being demonstrated in the previously Judeo-Christian West. He suggests that in the last sixty years, there has been a shift from the former more explicit transcendental framework in understanding who we are as people, to a more immanent understanding that is reflective of more ancient times.

"But," some may say, "people currently do not believe in anything sacred. Isn't that the difference today?" Smith carefully explains why he suspects this is not the case. He quotes Rabbi Sacks to explain that all human beings are meaning seekers, and this is what inevitably leads people to be religious—to respond to a call that is "outside us, a vocation, a mission."[3] Smith goes on to describe how modern people, while claiming a non-religious stance to life, still retain "a large stock of camouflaged myths and degenerated rituals."[4] He explains that these myths and rituals are paganism by other names.

What Might This Look Like in the Classroom?

Regarding our question of the reasons for what seems to be "strangers in our classrooms," Smith's basic framework may help us understand what Christian teaches and what these kinds of "pagan students" have in common and what is different. Firstly, what might seem to be utter rejection or ignorance of God and Christ may not be as irreligious as it looks. All humans have a "God shaped hole," and as Augustine noted,

---

2. Smith, *Pagans and Christians in the City*.
3. Smith, *Pagans and Christians in the City*, 28.
4. Smith, *Pagans and Christians in the City*, 44.

this restlessness of the soul only finds peace in God.[5] Perhaps, like the Christians of old, our work is to discern the heart of our pupils and to find a way to speak into that—and a good starting point is recognizing the "religious" nature of their world.

Some Possible Strategies

Perhaps we teachers should consider these kinds of questions as we prepare what to teach and how to teach it: What do our students find sacred? In other words, where are the baseline assumptions that give meaning to their lives? On what basis do they determine right and wrong, and how do they decide what is more valuable in their daily lives?

Nor should we assume that any of our young habits of mind will be the same. For example, while Smith notes that modern paganism lacks the more communal elements of the counter-cultural Christianity of the fourth century, he also noted three variants of paganism: Pagan secular, Christian secular, and positivistic secular.[6] We will review each of these in the next sections through the eyes of other authors.

Reality as Secular

It can be unusual to find someone who was publicly fixed on one way of thinking but then also became public about their change of mind and heart. Professor Mary Poplin is one such person. She is a fully tenured professor of education in the USA and was an avowed atheistic feminist. In that role, she went to India: "I went on sabbatical to Calcutta to find out what she [Mother Teresa] meant when she said, 'Our work is not social work; it is religious work.'"[7]

She found out, and wrote a book that asked the question *Is Reality Secular?* She observed that the public institutions like government-run colleges and universities were often avowedly atheistic, but underneath, spirituality of some kind often lurked. She gave her circle of friends as an example: "I was a material naturalist and secular humanist by day

---

5. Augustine, *Confessions*, 204.
6. Smith, *Pagans and Christians in the City*, 251.
7. Poplin, *Is Reality Secular?*, 24.

and a pantheist by night"[8] (and we will have a closer look at pantheism in the next section).

Poplin then outlined what she believes are the current main ways of viewing meaning for humans. Her first two descriptions are of types of atheism—they have no need for God (material naturalism and secular humanism). All of life is supposedly explained by physical matter plus time plus chance. Poplin[9] and others[10] have mapped how this has come to ascendency in Western thought.

What difference might such a dominance make for us in the classroom? C. S. Lewis, following on from others such as G. K. Chesterton[11] and A. J. Balfour,[12] wrote *The Abolition of Man*[13] to warn what new creatures might appear in front of us if the inherent relativism of secularism, or humanism, took hold within education.[14] Lewis noted that ideas of life that exclude a Creator are left with no coherent means of deciding what is ethically right and wrong in terms of how to live morally as human beings.

He, like Balfour before him, used the metaphor of pruning a tree. However, the branch on which one is sitting is the one being cut off. The result is that while opining that a good job is being done, the result is that like the branch, we fall down.

What Might This Look Like in the Classroom?

When we hear "my truth, your truth" as a reason for the decisions our young people have made, it reflects this relativistic dynamic. As Alan Noble has noted, this rhetoric is given under the pretence of being free from a transcendent being, but in fact, it is an exhaustingly impossible way to live.[15] The well-recognized Jeremy Adams summarized the conundrum that this brings to our children and young people as students: "Do

---

8. Poplin, *Is Reality Secular?*, 22.
9. Poplin, *Is Reality Secular?*, chs. 3 and 4.
10. For example, Moreland, *Scientism and Secularism*; and much earlier, Packer, *Knowing Man*.
11. Chesterton, *What's Wrong with the World*.
12. Balfour, *Theism and Humanism*.
13. Lewis, *Abolition of Man*.
14. Lewis and Chesterton both had this concern as a reoccurring theme in their writings, as have many from their generation, and since then.
15. Noble, *You Are Not Your Own*.

they see themselves as random specks of cosmic dust or as purposeful children of a loving and Almighty God?"[16]

If they wish to proclaim the freedom to be "specks of dust," then it is no wonder that they may seem different to those who have grown up in the context of believing that we humans are made in the image of God for a good purpose.[17] It is also therefore not surprising (although still disappointing) that these same pupils can on one hand be very demanding of their rights, but equally as fragile in being challenged to think differently or to work harder.[18]

Such a disposition has led to what has been called an "emotivist" environment,[19] where what we *feel* is the most central tenet for how we decide what is right and wrong. That way of approaching relationships is of course not easy in the classroom environment, where we are to be guides to truth that invite learners to accept what is good.

How might we respond to these competing assumptions about what is right and wrong? Noble explains this conundrum well, and perhaps his understanding can give us some direction in how to present the difficulties of relativism to our students:

> We are not free to pursue whatever brings us the most personal fulfilment. We are not free to define our identity in any way we wish. We are not free to use people or creation as tools for our own ends. We are limited. But it is in embracing and respecting these limits that we testify to our belonging to God and oppose the false promise of Self-Belonging. Rejecting the Responsibilities of Self-Belonging that so onerously burden us actually frees us to desire the good of others.[20]

Syncretism in the West

The term of "Christian paganism" used by Steven D. Smith might at first sound like an oxymoron.

How can one be a Christian and also a pagan? Yet there is some evidence that this is happening both in our Western society at large and even within Christian churches (and schools).

16. Adams, *Hollowed Out*.
17. Gen 1:26–27; Eph 2:8–10.
18. This is well explained in Lukianoff and Haidt, *Coddling of the American Mind*.
19. MacIntyre, *After Virtue*.
20. Noble, *You Are Not Your Own*, 181.

Part of Smith's work as a lawyer has been to describe that attempts to be "pagan secular" in our current Western context do not work very well. He outlines, similarly to Lewis, that systems of moral order collapse without a frame of reference that is greater than any individual or social group. However, the contemporary West (in his context, the USA) does not want to acknowledge the transcendent aspects of reality. The solution, according to Smith, is "smuggling."[21] The legal system holds onto tenets based on a Judeo-Christian metaphysic, but without admitting from where these ideas come.

Two social historians came to the same conclusion about other aspects of life which we hold as central to how we live together (including in our classrooms). Larry Siedentop's *Inventing the Individual* explains that ancient societies were not made up of a collection of individuals. As he described it, "Gods and groups marched hand in hand."[22] As an extension of this structure, Siedentop observed that inequality was the social norm. That is, in ancient cities, ancient tribes, and even into the Enlightenment, people were given a "category" that determined their level of worth. One of the implications was that the concept of people's capacity for rationality was determined by their social category.

Siedentop describes what changed—in summary, it was the radical message of the Jews that started the shift. Their law applied to everyone in the same way, which has become our basis of accepting equality before the law. The next counter-cultural moment was the life and ongoing influence of Jesus of Nazareth. In Siedentop's words, Jesus' crucifixion "provided the individual with a foothold in reality."[23] And the apostle Paul, in his letters, demonstrated how this reality could be applied in living together. Paul was consistent in his teaching that our response to this invitation to enact human agency toward love of God and others was individual—it was not by category or social label. Again, in Siedentop's words, "Paul's message is directed not merely to Jews, but to all humanity."[24]

Such a radical re-conceptualization of personhood was also described by Tom Holland in his *Dominion: The Making of the Western Mind*. He summarizes his journey in the introduction to the book: "Assumptions that I had grown up with—about how a society should properly be organised, and the principles that it should uphold—were not bred

21. Smith, *Disenchantment of Secular Discourse*, 26–27.
22. Siedentop, *Inventing the Individual*, 21.
23. Siedentop, *Inventing the Individual*, 58.
24. Siedentop, *Inventing the Individual*, 60.

of classical antiquity, still less of 'human nature,' but very distinctively of that civilisation's Christian past."[25]

Such research demonstrates that our treasured ideas about universal respect for each individual find their foundations in Moses, Jesus, and Paul. Moses introduced the idea. Jesus fulfilled the processes for reconciliation back into our relationship with God and others. And Paul explained what it looks like in the life of those "in Christ."

And now we expect such respect in our classrooms—it is even part of the Australian Professional Standards for Teachers (standard 4). However, there is no clear articulation of the basis for this belief. There appears to be, as Steven D. Smith noted, "smuggling."

This use of Christian ideas outside of the biblical understanding of faith has been described by Christian Smith. He (with others) has explored what he terms as the "true, functional, de facto religion of the vast majority of American teenagers: Moralistic, Therapeutic Deism (MTD)."[26] MTD can be summarized as believing that God is a mixture of a divine butler and therapist. He is there when we need him to help us physically or emotionally.[27]

However, it seems that when families and churches are faithful to their calling, as described by researchers such as Holland and Siedentop, there are apparently constructive results for our classrooms. Ilana Horwitz calls these "abiding" families—they believe and proactively belong to their faith commitments in their home and church.[28]

What Might This Look Like in the Classroom?

If you are a Christian teacher in a Christian school, then having "abiders" in your room will seem natural and, at many times, enjoyable. But what of those students who say they are "Christian" but believe in MTD? Or what if they are "cultural Christians," wanting to smuggle Christian ideas into their thinking, while pretending Christianity has nothing to do with what they believe?

25. Holland, *Dominion*, xxix.
26. Smith, Ritz, and Rotolo, *Religious Parenting*, 266.
27. McIntyre was referred to previously with reference to being in an emotivist social context in the West. The concept of the West becoming "therapeutic" was outlined by Reiff, *Triumph of the Therapeutic*.
28. Horwitz, *God, Grades and Graduation*.

Such varieties of understandings within the label "Christian" can indeed seem strange. And it is if we consider this as a unique time in history. The common mind of Western society was openly indebted to the Judeo-Christian worldview in times not too distant from today. While such thinking is burgeoning in the non-Western world, it is in apparent decline (publicly at least) in the West.[29]

What kind of teaching may be constructive to help our students consider their assumptions about what is good? Perhaps it is giving material that begs the question of "what is good and true for this situation?" For younger students, it may be celebrating that the Creator God has taught us what is good—doing justice, and loving mercy, before God.[30] We can even establish routines and expectations around this theme of doing what is right while helping others, as an act of service to God. All of these ideas focus on testing out the internal coherence of not only *what* is good, but *why*—and this includes why we should help others.

However, Christian paganism has a direct competitor beyond the simple pagan secular and confused Christian secular—it is the positivistic secular mindset that is sometimes called scientism.

Scientism

My son sometimes reminds me that I am closer to seventy than sixty. However you express it, I can remember when my primary (elementary) state-run education was openly accepting and appreciative of Christianity. We had Easter and Christmas displays at the appropriate seasons—more than that, we read and marveled at the actual Bible stories of Easter and Christmas.

By the time I went to secondary school, the debate was whether the Bible was compatible with science. The focus of this debate was how the universe began—was it spoken into being by a Creator, or by some evolutionary process that was purely physical? Much has been written on this topic in the ensuing decades.[31]

One philosopher who has sought to regularly critique the nature and implications of believing that life is only explained by physical matter

---

29. Stark, *Triumph of Faith*.
30. Mic 6:8.
31. Lennox's *Seven Days that Divided the World* is recommended reading from more recent literature.

in time and develops by chance is J. P. Moreland. His latest book on the topic explains the difference between science and scientism, and the implications of when the latter is confused with the former.[32]

Moreland describes some implications if science is replaced with scientism, where "scientism" is defined as "roughly the view that the hard sciences alone have the intellectual authority to give us knowledge of reality."[33] Such a view means that logic, philosophy, and theology are treated as personal preferences rather than as tools in the search for truth.

Scientism only succeeds if we ignore the realities of how we think as human beings. We are embodied souls, and this is demonstrated through our self-consciousness. This aspect of life—which falls within the category of "unseen aspects of reality"—cannot be explained by any materialistic descriptions of life.[34]

This issue is of no small import. As Moreland explains, if it is true, then our spiritual basis for morality becomes redundant. The need for Jesus' sacrifice and resurrection is unnecessary. The Bible becomes at most an interesting historical document, and Christians are to be pitied more than anyone else (to use the language of the apostle Paul[35]).

What Might This Look Like in the Classroom?

If a pupil and/or their family takes scientism seriously, they are likely to have very different morals and beliefs about what is true, what is good, and what freedoms they should be allowed.

What frame of reference becomes most central in this frame of thinking? It is the emotivist self, as noted in the sections above. Therefore, for such a person, how they *feel* is most important. That means that even asking an uncomfortable question can be seen as an aggressive act. Acting in this manner also means you are a bad person. And it also means that you probably fall into one of the categories of people who are defined, by their immutable characteristics, as oppressive—all regardless of your actual character and patterns of behavior.

---

32. Moreland, *Scientism and Secularism*.
33. Moreland, *Scientism and Secularism*, 23.
34. For example, see Swinburne, *Mind, Brain and Free Will*; and Dirckx, *Am I Just My Brain?*
35. 1 Cor 15:17–19.

Without a doubt, such thinking in our classrooms can usher in a strange new world. Carl Trueman summarizes these shifts in ideas about who we are as:[36]

- the transition from us being understood as an embodied soul, or person, to focusing on being a therapeutized self;
- that this new focus then results in assessment of ourselves moving from being about being of good character to being a fulfilled sexualized self; and then,
- this sexualized self, instead of being committed to the common good, becomes politicized toward more self-interest as a member of an identity group.

Each of the summary points above can potentially have an impact on *what* we teach and *how* we are expected to teach. This includes the *choice of content* and the *relational norms* that are to be reflected in our exchanges with our pupils. The debate in both areas is as contested as ever.

Part of the contest is very public. In 2014, the then prime minister asked two education professors to review the Australian National Curriculum. Drs. Wiltshire and Donnelly wrote a report[37] that outlined what had been achieved in introducing a national curriculum, but also explained two concerns:

a. That the emphasis in the "outcomes" approach to national curriculum was too focused on experiences and processes, and not on sequential core content; and

b. That there has been a progressive loss of understanding and appreciation of the Judeo-Christian heritage of our Western society.

The second point helps to educationally contextualize why the shift to individualistically emotivist orientation has filtered through to educational institutions and sectors. When a society forgets from whence their morals have been derived, newer ideas can more easily be accepted. This forgetfulness includes losing an external frame of reference for character and morality and replacing it with personal feelings as a platform for deciding right and wrong.

---

36. For a fuller description, see Trueman, *Rise and Triumph of the Modern Self.*
37. Wiltshire and Donnelly, *Final Report into the National Curriculum.*

An Australian case study of this dynamic has been described by Fiona Mueller, who claims that instead of education, Australian students (at school and university) are receiving "enstupidation."[38] Her discipline area is English literature, and she documents why she agrees with C. S. Lewis's warning in the *Abolition of Man* that young people will be more vulnerable to soft-headed propaganda because the commitments of their hearts have not been introduced to the deeper story of humanity via the classics of literature. Mueller dissects aspects of curriculum documents to demonstrate that inviting students to study historically proven literary texts (and not just extracts or simplified versions) has been replaced by a new cultural agenda—one of cultural neo-Marxists demonizing the past, and replacing it with the emotivist, sexualized, self-oriented agenda introduced above. She articulates how this leads not only to a distortion in understanding character, but also a sustained drop in competency in language use.[39]

Thankfully, it can be noted, many people who espouse the relativism of a politically sexually defined identity world still accept the order and beauty of a plane well built and medicine well done. However, the issue of what the controlling ideas are of how we make sense of life, and the purpose of any cleverness we discover, seems to be where the battles lines have been drawn. Roger Scruton describes the same history and outcomes as Trueman, and encourages us, in the spirit of 2 Cor 10:3–5, thus:

> The Old Testament warns against idolatry, which is the habit of investing mere things with a soul; modern psychology wants against addiction, in which the "dopamine fix" expels the long-term projects of the heart . . . our happiness depends on wanting the right things, not the things that happen to capture our attention or to inspire our lust. Overcoming temptation is a spiritual task. No political system, no economic order, no dictatorship from above could possibly replace the moral discipline that we each must undergo if we are to live in a world of abundance without putting everything that is most dear to us—love, morality, beauty, God himself—on sale.[40]

---

38. Mueller, "From Education to Enstupidation."

39. For another case study of educational impacts in other disciplines, see Walsh, *Fiery Angel*, 9.

40. Scruton, *Fools, Frauds and Firebrands*, 279–80.

How Might We, Therefore, Generally Respond?

How do we sustain what Scruton implores, if the strangeness in our classrooms appears bleak, and perhaps sometimes it is? We have a beautiful piece of ancient literature that warns us of such predicaments. It describes the struggle of our thinking and our collective souls. The apostle Paul sets the scene in Romans chapters 1 and 2, then explains why such difficulties arise over the next ten chapters. He then celebrates the hope that is still present for each of us when we look to Christ.

It is why Paul comes, at the end of chapter 11 of Romans, to a glorious song of praise to the One from whom and through whom and to whom are all things—that is, the one true Creator God, who has given us a ministry of reconciliation, through Jesus the Christ. Because of that mercy, we must be committed in our classrooms to worship him by serving others, while resisting being squeezed by the mold of our professional worlds. In that way we can humbly test out what God's good and pleasing will is for us in the classroom.[41]

Nancy Pearcey has written a whole book that applies these principles from the letter to the Romans so that she can help others in "unmasking atheism, secularism and other God substitutes."[42] It is suggested that her five prompt questions can help us in the face of the strange new world of ideas that we may encounter—either those described by the authors used in this chapter, or other idea frameworks that may unexpectedly become part of our classrooms:

> *Principle 1*—identify the idol. If humans do not worship the Creator, they will make a deity out of something in the created order.
>
> *Principle 2*—identify the reductionism. When one part of creation is deified, other aspects of creation will be suppressed, devalued, dismissed, or denied. Reductionism is always dehumanizing. When reductionistic worldviews gain political power, the consequences are oppressive, coercive, and inhumane.
>
> *Principle 3*—test the alternative worldview against the facts of experience and the truth of general revelation. Every idol-based worldview will contradict the knowable facts of general revelation.

---

41. This paragraph is an amplified and targeted paraphrase of Rom 11:36—12:3.
42. Pearcey, *Finding Truth*.

Principle 4—every reductionist worldview is self-defeating. That's because it reduces reason to something less than reason.

Principle 5—make the case for a Christian worldview. We can do this by addressing the heart concerns and interests of our students. If we believe that the Bible has the best "explanatory power"[43] for faith and life, what can we do for our students to see this explicitly and implicitly in what we teach and how we teach?[44]

Decades before these salient suggestions, J. I. Packer, in his less well-known 1979 book *Knowing Man*, explained the choices we have as follows:

> If, therefore, Christians lack power to exert Christianising influence, they should consider before God how they might acquire it . . . to create alternative patterns of communal living in homes, extended families, local churches and ad hoc "task force" associations [like Christian schools] which will function in society as a city set on a hill, demonstrating to the world the power of Christ in action . . . . Most of all, Christians should labour to understand the secularization that goes on around them—what arguments and hurts (usually the latter rather than the former) lead people to embrace secularism. . . . It is time to seek the Lord, and to do some homework.[45]

May we do our homework well as we continue to seek the Lord.

Questions for Discussion

1. Do you know what "ideologies" are popular among your students? (Ideology = a belief system in which we put our faith.)

2. Which belief system works to ignore God the most among your students? Why do you think it works?

3. Are there students who have a "watered down Christianity" (like a "therapeutic Christianity") in your classes? Why do you believe this has an attraction for them?

4. Do you hear the phrase "But the research says" very often? How do you decide if it is reasonable science or scientism?

---

43. Dowson, "Biblical Philosophy of Education."
44. Based on Dowson, "Biblical Philosophy of Education," 256–57.
45. Packer, *Knowing Man*, 97–99.

5. On what aspect of classroom practice might you need to use Pearcey's five questions to check for professional idolatry?

References

Adams, Jeremy S. *Hollowed Out: A Warning About America's Next Generation*. Washington, DC: Regnery, 2021.
Augustine. *The Confessions*. Translated by E. M. Blaiklock. London: Hodder and Stoughton, 1983.
Balfour, Arthur James. *Theism and Humanism: The Gifford Lectures*. London: Hodder and Stoughton, 1914.
Chesterton, G. K. *What's Wrong with the World*. Cavalier Classics: n.p., 2015.
Dirckx, S. *Am I Just My Brain?* Oxford: The Goodbook Company, 2019.
Dowson, Martin. "A Biblical Philosophy of Education." In *Teaching Well: Insights for Educators in Christian Schools*, edited by K. Goodlet and John Collier. Canberra, Australia: Barton, 2014.
Holland, Tom. *Dominion: The Making of the Western Mind*. London: Abacus, 2019.
Lennox, J. C. *Seven Days That Divided the World: The Beginning According to Genesis and Science*. 10th anniversary ed. Grand Rapids, MI: Zondervan Reflective, 2021.
Lewis, C. S. *The Abolition of Man*. Collins, UK: Fount, 1982.
Lukianoff, Greg, and Jonathan Haidt. *The Coddling of the American Mind: How Good Intentions and Bad Ideas Are Setting Up a Generation for Failure*. London: Allen Lane, 2018.
Horwitz, Ilana M. *God, Grades and Graduation: Religion's Surprising Impact on Academic Success*. Oxford: Oxford University Press, 2022.
MacIntyre, Alisdair. *After Virtue*. 3rd ed. Notre Dame, IN: University of Notre Dame Press, 2007.
Moreland, J. P. *Scientism and Secularism: Learning to Respond to a Dangerous Ideology*. Wheaton, IL: Crossway, 2018.
Mueller, Fiona. "From Education to Enstupidation: Teaching English Language and Literature in Australia." In *Cancel Culture and the Left's Long March*, edited by Kevin Donnelly, 65–81. Melbourne, Vic: Wilkison, 2021.
Noble, Alan. *You Are Not Your Own: Belonging to God in an Inhuman World*. Wheaton, IL: InterVarsity Press, 2021.
Packer, J. I. *Knowing Man*. Westchester, IL: Cornerstone, 1979.
Pearcey, Nancy. *Finding Truth: 5 Principles for Unmasking Atheism, Secularism and Other God Substitutes*. Colorado Springs: David Cook, 2015.
Poplin, Mary. *Is Reality Secular? Testing the Assumptions of Four Global Worldviews*. Downers Grove, IL: InterVarsity Press, 2014.
Reiff, Philip. *The Triumph of the Therapeutic: Uses of Faith After Freud*. 40th anniversary ed. Wilmington, DE: ISI, 2007.
Scruton, Roger. *Fools, Frauds and Firebrands: Thinkers of the New Left*. London: Bloomsbury Continuum, 2019.
Siedentop, Larry. *Inventing the Individual: The Origins of Western Liberalism*. London: Penguin, 2014.
Smith, Christian, B. Ritz, and M. Rotolo. *Religious Parenting: Transmitting Faith and Values in Contemporary America*. Princeton, NJ: Princeton University Press, 2020.

Smith, Steven D. *The Disenchantment of Secular Discourse*. Cambridge, MA: Harvard University Press, 2010.

———. *Pagans and Christians in the City: Culture Wars from the Tiber to the Potomac*. Grand Rapids, MI: Eerdmans, 2018.

Stark, Rodney. *The Triumph of Faith: Why the World Is More Religious Than Ever*. Wilmington, DE: ISI, 2015.

Swinburne, Richard. *Mind, Brain and Free Will*. Oxford: Oxford University Press, 2013.

Trueman, Carl R. *The Rise and Triumph of the Modern Self: Cultural Amnesia, Expressive Individualism, and the Road to Sexual Revolution*. Wheaton, IL: Crossway, 2020.

Walsh, M. *The Fiery Angel: Art, Culture, Sex, Politics and the Struggle for the Soul of the West*. New York: Encounter Books, 2018.

Wiltshire, Kenneth, and Kevin Donnelly. *Final Report into the National Curriculum*. Australian Federal Government, 2014.

CHAPTER FIVE

The Buffered Learner and Religious Conviction

Matthew Etherington

> He, who will not reason, is a bigot; he, who cannot, is a fool; and he, who dares not, is a slave.—William Drummond of Logiealmond

Introduction

This chapter is dedicated to the identities that persuade learners to perceive themselves, their interaction with others, and their faith in specific ways. The two identities explored in this chapter are the *buffered* and *porous* identities, coined by Canadian historian and philosopher Charles Taylor.[1]

The two identities are professionally interesting, but more importantly, they are relevant today because the present-day focus on one's "identity" is culturally germane, as observed in the mainstream media, academic conferences, and inclusive education curricula, affiliated with elementary, secondary, and higher education.

1. Taylor, *Secular Age*.

The aim in this chapter is modest. First, I will sketch out and build upon Taylor's ideas, focusing on his published work *A Secular Age*, written nearly two decades ago. The book's length can strike potential readers with fear due to being over 850 pages of detailed analysis. However, Taylor's work on identity is worth exploring because it details how people's identities have changed over time from collective agencies to expressive individuals. Taylor coined the terms to describe one's identity as *buffered* or *porous*. These two identities are considered in relation to students' learning in faith-based religious schools.[2] The *buffered* and *porous* learner has implications for faith-based schools prioritizing learning communities because community requires collective responsibility. Similarly, Todorov's essay "Living Alone Together" challenges us to "rethink the thesis that each of us is a purely autonomous individual and yet individuality is humankind's highest achievement."[3]

The Challenge

In a similar vein to Taylor, I contend there has been a consistent drift away from orthodox Christian conceptions of God as an agent interacting with humans and intervening in human history and toward God as a benign architect of the universe. Since God no longer interacts with humans, we can no longer take the truths we learned on trust but must generate them ourselves. Charles Taylor refers to this as "disengagement," and the consequence is a "buffered self" identity. Disengagement is a self-stultifying strategy as it is unable to generate open-mindedness[4] while distracting us from understanding what someone is trying to tell us in a conversation or grasping how an individual or a group of people perceives the world.[5]

On Being Open-Minded

The direct quote at the opening of this chapter is by William Drummond of Logiealmond. The idea is that individuals who lack the ability

---

2. Concentration on "buffered" and "porous" learners in faith-based education typically refers to the educational systems of Western countries, such as the United States, Canada, and Australia, but also in European Western countries.
3. Werhane, "Community and Individuality," 16.
4. Taylor, *Secular Age*, 270, 285, 286.
5. Taylor, *Secular Age*, 285.

or willingness to engage in rational thought or logical reasoning seeking earnestly to understand (but not agree) lose the treasures of wisdom since understanding, knowledge, and liberty can advance wisdom. Of course, the Bible says many things which pertain to wisdom. God's nature and character define wisdom, and the faithful are called to follow Wisdom. We are to act in this world as God desires, not as we desire.

Individuals who can reason to pursue understanding but actively choose not to do so lack the open-mindedness and disposition to examine alternate viewpoints and challenge themselves, which are essential for intellectual maturity and personal growth. Individuals with the ability and willingness to reason and pursue understanding but who refrain from doing so have yet to show the magnitude of intellectual courage to think autonomously, free from undue influence or coercion.

I have interacted with individuals who wish others would perceive them as open-minded people. That is, someone who can consider knowledge claims cautiously, who can discuss the validity of the claims, and who is willing to seek understanding about the beliefs and worldviews that are not their own. The ideal outcome is respect for the person and tolerance for the belief. In this example, tolerance is a disagreement with a belief or behavior but a full endorsement of a person's right to hold and express their belief or behavior.[6]

Open-minded people value intellectual and personal growth advancement when alternatives are studied thoroughly and sincerely because examining ideas and practices is considered genuinely important. We would like this trait displayed in others, so we should expect it from ourselves. Of course, we want the freedom to make our own decisions, but our actions are never absolute; other conditions, such as objective reality, always constrain them. Reality has a habit of thrusting truths and limitations upon our volitions. In contrast, subjective reality is equally predicable of all feelings and thoughts, whether the content or objective reference of these feelings and thoughts is objectively valid.[7] We must also remember that open-mindedness means holding fast to what is good and being willing to evaluate alternative beliefs and worldviews. So, which identity is favored for being more open-minded, the buffered or porous self? This chapter explores this question.

---

6. It should be clear that any psychologically or physically harmful action should not be tolerated but extinguished.

7. Ritchie, "What Is Reality?," 266.

Human Agency and Identity

Reflection on human agency and identity has dominated education over the last two decades. One of the significant global conversations in education is about one's identity. Although social media has a substantial part to play, neuroscience has expanded the importance of the self. Although there are many aspects of one's identity, human agency is inherent in students' ability to regulate, control, and monitor one's life and learning journey. Consequently, students are encouraged to act on their agency via self-reflection and discover the various influences and causes most supportive of their identity.

A modern sense of self, human agency, and identity occupy, among other entities, particular language sets, which have a significant share with what it means to be "true to oneself." Taylor submits that the human is a "language animal" where human consciousness comes to be. Being a human is being an "individual" and making your own choices in life unfettered by external influences.

Learners are individuals and are encouraged to take control of their learning choices. A focus on the self and having agency is high on the education agenda, and learners are awake to this experience. This leads to what Charles Taylor coined as the "buffered" and "porous" self. The "buffered" and "porous" identities influence how learners perceive themselves and behave as individuals and community members.

The Buffered and Porus Self

What is a *buffered* identity? Charles Taylor describes *bufferedness* as an identity closed off to others, a self-defined "product" composed of multiple selves. A helpful analogy is the many "coats" displayed on a Russian doll.

Figure 1. Matroshka: The Russian Nesting Dolls[8]

8. https://transfurniture.wordpress.com/2010/12/22/matroshka-the-russian-nesting-dolls-concept/.

The doll uncovers multiple related and separate "coats" that form the whole doll. The Russian doll is small but solid when the layers are removed, exposing the core. In the same way, the individual must remove their "layers" to recover their inner core identity.[9]

The analogy provides an image of what it means to be *buffered*. The *buffered* self carries multiple identities, with layers that, when removed, result in a solid but also unstable core identity. Taylor suggests that being a modern individual does not mean ceasing to belong but instead imagining oneself belonging to even wider and more impersonal entities such as the State, the "movement," and the "community" of humankind. In terms of diversity, this would mean that modern societies are more homogeneous than pre-modern ones.[10]

Concerning the *porous* identity and human relationships, people experience the *innermost* layer as the pinnacle of intimacy and vulnerability. The *porous* identity is visible and vulnerable in that it is open to the existence of a transcendent being, and any self-improvement is vetted through one's community and its members rather than oneself. The *porous* identity depends on intimate interactions with the community, involving family, friends, and the spiritual. The *porous* identity allows full transparency, exposing vulnerabilities, fears, and aspirations. This occurs through close attachments, as friendships can access the "hidden" layers, preserving the *porous* self as an open and transparent being.

This compares with the *buffered self*, which Taylor explains through social exchanges and value assessments:

> . . . social interactions and value judgments defined by the commitments and identifications which provide the frame or horizon within which *I* can try to determine from case to case what is good or valuable.[11]

Consequently, the *buffered* identity is capable of disciplined control and benevolence but is generated by one's sense of dignity and power, that is, satisfaction.[12] Although each identity interacts with the former layer, the interactions are minimal and superficial, with a trivial or

---

9. What are some of the identities that could lead to bufferedness? These can include environmentalism, human rights, anti-capitalism, socialism versus capitalism, gender, and social justice issues. These are important identities with significant outcomes.

10. Taylor, *Secular Age*, 207.

11. Taylor, *Sources of the Self*, 27.

12. Taylor, *Sources of the Self*, 262. Taylor suggests the buffered self can display disciplined control and benevolence but only in agreement with exclusive humanism.

non-existing association with the *transcendent*.[13] In other words, the *buffered self* has overcome the "irrationality" of belief—they are self-made but disenchanted.

In contrast, the *porous* self is affirmative; that is, the identity is open to a life *with* the *transcendent*, including the existence of spirits, magic forces, and evil.[14] The *buffered* self is not only disenchanted but hostile to the *transcendent*, which may also require a lessening of autonomy, which is a core belief of the *buffered* self. The identity is disinterested with an enchanted cosmos, closed off to others, and with truth simply recycled in one's own mind.

Although responsive to the surrounding culture, the layered identities of the *buffered* self are impervious to anything "higher" than oneself. The *buffered* individual reflects the surrounding culture as she adopts causes and convictions of the culture, which the individual then absorbs. The *buffered* identity is impervious to the enchanted cosmos or a reality that offers truths that would typically limit the self and do not have any effect.

Writing on what it means to be a fully functioning person, Sokolowski[15] explains how reality always presents truths to us, even unwelcome truths, and to be fully human, we must acknowledge those truths. With the adoption of multiple identities, together with an insular presence, the *buffered* self is isolated to additional truths and, therefore, deprived of learning. The *buffered* identity resembles the self-declaration of the individual, firm with opinions and believing others should think identically as they do, succumbing to the ethics of the surrounding culture of the day.

The *porous* identity displays the self-denial characteristic of any strong community. The *porous* self can pass over one's self-interests and tolerate ideas outside one's inclinations. Their barriers are down as they take the truths of reality and the emotions and convictions of others seriously. They deny themselves the ability to fulfill a commitment to the

---

13. As previously noted, some of these identities could include individualism, benevolence, autonomy, environmentalism, gender, race, social justice, and so forth.

14. The *Transcendent* is also known as God, Creator, or a Spiritual force that acts in the world and through human beings. With an understanding of the transcendent comes an awareness that there is something in the world that is epistemologically, ethically, and ontologically greater than any human being.

15. Sokolowski, *Phenomenology of the Human Person*.

transcendent while being more likely to rally against self-centeredness, pride, and egoism.

When a faith identity is the central identity, which is representative of the *porous* self, being sensitive and acting to uphold the ethical treatment of others becomes more evident. They can evaluate if the dominant ethic of the day is at odds with a transcendent sense of being human. For example, when people with a strong sense of the *transcendent* detected the incompatibility of their faith with slavery, although this might have been the ethic of the day, they did not adopt the ethic of the day.

One famous example is William Wilberforce, who converted to evangelical Christianity in 1784 and advocated against the slave trade. Though this was the ethic of the day, he cofounded the Anti-Slavery Society. Wilberforce's political views were guided not by the ethics of the day but by his faith in a transcendent God and his desire to promote an ethic, not of the surrounding culture, which would have been far easier to do, but consistent with his faith and lifelong concern with social reform.

In contrast, the person with the *buffered* identity who may also ally with the Christian faith could, without difficulty, perceive Christianity as the enemy. When faith calls for a more demanding life than just human flourishing, a life of denial would be a denial of oneself. Yet, this is the identity and lifeworld of the Christian transcendent. The verse in Matt 16:24–25 is not ambiguous. Jesus told his disciples, "If anyone would come after me, let him *deny* himself, take up his cross, and follow me. For whoever would save his life will lose it, but whoever loses his life for my sake will find it."

When human flourishing is the ethic of the day, a human good, Christianity becomes the enemy, notably for the *buffered* individual. Taylor describes this as *exclusive humanism*;[16] if Christianity does not advance human flourishing as the highest central ideal, it must be the enemy. For those of faith, human flourishing is not the highest goal in life. So, the *buffered* identity is the outcome of *exclusive humanism*.

What are the possible consequences of these two *selves* concerning learning? For the *buffered* self, God is perceived as a grudging, vindictive, excessively restrictive being, harmful to my identity,[17] and so, in my search for God, I find "yours truly." The *buffered* individual perceives God as a being that wants to rob them of something good or at least

---

16. Taylor, *Secular Age*, 264.
17. Moser, "Reorienting Religious Epistemology," 60.

something rightfully theirs. Consequently, the *buffered* learner refuses to take God seriously.

The consequence is a *buffered* individual, protected by layers of identities that create an imperviousness to anything higher than oneself. Consequently, there is an impermeability to outside direction and correction, and working together to solve problems results in conformity rather than critical thinking.[18]

These markers or identities have their place in teaching and learning; however, the question is how young people today, in their school years and beyond, *imagine* themselves as learners together with other learners and what features of Western modernity have influenced how they imagine themselves to behave with their neighbors as individuals, citizens, and community members.

Porous Faith to Buffered *Virtues*

In eighteenth-century Europe, intellectuals adopted a view that practice and adherence worthy of God through virtues were the only forms of practice and became the adopted interpretation. This view had a humanizing trend in that the transcendent dimension of life became less critical, forming what Charles Taylor calls an "anthropocentric shift."[19] As a result, faith became less central, and a decline in the mystery of God faded. "True" faith was polite and civilized.[20]

The eighteenth century saw an "obvious" anthropocentric shift in God's plans for human beings. The "plan" reduced one's life to happiness and well-being. This plan manifests in education in the twentieth and later part of the twenty-first centuries. The student who *was* the learner is now at the center of their learning, guiding and, in some cases, the primary assessor of their knowledge and learning.[21] Although a student-centered

---

18. Although there are "types" of critical thinking which can be distinguished, the definition I promote here is the sociocultural approach. This approach considers how thinking processes are influenced by cosmologies, ontologies, and epistemologies. Sociocultural critical thinking is advantageous because people work together to solve problems; meaning, they "do not only interact, they 'interthink'" by combining their intellects in creative ways that may achieve more than the sum of the parts. Imperio, Staarman, and Basso, "Relevance of the Socio-Cultural Perspective."

19. Taylor, *Secular Age*, 222.

20. Taylor, *Secular Age*, 264.

21. In his writings and lectures from the 1940s, John Dewey raised awareness of the concept of the student-centered learner. The student is at the center of the pedagogical

theory of learning correctly resisted an insalubrious teacher-centered practice, the difference now is that the learner perceives individual flourishing as an essential outcome of education and schooling.

Virtue education has been a stable feature in schools ever since humans first became aware that their attitudes and behaviors can influence people and the external world in good and bad ways. Today, Christian virtues and their implementation in the classroom are a topic of relevance, discussion, and application. With the new humanism, people are motivated to act on behalf of their fellow human beings. Acting on behalf of others who are less than able is virtuous; however, the transcendent and the motivation to act on behalf of a God of justice is replaced with a "community transcendent."

With the adherence to virtues, Christian institutions adopt a focus on teaching the virtues. The importance of virtue education for teacher preparation in this area is expected. Horowski considers virtue practice in religious schooling:

> In its moral aspect, if teachers and school education are to lead to virtue development, the teachers' challenge at school is a deliberate incorporation of maturing people into a school community life in such a way as to face moral dilemmas, seek solutions that would be and learn to forgo simple pleasures.[22]

There is much to consider in this hope. One must forgo simple pleasures in acknowledging others and be mature, tolerant, and prepared to face moral challenges. However, if Taylor is correct, then the *buffered* individual may have the information but cannot practice the virtues. Although the practice of virtues is a worthy and vital core in education, the problem for the *buffered* individual is an overriding view that God's purposes are only for our good. We become centered on the self—self-love, pride, and social life are identical. The discourse of *pride* becomes ordinary while individuals distance themselves or disengage from others who might threaten the focus on the self, which is why this emotion may be evaluated less positively in cultures and sub-cultures. One example is religious education,[23] where social relations are anticipated, humility is encouraged, and community is expected.

---

act, which emphasizes the student's personality, interests, and skills.

22. Horowski, "Christian Religious Education," 453.

23. This is true with the religious education of Jews, Christians, and Muslims.

The *porous self* can practice humility since courage and risk are needed to go against conformity in a counter-cultural role. For a practice of fortitude, the *porous* self is in a daily and worthy adventure against hardships, corruption, groupthink, pride, oppression, and fatigue.

The Challenges with a Buffered Identity

Taylor suggests that individuals who adopt a *buffered* identity express disengagement and a loss of the *transcendent*, i.e., God. The *buffered* identity generates self-truths, lacks an adventurous, risk-taking spirit, and ignores the education that can arise from learning from others who have a unique way of perceiving the world and its events.

As such, the disengaged *buffered* identity will likely bypass critical learning moments. When we want to know what someone is trying to tell us, grasp how someone sees the world, or even what motivates them, disengagement will undoubtedly be a self-stultifying strategy. To learn, we must be open-minded, patient, risk-taking, adventurous, and tolerant of the person or event.[24]

Conclusions

We all need understanding to help students and ourselves become more *porous* and less *buffered*. The *buffered* learner seeks a simpler world. They do seek to understand, but for the *buffered* learner to understand, they must accept that complicating things is critical in developing reliable insight and knowledge. I remember when a new school song was introduced to the teaching staff in my early teaching days. It was titled "The Mystery of Christ," founded on Eph 5:32: "This is a profound mystery—but I am talking about Christ and the church."

It was a beautiful composition, and as the songwriter sang and played the song on the piano, we were mesmerized by the beauty of the words and the way it was sung. However, when the song concluded and the staff was invited to comment, some reacted disappointedly. They rejected the notion that Christ is a mystery. Christ, they asserted, is not a mystery but transparent and understandable. As I think about that moment, I realize that we have a human need to simplify. Simplifying things enables us to find our way in life and helps us navigate a complex

---

24. Taylor, *Secular Age*, 285.

world. The notion of "complexity" resonates with me because it rests on acknowledging a lack of complete knowledge but desiring to understand. People, including myself, often deal with complexity by trying to simplify things.[25] Consequently, I am aware of why using *buffered* and *porous* identities could be another attempt to simplify a complex phenomenon by constructing caricatures from myths or personal feelings. While this might be a valid criticism, the two identities describe how and why people react and behave as learners. As such, they offer a point of discussion and evaluation, which are important cognitive exercises. They are also self-reflective concepts that force us to ask ourselves—*to what degree have I become buffered or porous?* Of course, we are always encouraged to look deeper and be suspicious of categories that classify us.

If understanding is one of the primary goals of education, the Christian community has an obligation to recognize how people will learn as *buffered* identities and continually investigate how faith influences that learning. How do the two identities discussed support or impede living a life of faith and conviction? How do the *buffered* and *porous* selves increase a pursuit of God? Which one will fare better over time?

If what has been described in this chapter is possible, the *buffered* self is already at maximum capacity, just as a soaking water sponge cannot endure more liquid. The *buffered* identity places trust in the individual who has absolute freedom, and anything that challenges this belief is oppressive, including God. Consequently, for faith-based and religious schooling, the *buffered* and *porous* selves experience the Bible's teaching on self-denial or repentance differently because these are expressions of love for others and for trusting God.

However, trust must also be navigated in a landscape of uncertainty. The "layers" of the *buffered self* must be removed to reveal the inner being—the *porous* self. By shedding the layers of multiple identities and attachments, individuals pave the way, albeit one full of risk and adventure, for the ultimate passage back to the "source," that is, the transcendent realm.

Questions for Discussion

1. Do you think there are other reasons for the drift away from orthodox Christian concepts of God?

25. Roeland, "Why We Need to Complicate Things," 146.

2. Have you experienced a *buffered* Christian identity? How have you become *porous*?

3. How might the individual experience the learning journey in Christian education with a *buffered* or *porous* identity?

4. In what ways does the Christian community negotiate personal identity and corporate identity in relation with a Christian identity?

5. Are the *porous* and *buffered* identities natural or artificial categories?

References

Bromley, Patricia, et al. World Education Reform Database (WERD): A Global Dataset on Education Reforms, version 2. 2023.

Cech, Erin A. *The Trouble with Passion: How Searching for Fulfilment at Work Fosters Inequality.* Berkeley: University of California Press, 2012.

Díaz-Díaz, Claudia, and Mona Gleason. "The Land Is My School: Children, History, and the Environment in the Canadian Province of British Columbia." *Childhood* 23 (2016) 272–85. https://doi.org/10.1177/0907568215603778.

Horowski, Jarosław. "Christian Religious Education and the Development of Moral Virtues: A Neo-Thomistic Approach." *British Journal of Religious Education* 42 (2020) 447–58. https://doi.org/10.1080/01416200.2020.1752618.

Imperio, Alessandra, Judith Klein Staarman, and Demis Basso. "Relevance of the Socio-Cultural Perspective in the Discussion About Critical Thinking." *Journal of Theories and Research in Education* 15.1 (2020) 1–19.

Moser, Paul. "Reorienting Religious Epistemology." In *For Faith and Clarity*, edited by James K. Beilby, 65–85. Grand Rapids, MI: Baker Academic, 2006.

Nickerson, Raymond S. "Understanding Understanding." *American Journal of Education* 93 (1985) 201–39.

Ritchie, David G. "What Is Reality?" *The Philosophical Review* 3 (1892) 265–83. https://doi.org/10.2307/2175783.

Roeland, Johan. "Why We Need to Complicate Things: The Teaching and Learning of Religion Beyond Simplification." *Teaching Theology and Religion* 26:4 (2023) 144–50. https://doi.org/10.1111/teth.12654.

Sokolowski, Robert. *Phenomenology of the Human Person.* Cambridge, UK: Cambridge University Press, 2012.

Taylor, Charles. *A Secular Age.* Cambridge, MA: Harvard University Press, 2007.

———. *Sources of the Self: The Making of the Modern Identity.* Cambridge, MA: Harvard University Press, 1989.

Tracy, Jessica L., and Richard W. Robins. "Putting the Self into Self-Conscious Emotions: A Theoretical Model." *Psychological Inquiry* 15 (2004) 103–25. DOI: 10.1207/s15327965pli1502_01.

Werhane, Patricia. "Community and Individuality." *New Literary History* 27 (1996) 15–24.

CHAPTER SIX

The Promise of School Choice Policies for Cultivating an Educational Ecosystem

Albert Cheng

Introduction

IN 2019, CARDUS AND the Barna Group conducted a poll of clergy in the United States. They found that two-thirds of Protestant pastors and half of Catholic priests perceived school to be a negative influence on a child's spiritual formation. Nevertheless, half of the respondents said they have not addressed the topic of school choice, and only one out of five clergy reported that they prioritized training parents for the spiritual formation of their children.[1] In other words, despite an awareness of a lack of quality educational opportunities for many of the children in their congregations, members of the clergy have not engaged parents in their congregations about how to respond. The executive vice president of Cardus, Ray Pennings, suggested that those findings indicated "a disconnect (or perhaps just ignorance) among church leaders, parents,

---

1. Barna Group and Cardus, *Who Is Responsible*.

and schools when it comes to the question of how schooling potentially affects students' spiritual formation."[2]

The findings from that survey conducted by Cardus and the Barna Group underscore a conventional way of thinking about education as it relates to the home and to the church. Insofar as the three spheres of school, home, and church are not viewed in complete isolation from one another, education is often viewed to be under the purview of home and school but not church. After all, if the aim of education is, as it is commonly held in much of the modern world today, the acquisition of skills such as literacy and numeracy so that children can be economically productive in adulthood, then what does the church have to say about math and language arts curriculum? On such topics, deference to the authority of schools in partnership with the home should be given.

Spiritual formation, on the other hand, is often relegated to the spheres of home and church but not the school. After all, religious, moral, and other matters pertaining to how one ought to live belong in the private realm of the home and the church and especially not in the public realm of schools funded and, in many cases, operated by the state. The public realm, the argument goes, should restrict itself to considering secular matters such as literacy, numeracy, and economic productivity. In general, the siloing of home, church, and school naturally flows from a narrowed understanding of education limited to skills development and exclusive of other aspects of human formation.

There are exceptions to this delimited understanding of home, school, and church as well as this reductive view of education. For instance, some Christian schools aim to partner with home and church, while also espousing a view where both spiritual formation and skills development are understood as constitutive of education. However, it is not necessarily the case that Christian schools are guided by that vision, especially when there are pressures for them to resemble other kinds of schools.[3] On top of that, enrollment in independent Christian schools is relatively rare in the United States, the country that is the subject of this chapter. According to 2019 data from the U.S. Department of Education, 56 million children were enrolled in school. Yet only about 2.6 million students, or roughly 5 percent of children who were enrolled in school, were enrolled in a Catholic or Evangelical Protestant school.

2. Pennings, "Cardus' Cofounder Ray Pennings."
3. Ford and Andersson, "Sources of Isomorphism."

An even smaller proportion of students are enrolled in schools of other religious traditions.[4]

School choice, however, has rapidly expanded since 2019 in many US states, increasing families' access to a variety of educational options for their children, including Christian schools. According to EdChoice, 59 school voucher, tax-credit scholarship, or education savings accounts programs existed in the United States in 2019. At the time of this writing in 2024, there are 69 such programs with many more under consideration in numerous state legislatures. Moreover, no programs in 2019 offered universal access; programs were typically restricted to families below a household income threshold or children with disabilities. Currently, there are 12 universal programs. All of these programs provide funds to families for the cost of private school tuition. Education savings accounts additionally allow families to use those funds to pay for educational expenses besides private school tuition, such as tutoring and curriculum. EdChoice estimates that the number of students who participate in these programs has more than doubled from 482,000 in 2019 to 982,000 today.[5]

These changes present an opportunity for school, home, and church to come together to provide an education that is distinctively Christian and will promote the flourishing of our communities. How such an opportunity might be seized is the focus of this chapter. In the subsequent section, I offer a more thorough discussion of the role of home, church, and school as it pertains to education. I specifically draw upon *paideia*, the classical conception of education, and propose it as an alternative to the reductive conceptions of education typical to modernity. I additionally suggest that *paideia* is aligned with a Christian vision of education. After that, I offer a brief overview of how school choice policies work. Next, I argue that these policies offer opportunities to practice education understood as *paideia*. I conclude by offering some practical suggestions for Christians to consider in light of those opportunities. In general, I argue that Christians are called to cultivate a vibrant educational ecosystem—defined not only as the set of schools of which families may avail themselves but also the supporting institutions such as government policies, school associations, parent

---

4. U.S. Department of Education, *Digest of Education Statistics*
5. EdChoice, *ABCs of School Choice*.

associations, school boards, curriculum developers, accreditors, and educator preparation or professional development programs.

Paideia and a Christian Vision for Education

Because of the many competing visions of education, the purpose of education is vigorously debated. For example, the utilitarian vision of developing human capital to ensure that children will be economically productive as adults is one view that has inspired much of school reform for the past forty years.[6] Especially since the COVID-19 pandemic, though even beforehand, another educational vision seeks to ensure children's psychological well-being.[7]

Uniting the two respective visions of economic and psychological well-being is a broader vision in which the purpose of education is to ensure that all children can be autonomous. In this view, autonomy is understood as the capacity to evaluate and revise conceptions of a worthwhile life and then to choose among the options.[8] Economic and psychological well-being are constitutive of realizing autonomy. Consider, for example, why children are encouraged to obtain a college degree. They are told that with requisite skills and credentials, they can go anywhere,[9] pursue any opportunity, follow their true passions, realize higher earnings,[10] and in the end, be happy. In other words, children are told that the rewards from earning a college degree will make them into, as political philosopher Rita Koganzon described, "the secular, upwardly mobile professional who can succeed in the globalized economy" who is "maximally autonomous because they have access to the greatest number of lifestyle choices available . . ., among the greatest variety of careers, hobbies, friends and potential spouses, residences, and consumer goods."[11] In other words, education for autonomy helps children find freedom, at least freedom understood as being able to do whatever they want to do, freedom understood as being unencumbered by any external constraint, and freedom to

---

6. Hanushek, Peterson, and Woessmann, *Endangering Prosperity*.
7. Kristjánsson, "Positive Psychology."
8. Levinson, "Liberalism, Pluralism, and Political Education."
9. Berry, "Higher Education and Home Defense."
10. Autor, "Skills, Education, and the Rise."
11. Koganzon, "Pork-Eating Is Not a Reasonable," 36.

find that so-called independent, authentic self. These are the conditions of the ideal life, according to this vision.

However, the conception of freedom as autonomy is inconsistent with Christian tradition in which freedom is not properly understood as realizing the autonomous self to do as one pleases but includes submission and conformity to God and the order that he has ordained. Augustine famously articulated this view in his *Confessions*: "In yourself you rouse us, giving us delight in glorifying you, because you made us with yourself as our goal, and our heart is restless until it rests in you."[12] Freedom, in other words, has boundaries. It is constrained by human nature and the purpose for which God created humans, union with him.

Christian tradition, then, challenges modern notions of freedom and narrowed conceptions of education. Education is not primarily about being able to pursue anything but about pursuing the right things. Education is not about choosing to love whatever one wants but about choosing to love the things one ought to love. Education is not about providing the requisite information and skills so that one can do whatever one wants but about providing the requisite formation and habits so that one can be the kind of person one should be. It encompasses more than attaining economic or psychological well-being.

Instilling proper affections and character is a critical part of education, a claim that can be found in classical Greek thought. Plato, for example, described the educated person as "having the right kinds of dislikes," and as a result, "would praise the fine things; and, taking pleasure in them and receiving them into the soul . . . . He would blame and hate the ugly in the right way." Plato goes on to call such a person a *kaloskagathos*—literally, beautiful and good.[13] Aristotle likewise asks what is the highest good that all humans should aim for. In other words, what is the ultimate purpose, or *telos*, of being human? His answer is *eudaimonia*, which is typically translated as flourishing. Aristotle, more importantly, considers how one can attain *eudaimonia*. The answer is by being virtuous, or literally, being excellent in the art of being human.[14]

Plato and Aristotle used term *paideia* to denote the formative project that they understood education to be. *Paideia* connotes rearing a child to form attachments to a particular community together with its shared vision of a worthwhile life. Put another way, education

12. Augustine, *Confessions*, 3.
13. Plato, *Republic*, 80.
14. Aristotle, *Nicomachean Ethics*.

understood as *paideia* is concerned with passing on a particular culture, not merely with what it takes to be economically productive, psychologically adjusted, or autonomous. To understand the scope of this kind of education, it is helpful to recognize that the word *culture* is etymologically connected to the word *cult*. In contemporary times, *cult* has a negative connotation and refers to small groups often led by a charismatic but deceptive leader who exercises tight control over its members and demands unquestioned submission to a set of beliefs and practices. However, in earlier times, *cult* was a positive term and connected to worship and devotion. Understood in this way, to bequeath a culture to children is to point them toward what they ought to worship. Education, understood as *paideia*, is about shaping children so that they have reverence for and devotion to the things they ought to have such reverence and devotion. Per Christian tradition, this object—or person, really—is the triune God. For the greatest commandment is to love God with one's entire being.[15] Or to use the words of the Westminster Shorter Catechism: "Man's chief end is to glorify God and enjoy him forever."[16] If education is ultimately about worship, then *paideia* accurately captures the kind of education God calls one generation to provide to the next. Such an education is the essence of Christian discipleship.

Although the Greeks did not have the special revelation of the Christian God, they had a proper understanding of the nature of education. Christianity completes Greek insight. While Aristotle says that true flourishing comes from living a life of virtue, Christianity asserts that the abundant life comes from having our entire being conformed into the image of Christ, who being the Word made flesh is the perfect embodiment of virtue. While Plato says that the good and beautiful person has his affections cultivated toward the true, good, and beautiful, the author of Hebrews writes that the "mature," or individuals who have been made complete, are "those who have their powers of discernment trained by constant practice to distinguish good from evil."[17] *Paideia*, then, conveys the kind of education for bringing about Christian maturity.

Home, church, and school all must be in the business of education and shaping future generations. The task of *paideia* cannot be left to a two-legged stool of church and home, to speak metaphorically. The third leg, that is, the school has often been severed by adopting a reductive vision

---

15. Matt 22:34–40. All Scripture quotations in this essay are from ESV.
16. Westminster Assembly, *Westminster Shorter Catechism*, question 1.
17. Heb 5:14.

of education that is mutually exclusive from the work of the church and home. In some cases, the third leg of the school has not been completely severed but is warped in some other way because the kind of formation that children experience at school does not align with the kind of formation intended by church and home. As a case in point, education aimed at economic productivity, psychological adjustment, or autonomy is inconsistent with the Christian vision of humanity's ultimate purpose.

Fortunately, the rapid expansion of school choice programs across the United States presents an opportunity to recover an understanding of education as *paideia* as well as an alignment between church, home, and school in the education of children.

A Primer on How School Choice Policies Work

School choice is a policy arrangement where families have the ability to send their children to a learning environment of their choice. Practically, there are many policy arrangements to enable families to send their children to a learning environment of their choice. Specific policies will differ in three important regards: (a) the learning environments that are available for families to access, (b) how the financial means to enable access to those options are provided, and (c) which families will be able to avail themselves of the means of access. These aspects that differentiate different school choice programs and policies are summarized in table 1. I will discuss each of these three aspects of school choice policies in turn.

Table 1. Taxonomy of Forms of School Choice

	Traditional Public Schools	Charter Schools	Private Schools	Homeschooling
Learning Environment: Where does the child's schooling take place?				
Financial Means of Access: How do families cover the costs of attending the learning environment?	Local, state, and federal funding; free to families who enroll their children, though families must live in the catchment area of their preferred traditional public school.	Primarily state funding; minimal local and federal funding; free to families who enroll their children.	1. Families who can cover the cost of tuition. 2. Some states offer voucher, tuition-tax credit, or education savings accounts programs to help families cover the cost of tuition.	1. Families cover the cost of providing education. 2. Some states offer education savings accounts programs to help families cover the costs for homeschooling.
Eligibility: Who can access the learning environment?	1. Families who can afford to purchase a home in the catchment area of their preferred traditional public school. 2. Families who participate in interdistrict or intradistrict choice programs.	Families who live in areas where charter schools exist.	1. If no tuition-assistance programs exist, only families who can cover the cost of tuition have access to private schools. 2. Some states offer means-tested programs that provide financial aid to low-income families or families with children with special needs. 3. Some states offer universal programs that provide all families with financial aid for private school tuition.	1. If no financial-assistance programs exist, homeschooling is only families who can cover the real and opportunity costs of homeschooling. 2. Some states offer education savings accounts that provide families with funds to spend on eligible education expenses on which homeschooling families typically rely.

Learning Environments

Different school choice policy arrangements expand access to a different range of learning environments. These learning environments in the United States include traditional public schools, a charter school, a private school—faith-based or secular—or homeschooling.

The vast majority of children in the United States attend the traditional public school to which they are assigned based on their place of residence. In 2019, approximately 90 percent of children enrolled in school attended a traditional public school.[18] This proportion has dropped by 2.5 percent in the 2021–22 school year, according to some estimates.[19] Some large urban school districts allow parents to attend any traditional public school within the district instead of the one they are assigned to by their place of residence—a system called intradistrict choice. Other districts allow parents who do not live within the school district boundaries to attend their traditional public schools—a system called interdistrict choice.

Meanwhile, forty-six states and the District of Columbia offer charter schools as an additional learning environment to their families. Charter schools are primarily funded by state governments and rarely get funding from local governments.[20] They are also free from typical regulations that traditional public schools face but are held accountable by an authorizing body for meeting goals that are outlined in their charter, hence the name *charter* school.

Independently run private schools, whether they are faith-based or non-sectarian, offer families additional options of learning environments. Families can also opt for learning environments outside conventional brick-and-mortar schools. Homeschooling and newer arrangements like microschools and hybrid schools have gained more traction since the COVID-19 pandemic.[21]

---

18. U.S. Department of Education, *Digest of Education Statistics*.
19. Dee, *Where the Kids Went*.
20. Johnson et al., *Charter School Funding*.
21. Wearne, "School Sector in Search of a Name."

Financial Means to Access Learning Environments

The existence of learning environments does not guarantee families access to them. For example, although all traditional public schools are funded by local, state, and federal taxes and free to families who enroll their children in those schools, families who cannot afford to live in the catchment area for their desired traditional public school cannot access that learning environment. Only the families who have purchased a home in the catchment area of their desired traditional public school have exercised a choice to attend that school, and many families do.

Some families rely on intradistrict and interdistrict choice policies to enroll their children in their preferred traditional public school. However, intradistrict and interdistrict choice systems are not ubiquitous, nor does the existence of intradistrict or interdistrict choice systems guarantee access to preferred traditional public schools, as the number of available transfers is limited. Meanwhile, charter schools are free of charge to families like traditional public schools, but a few states do not have charter schools. Even within states that have laws allowing charter schools, charter schools are not present in every community or have enrollment caps.

Some families prefer the distinctive education offered by independently run private schools, but access to those schools is restricted by the ability of families to pay the cost of tuition. Homeschooling offers families the opportunity to provide a particular type of education, but there are also financial constraints to homeschooling—both real costs such as expenses for curriculum and tutors and opportunity costs such as the parents' time and the inability for one parent to be employed full time.

School choice policies attempt to lower these financial barriers in a variety of ways. For example, intradistrict and interdistrict choice programs enable families to attend a preferred public school without having to pay the cost of residing in its catchment area. Private school choice programs offer funding to families to offset the cost of tuition. For instance, through the Milwaukee Parental Choice Program, the nation's first urban private school choice program established in 1990, the state of Wisconsin provides a voucher that low-income parents can use toward tuition at any participating private school in Milwaukee.

In 1997, Arizona launched the first tax-credit scholarship program in the United States, which, like voucher programs, provide families with funds to pay for private school tuition. The only difference from a voucher program is that the funds come do not come from the state but from individuals or businesses who make a charitable donation to a scholarship-granting organization and receive full or partial tax credits for that gift.

A few years later in 2011, Arizona launched the nation's first education savings accounts program. Unlike a voucher or tax-credit scholarship program, the state deposits funds into a savings account that families draw from to cover eligible education expenses. Eligible expenses include but are not limited to private school tuition. Funds can be used for tutoring, curricular materials, and even therapy. Almost all of the newest school choice programs are education savings accounts.

Eligibility Requirements to Participate in School Choice Programs

So far, I have discussed how school choice policies rely on different funding arrangements to provide families with access to a variety of learning environments for their children. A third way that school choice polices vary from one another is eligibility requirements to participate. For instance, in the traditional public school system where choice is exercised by choosing where to reside, only families with the economic means to exercise residential choice can have school choice. Eligibility to participate in private school choice programs also varies. All of the earliest voucher, tax-credit, and education savings accounts programs were only available for a small segment of the population. Many of the programs were means-tested, meaning the funds were only available to families below a certain household income threshold. Other programs were only available to families with children with special needs.

However, almost all programs established since 2021 have included a universal-eligibility provision allowing all families to participate. Meanwhile, many states have expanded their existing means-tested programs to universal or near-universal eligibility, granting access to many more families.

School Choice as a Means for *Paideia*

The Equity Argument for School Choice

The earliest school choice programs did not have universal eligibility because school choice itself was framed as an equity issue. At that time, advocates of school choice argued that it was inequitable that some families were able to send their children to their preferred traditional public or private school while other families could not, especially if they had no recourse to exit their residentially assigned traditional public school if they were unsatisfied with it. Because access is greatly constrained by finances, the families who were unable to exercise school choice typically came from lower socioeconomic backgrounds. To rectify this inequity, advocates reasoned, school choice policies ought to make it possible for families without the means to exit their assigned public school to enroll in a charter school where attendance is not determined by place of residence or to enroll their child in a private school with the help of a financial subsidy.

Relying on principles of equity, then, policymakers ought to encourage the founding of new charter schools near low-performing public school districts or to pass means-tested private school choice programs, targeted only to the neediest families rather than universal programs where everyone regardless of need can participate. This is why until only the last few years, voucher, tax-credit scholarship, and educational savings accounts were not available to all families but only targeted to a segment of the population—typically families from lower-income backgrounds or families with children with special needs.

This equity framing of choice was also a practical result of politics. Those on the political right—especially those with business interests and a predilection for free market policies—were drawn to the prospect that charter and private schools could be more efficient at improving educational outcomes. Those improvements, in turn, would improve human capital and benefit the US economy. They also reasoned that the existence of educational alternatives would induce competitive market pressures causing all schools to improve. But to build a coalition to pass school choice policies, there was a need to include advocates on the political left, who were intrigued by the potential of school choice policies to rectify the inequities in the education system. The prospect of historically under-served families accessing better schools and realizing economic advancement was attractive to those on the political left.

As it turns out, the best social scientific evidence about the effectiveness of school choice programs on participants is, on balance, positive. Achievement on standardized tests,[22] educational attainment,[23] and parent satisfaction[24] all generally improve for families who participate in school choice programs. Other research further demonstrates that traditional public schools improve in the presence of these school choice programs, presumably because they can no longer take it for granted that dissatisfied families cannot exit for other educational options.[25] In general, school choice policies were an efficient means of achieving more equity between more and less advantaged families.

The Values Argument for School Choice and the Connection to *Paideia*

Since 2019, however, rising alongside the equity-based argument for school choice is the values-based argument for school choice. The values-based argument for school choice recognizes the formative role that families together with schools and other associations within civil society, such as churches, play in educating their children. It recognizes the inherently human activity of pondering ultimate moral questions, living according to discerned answers to those questions, and living according to the dictates of conscience. Forcing individuals or communities to stop asking these questions, coercing them to arrive at particular answers, or restraining them from following their best judgments of conscience would diminish their humanity. Given these premises, the values-based argument for school choice states that families ought to be able to choose a learning environment that espouses values that align with the values they wish to pass on to their children. School choice, by granting families access to a larger and more diverse set of schools, would enable families to access such a learning environment, the argument goes.

The values-based argument is currently growing in salience, but that development does not mean it was never at play in the past. Families,

22. Shakeel, Anderson, and Wolf, "Participant Effects of Private School Vouchers."
23. Foreman, "Educational Attainment Effects."
24. Rhinesmith, "Review of the Research on Parent Satisfaction."
25. Jabbar et al., "Competitive Effects of School Choice."

religious schools, and some clergy have long recognized that no school can be neutral toward ultimate questions.[26] Every curriculum inherently takes a position on what is true or false, what is good or evil, and what is beautiful or ugly. In deciding what to cover, it deems certain things worthy of attention, and in deciding what to omit, it deems other things unworthy of attention. Every curriculum has answers to ultimate questions such as the origins, meaning, and purpose of life, making every educational enterprise inherently value-laden. For these reasons, families have historically chosen to enroll their children in religious private schools because of the availability of religious and moral instruction that aligns with the values they wish to pass on to their children.[27] Framed this way, school choice is both a means for educational equity and *paideia*.

Cultivating the Educational Ecosystem

The Necessity of an Educational Ecosystem

Despite its success, school choice policies have fallen short of what some supporters have expected. In 2014, Michael McShane, who is the director of national research at EdChoice, wrote an essay in *National Affairs* in which he explains why school choice policies have not fully delivered on their promises. He writes:

> School choice has just not lived up to the hype. Why is this the case? In theory, school-choice programs can cause three things to occur in education systems. They can fill empty seats in existing high-quality private schools, encourage existing private schools to grow to serve more students, or drive the creation of new high-quality schools. But a gap has opened up between the theory of school choice and policymakers' ability to implement it. School-choice programs have been great at filling in existing space in private schools, but they have not helped these schools expand or encouraged the creation of new schools. As a result, there has been a stubborn upper bound on the amount of change any of these programs can effect in the American education system. In short, school-choice policies have failed to create a vibrant marketplace for private educational options, so

---

26. Shuls, "Father of the School Choice Movement."
27. Erickson, "How Do Parents Choose Schools?"

the idea's potential to dramatically revolutionize K-12 schooling has so far gone unfulfilled.[28]

In the ten years since McShane wrote that essay, the passage of many more school choice programs that further lowered the financial barriers that prevented families from exercising school choice demonstrates the additional strides that have been made in improving educational opportunity. However, and to invoke market metaphors once more, the passage of new programs has only addressed the demand-side of the equation, that is, providing families the means of accessing learning environments. As McShane has contended, the supply-side problem has not been adequately addressed. Families can exercise school choice, but the supply of options from which they have to choose has been outstripped by demand.

When Milton Friedman first articulated an economic theory about school choice, he posited that free-market dynamics would ensure a steady supply of high-quality schools as they responded to the demand of parents.[29] School choice advocates since then presumed that once school choice policies were set, those free-market dynamics would necessarily follow, but McShane's observations suggest that educational opportunities do not arise ex nihilo because school choice has been expanded by a new policy. The mere existence of school choice policy does not guarantee that it will deliver on its presumed promise. Some scholars suggest that the lack of educational supply is attributable to the fact that there is no genuine free market in education.[30] Be that as it may, I would like to point to another issue that has limited the supply side. Although school choice programs potentially unleash some free market forces in education, Adam Smith's invisible hand is not entirely invisible. There are real people who must labor to create things that make for a vibrant market. New schools have to be built. Existing schools have to not only fill a few empty seats but be taken to a greater scale. Teachers and leaders have to be trained and recruited. Curriculum has to be developed. In short, meeting the demands and needs of families requires an educational ecosystem, that consists of schools, other educational service providers, and the supporting institutions that enable them to be sustainable and to fulfill their educational mission: government policies, school associations, parent associations, school boards,

---

28. McShane, "Helping School Choice Work," 22.
29. Friedman, "Role of Government in Education."
30. Merrifield, *School System Reform*.

curriculum developers, accreditors, and educator preparation or professional development programs. How to cultivate this educational ecosystem is the focus for the remainder of the chapter.

The Gandalf Option and the Educational Ecosystem

To help us think metaphorically about school choice in terms of an ecosystem rather than a market, let us turn back to the word *culture*. I mentioned earlier that the word *culture* is connected etymologically to worship. There is a second etymological connection to the word *culture*, namely, to care for. The word *cultivate* arises out of that second connection, which is precisely what is required if school choice policies and programs are to fulfill their potential. A rich, robust educational ecosystem has to be cultivated. Like a garden, it has to be diligently cared for. It needs to be tended and given attention. One must ask what that garden needs and be willing to meet that need.

To better understand the work of cultivation, it is helpful to invoke commentary from Baylor University's Alan Jacobs about a scene from Tolkien's *The Return of the King*.[31] The scene occurs on the eve of the siege of Minas Tirith, the capital city of Gondor. Gandalf visits Lord Denethor, who is the steward of Gondor until its true king returns. At this point of the story, it is clear that Lord Denethor is neglecting his duties as a steward, not only because Mordor is about to overrun Minas Tirith but also because he desires to keep power for himself. As a result, when Gandalf confronts Denethor about the impending siege, Denethor accuses Gandalf of trying to usurp his power. He says to Gandalf:

> You deal out such gifts according to your own designs. Yet the Lord of Gondor is not to be made the tool of other men's purposes, however worthy. And to him there is no purpose higher in the world as it now stands than the good of Gondor; and the rule of Gondor, my lord, is mine and no other man's, unless the king should come again.[32]

Gandalf then responds:

> Unless the king should come again? . . . Well, my lord Steward, it is your task to keep some kingdom still against that event,

---

31. Jacobs, "Crisis and Christian Humanism."
32. Tolkien, *Return of the King*, 30.

which few now look to see. In that task you shall have all the aid that you are pleased to ask for. But I will say this: the rule of no realm is mine, neither of Gondor nor any other, great or small. But all worthy things that are in peril as the world now stands, those are my care. And for my part, I shall not wholly fail of my task, though Gondor should perish, if anything passes through this night that can still grow fair or bear fruit and flower again in days to come. For I also am a steward. Did you not know?[33]

Note how Gandalf understands his role as a steward and the gardening metaphor that he uses. He calls "all worthy things that are in peril as the world now stands" his "care."[34] Given the connection between the words *cultivate* and *care*, one can understand Gandalf's role as a steward is to cultivate all worthy things—a role that resonates with what God originally charged Adam and Eve and, by extension, everyone else to do.

Gandalf then goes on to say that he "shall not wholly fail . . . if anything passes through this night that can still grow fair or bear fruit and flower again in days to come."[35] Such a statement evinces his hopefulness and courage. When all the world as he knows it seems bleak and likely to be covered in the darkness of Mordor, Gandalf still faithfully pursues his calling. He recognizes that he will be successful if anything good—no matter how small—will sprout in an otherwise darkened world. Gandalf is tending the garden over which he has influence so that it might flourish and bless all those who pass by. I suspect that Gandalf's posture is the kind that deserves the words: "Well done, good and faithful servant. You have been faithful over a little; I will set you over much. Enter into the joy of your master."[36]

An educational ecosystem that will flourish and be a conduit of God's grace to families and their children needs to be similarly cultivated. But how might this work be done? How can this ecosystem support the work of home, church, and school in the task of *paideia*?

---

33. Tolkien, *Return of the King*, 30–31.
34. Tolkien, *Return of the King*, 30.
35. Tolkien, *Return of the King*, 31.
36. Matt 25:21.

Practical Steps

I will conclude this chapter with some practical suggestions for leaders in primary and secondary Christian schools, leaders in higher education, members of clergy, and others. Before I do, I wish to emphasize that I am not suggesting that one should only support Christian schools. People often sort into camps that support a specific sector whether it is a traditional public school, charter school, private school, or homeschooling. Instead of throwing one's support for a particular sector, it is more helpful to recognize that every school or educational provider—whether they are operated and funded by governments, independently, or a mixture of two—serve the public, that is, the people—everyone. Each school sector contributes to the common good in a variety of ways, as the Cardus Education Survey has demonstrated for over a decade. Based on numerous surveys of adults in the US,[37] Canada,[38] and Australia,[39] some sectors excel at forming citizens who are civically engaged. Others set up students for successfully completing postsecondary education and professional careers. Still others prepare their graduates to have a sense of life purpose and vibrant religious lives. All of this formation promotes the flourishing of communities. All schools are part of the educational ecosystem. The goal in cultivating the educational ecosystem is to ensure that all children and their families are served well.

For Primary and Secondary School Leaders

If you are a leader in a private school, consider participating in a school choice program if your state or province offers it. Familiarize yourself with the program requirements and assess whether your school is able to comply with those requirements without undermining the integrity of its work. On the one hand, avoid categorically rejecting the possibility of participating in a school choice program. On the other hand, count the cost of participation. Exercise wisdom and discuss the possibility of participation with teachers, parents, board members, and other leaders. If your school is considering participating in a school choice program talk to leaders at schools that do and seek their wisdom. Conversely, if your school currently

---

37. Casagrande, Pennings, and Sikkink, *Cardus Education Survey 2018*.
38. Green et al., *Educating to Love Your Neighbour*.
39. Cheng and Iselin, *Cardus Education Survey Australia*.

participates in a school choice program, consider connecting with other leaders and sharing the lessons you have learned. On a related note, school associations should consider how they could facilitate these kinds of conversations between leaders, and accrediting agencies should consider how to come alongside schools to support their participation.

Regardless of whether your school participates in a school choice program, do not lose sight of their missional purpose. Christian schools, in particular, vary in their levels of intentionality toward and ability to serve disadvantaged populations. Although the degree to which each school can be missional depends on factors, such as whether they are equipped and strategically ready to do so, some reflection about which families a school currently serves and which families that school could serve could be fruitful. If you as a school leader believe that a Christian education is the kind of education that should be more widely accessible, there ought to be some strategizing for how to expand their school's reach, especially to populations that typically do not have access to them. More generally, ask the questions of how you can fill empty seats that you currently have, how you might scale up your operations, and how you might even help build a new school in the same way that existing churches often plant new churches. As a school leader, you play a pivotal role in cultivating the educational ecosystem by directly affecting the supply of schools that are available for families.

For Leaders in Higher Education

If you are a leader in higher education, consider the pivotal role your institution plays in advising and preparing educators and school leaders. Most educator preparation programs are set up to prepare candidates for working in traditional public schools.[40] After all, postsecondary institutions often need to organize programs so that they capture the greatest market share of potential teacher candidates, and the vast majority of teachers in the United States teach in traditional public schools. However, the lack of adequate preparation to teach in settings besides traditional public schools has led to an educator pipeline problem in those alternative educational settings. Private school and charter school leaders face challenges of recruiting and hiring educators that apprehend the particular pedagogical approach and educational philosophy

---

40. McShane, *Surfing the Pipeline*.

of their schools.[41] Often times, private and charter school leaders have to spend considerable resources to train their teachers. A similar issue exists for school leaders who sometimes do not feel that their leadership preparation programs have adequately trained them for their responsibilities in their respective schools.[42]

As a leader in higher education, you have a critical role to play in addressing the teacher and school leader pipeline. New preparation or alternative certification programs need to be developed to equip teachers and leaders to serve in educational settings besides traditional public schools. Consider undertaking the challenge of modifying their existing educator preparation programs or creating new ones. Schools are unsustainable without a stable teacher and leader pipeline. Aside from replacing teachers and leaders who leave their positions, new teachers and leaders need to be hired if schools are to scale up their operations or if new schools are to be founded. A robust educational ecosystem requires strong pipelines of teachers and leaders. Because of its outsized role in training future teachers and leaders, higher education has the potential to address the challenges with teacher and leader pipelines. As you envision solutions for educator preparation that postsecondary education institutions can undertake, consider partnerships with schools and school associations to coordinate these efforts. Communicate with accrediting agencies as well to find ways to give schools the flexibility to hire staff that emerge from these alternative teacher and leader preparation programs. Finally, along with your faculty and staff, get to know more of your students and encourage them to pursue a profession or vocation in education.

For Members of Clergy

If you are a member of the clergy, start by talking about education with families in your congregation and discuss how school, home, and church are connected in the larger project of *paideia* and Christian discipleship. As evidenced in the survey of clergy in the United States conducted by Cardus and Barna, those conversations are not happening nearly as much as they should. Moreover, familiarize yourself with the educational options that exist in your community and counsel your parents as they navigate the task of educating their school-aged children. For members of

---

41. Foley and Torres, "Big Picture."
42. Lee and Cheng, "Preparation and Practice of Protestant School Leadership."

your congregation that do not have school-aged children, exhort them to invest in the lives of the children in your congregation. Bringing children up in the nurture and admonition of the Lord is the responsibility not only of their parents but other congregants.

Encourage families in your congregations to consider all educational options that are available to them and to avail themselves of the one that will be best for their children. In fact, some families might even need to use separate options for separate children based on their respective needs. Shepherding your families regarding the education of their children, of course, also requires you to learn about the educational opportunities in your own local community. Spend some time getting acquainted with the schools and homeschooling groups that exist so that you can refer them to your families. Perhaps a relationship with school leaders in your community will lead to new partnerships or occasion other ways for you to invest in children, such as an invitation to give a short homily for a chapel session at your local Christian school.

In addition to referring families to schools, mention the school choice programs that exist in your state. Telling families about a school is one thing; to help them cover the cost of enrolling in that school is another. Helping your families avail themselves of the resources that school choice programs offer also requires you to be familiar with how those programs work. Even if no school choice programs exist in your state, consider how the church might offer scholarships and other forms of financial assistance for families to cover the cost of private school tuition. This is a practice that some church leaders have adopted to support members of their congregation.

Finally, consider renting, or even offering at no cost, your church property for schools or homeschooling families that need meeting space. Especially if your church property sits empty during the week, consider allowing others to use it. Having physical space available is one of the most significant challenges faced by educational entrepreneurs who want to start a new school. Capital campaigns take time to execute, and new schools typically cannot raise sufficient capital for new buildings. A vibrant educational ecosystem requires capital, an issue that churches that already own their properties can address. And if you lead a church that does not yet own its own property, consider how you might build or find a property that could eventually house a school.

For Everyone Else

Finally, if you are not a member of the clergy or a leader in primary, secondary, or tertiary education, you still have a role to play. My general suggestion for you is to get involved and support the work of schools and other educational providers in your community. Schools, especially new start-ups or ones that are attempting to scale up their operations, are always looking for volunteers. Teachers could use assistance in their classrooms. School leaders could use additional administrative help. Schools often need substitute teachers when emergencies arise. If interacting with schoolchildren causes anxiety, consider volunteering in other capacities. Schools often need assistance organizing events for athletics, fundraising, and performing arts. Aside from volunteering for these events, consider attending them and encourage others to do so. Your presence at these events signals your support for these schools and is an encouragement. In addition to giving your time, give your treasure and provide the financial resources that will enable schools to successfully expand their operations. Inspire others to be generous with their time and money. For those who are contemplating ways to become even more involved, consider serving on the school board. Schools will not be viable without the leadership of governing boards. However, being a suitable board member requires building trust with the school community and getting to know the school. Simply get involved, no matter how modest the manner, so that existing board members can get to know you and so that you will be ready for that position if the opportunity comes.

Short of becoming involved in the operations of a school, be a good neighbor and get to know the families with school-aged children in your neighborhood and communities. Especially if they are discerning how to educate their children, be ready to tell them about the different options that are available to them. If they are eligible for financial assistance from a private school choice program, help them avail themselves of those resources. On a related note, private school choice programs are often managed by charitable organizations. Consider volunteering your time for those organizations so that they can administer those programs effectively.

If one generation is to commend God's work to another generation, we must roll up our sleeves and get our hands dirty cultivating an educational ecosystem that will sustain that task.[43] The ultimate goal is to

---

43. Ps 145:4.

bequeath to eternal souls, many of whom do not yet exist, a better world filled with things that, as Gandalf said, "grow fair or bear fruit and flower."[44] We are to care for, or cultivate, our civilization so that it is filled with true, honorable, just, pure, lovely, commendable, excellent, praiseworthy things.[45] Everything around us should radiate as much as possible with God's beauty and goodness. We are to disciple people and build institutions that promote the flourishing of believer and unbeliever alike. All of these are vehicles of God's grace that bear witness to his redemptive and restorative work in a world tainted and broken by sin. Let us envisage and cultivate an educational ecosystem that lives up to these purposes.

Questions for Discussion

1. Is *paideia* aligned with a Christian vision of education? Assess the argument regarding the connection between *paideia* and a Christian vision of education articulated in this chapter.

2. What school choice programs exist in your state? Familiarize yourself with the programs and how they work. How can you help families access that program? What role can you play in sustaining the program? If your state does not have a school choice program, what can you do to provide families with more educational opportunities?

3. How might schools, churches, and homes better partner with one another to educate children?

4. What can we learn about Christian stewardship from the exchange between Gandalf and Lord Denethor cited in this chapter?

5. What is something you will begin doing to cultivate the educational ecosystem in your community?

References

Aristotle. *Nicomachean Ethics*. Translated by Terence Irwin. Indianapolis: Hackett, 2019.
Augustine. *Confessions*. Translated by Sarah Ruden. New York: Modern Library, 2017.
Autor, David. "Skills, Education, and the Rise of Earnings Inequality Among the 'Other 99 Percent.'" *Science* 344 (2014) 843–51.

---

44. Tolkien, *Return of the King*, 31.
45. Phil 4:8.

The Barna Group and Cardus. *Who Is Responsible for Children's Faith Formation?* Mar. 19, 2019. https://barnadev.wpengine.com/research/children-faith-formation/.

Berry, Wendell. "Higher Education and Home Defense." In *Home Economics*, 49–53. Berkeley, CA: Counterpoint, 2009.

Casagrande, Marisa, Ray Pennings, and D. Sikkink. *Cardus Education Survey 2018: Rethinking Public Education*. Hamilton, ON: Cardus, 2019.

Cheng, Albert, and Darren Iselin. *Cardus Education Survey Australia: Australian Schools and the Common Good*. Hamilton, ON: Cardus, 2020.

Dee, Thomas. *Where the Kids Went: Nonpublic Schooling and Demographic Change During the Pandemic Exodus from Public Schools*. Washington, DC: Urban Institute, 2023.

EdChoice. *The ABCs of School Choice 2024 Edition*. Indianapolis: EdChoice, 2024.

Erickson, Heidi H. "How Do Parents Choose Schools, and What Schools Do They Choose? A Literature Review of Private School Choice Programs in the United States." *Journal of School Choice* 11 (2017) 491–506.

Friedman, Milton. "The Role of Government in Education." In *Economics and the Public Interest*, edited by Robert A. Solo, 123–44. New Brunswick, NJ: Rutgers University Press, 1955.

Foley, Brenna, and Amanda Torres. "The Big Picture: Hiring and Retention in Independent Schools." *Independent School Magazine*, 2024. https://www.nais.org/magazine/independent-school/spring-2024/the-big-picture-hiring-retention-in-independent-schools/.

Ford, Michael R., and Fredrik O. Andersson. "Sources of Isomorphism in the Milwaukee Voucher School Sector." *Public Policy and Administration* 36 (2021) 89–114.

Foreman, Leesa M. "Educational Attainment Effects of Public and Private School Choice." *Journal of School Choice* 11 (2017) 642–54.

Green, Beth, et al. *Educating to Love Your Neighbour: The Full Picture of Canadian Graduates*. Hamilton, ON: Cardus, 2016.

Hanushek, Eric A., Paul E. Peterson, and Ludger Woessmann. *Endangering Prosperity: A Global View of the American School*. Washington, DC: Brookings Institution Press, 2013.

Jabbar, Huriya, et al. "The Competitive Effects of School Choice on Student Achievement: A Systematic Review." *Educational Policy* (2022) 247–81.

Jacobs, Alan. "Crisis and Christian Humanism with Alan Jacobs" [webinar]. Washington, DC: The Trinity Forum, 2020.

Johnson, Alison H., et al. *Charter School Funding: Little Progress Towards Equity in the City*. Fayetteville, AR: School Choice Demonstration Project, University of Arkansas, 2023.

Koganzon, Rita. "Pork Eating Is Not a Reasonable Way of Life: Yeshiva Education vs. Liberal Educational Theory." In *Religious Liberty and Education: A Case Study of Yeshivas vs. New York*, edited by Jay P. Greene et al., 31–46. Lanham, MD: Rowman and Littlefield, 2020.

Kristjánsson, Kristján. "Positive Psychology and Positive Education: Old Wine in New Bottles?" *Educational Psychologist* 47 (2012) 86–105.

Lee, Matthew H., and Albert Cheng. "The Preparation and Practice of Protestant School Leadership: Evidence from a Nationally Representative U.S. Sample." *Journal of Research on Christian Education* 30 (2021) 244–69.

Levinson, Meira. "Liberalism, Pluralism, and Political Education: Paradox or Paradigm?" *Oxford Review of Education* 25 (1999) 39–58.

McShane, Michael Q. "Helping School Choice Work." *National Affairs* 20 (2014) 21–35.

———. *Surfing the Pipeline: Understanding Pathways into Teaching in Alternative Models of Schooling*. Indianapolis: EdChoice, 2024.

Merrifield, John. *School System Reform: How and Why Is a Price-Less Tale*. Murrells Inlet, SC: Covenant Books, 2019.

Pennings, Ray. "Cardus' Cofounder Ray Pennings on Schooling and Spiritual Development." Barna (blog), Mar. 19, 2019. https://www.barna.com/schooling-spiritual-development-ray-pennings/.

Plato. *The Republic*. Translated by Alan Bloom. New York: Basic Books, 1991.

Rhinesmith, Evan. "A Review of the Research on Parent Satisfaction in Private School Choice Program." *Journal of School Choice* 11 (2017) 585–603.

Shakeel, M. Danish, Kaitlin P. Anderson, and Patrick J. Wolf. "The Participant Effects of Private School Vouchers Around the Globe: A Meta-Analytic and Systematic Review." *School Effectiveness* 32 (2021) 509–42.

Shuls, J. V. "The Father of the School Choice Movement." *Journal of School Choice* 18 (2024) 334–50.

Tolkien, J. R. R. *The Return of the King*. Boston: Houghton Mifflin, 1955.

U.S. Department of Education. *Digest of Education Statistics, 2021*. Washington, DC: Institute for Education Sciences, 2023.

Wearne, Eric. "A School Sector in Search of a Name." *Education Next*, 2023. https://www.educationnext.org/a-school-sector-in-search-of-a-name/

Westminster Assembly. *The Westminster Shorter Catechism*. 1647.

CHAPTER SEVEN

How the Bible's Narrative Framework Is the Basis for a Holistic and Integrated Approach to Scripture

Alan Gilman

Introduction

In this chapter, we will explore how viewing Scripture as an integrative whole unlocks great depths of teaching potential so often missed due to common tendencies toward reductionism and fragmentation.

In Paul's first letter to his protégé Timothy, he provides this reminder:

> All Scripture is breathed out by God and profitable for teaching, for reproof, for correction, and for training in righteousness, that the man of God may be complete, equipped for every good work. (2 Tim 3:16–17)[1]

According to Paul, Scripture is God's equipment to enable his servants to live effective godly lives. But what *Scripture* is he referring to? Since the collections of writings which would later be called "the New

---

1. Unless otherwise indicated, all Scripture quotations in this essay are from ESV.

Testament," including Second Timothy, were not for the most part written yet, much less compiled, he obviously meant the Hebrew Scriptures, the "Old Testament."[2] This is not to say that the New Testament isn't inspired scripture. It's that we discover here that, according to Paul, the Hebrew Scriptures were sufficient to effectively instruct Jesus followers.

The sufficiency of the Hebrew Scriptures in no way undermines the need for the New Testament. The New Testament is a record of the teachings of Jesus and his early messengers, which in Paul's day were accessible through them in person. Their teaching, first verbally and through letters like Second Timothy, established what the Hebrew Scriptures anticipated—that the Messiah of Israel had come in the person of Jesus of Nazareth and that through him God's purposes for Israel and the whole creation come to their fullest expression (see my explanation on "fulfillment" below). Moreover, the New Testament provides the bridge between Hebrew Scripture as the exclusive possession of the people of Israel and those from among the nations who would entrust themselves to the God of Israel through the Jewish Messiah.

Despite Paul's assertion of the sufficiency of Hebrew Scripture, readers of the New Testament have historically regarded it as the new and improved testament in contrast to the apparently old and obsolete one. The common English titles of these two major sections of Scripture (Old Testament/New Testament) were ascribed to them many years after the completion of each. The English term *testament* is related to the idea of covenant and applied as such to emphasize the differing functions of the old and new covenants as detailed in the Bible. However, labeling what Paul calls "Scripture" as the Old Testament or old covenant gives the wrong impression as to its contents. While the old covenant as given to Israel through Moses at Mount Sinai is central to this section of Scripture, there is more to what is normally called the Old Testament than the old covenant alone. I will explain.

---

2. I will be explaining the historical confusion due to the term "Old Testament," preferring "Hebrew Scripture" or "the Hebrew Scriptures." I am aware that a small percentage of this section of the Bible is written in Aramaic, but the predominant nature of Hebrew warrants such a designation. Even better would be the Hebrew acronym "Tanakh," standing for the three traditional Jewish divisions, "*Torah* (Instruction), *Nevi'im* (Prophets), and *K'tuvim* (Writings)" as this is more in line with Jesus's own reference to Scripture: "Then he said to them, 'These are my words that I spoke to you while I was still with you, that everything written about me in the Law of Moses and the Prophets and the Psalms must be fulfilled'" (Luke 24:44).

First, there is much essential material prior to the giving of the old covenant at Mount Sinai, including creation: our first parents' rebellion against God and its consequences; Noah; Babel; all that God established through the patriarchs Abraham, Isaac, and Jacob; plus Moses and the deliverance of Israel from slavery in Egypt.

Second, the covenantal promises given to the patriarchs, while foundational to Israel's deliverance from Egypt and the subsequent covenantal system given through Moses at Sinai centuries later, are distinct from the old covenant itself. This is evident in the book of Hebrews, where the writer contrasts the new covenant established through Jesus and the older one through Moses, a contrast based upon the prophet Jeremiah foretelling of a new covenant, "not like the covenant that I made with their fathers on the day when I took them by the hand to bring them out of the land of Egypt" (see Heb 8:7–9; cf. Jer 31:31–33). Misunderstanding the distinction between the Abrahamic and Sinai covenants undermines the eternal nature of the promises given to the patriarchs and how they continue to function through to our day. In fact, core to God's promises to Abraham is God's determination to bring blessing to the nations (Gen 12:3), a promise that Paul will later call "the gospel" (Gal 3:8). Certainly, this indicates that Hebrew Scripture in general, as opposed to the Sinai covenant in particular, is anything but obsolete,

Third, despite the obsolescence of the Sinai covenant as a covenant, much of its events and teaching are universal. By universal, I mean they extend beyond the strict confines of the covenantal system itself. While there are specific directives given by God to the people of Israel alone that are limited to a particular place and time, it is within that same context that we learn eternal truths about God, his nature and character, as well as his general will for human beings. It also anticipates the eventual extension of his redemptive mission to all nations and the renewal of the whole creation. In fact, New Testament teaching, far from contradicting or replacing Hebrew Scripture, affirms and develops what was previously revealed.

A Fragmented Bible

The Bible is a collection of various types of writing written over the course of at least sixteen hundred years by about forty different authors in three languages covering a vast geographical region. Yet, it is surprisingly cohesive in the development of its overall narrative (more on that below) and common themes. However, that cohesion has often been fragmented by various assumptions and assertions. These assumptions and assertions may be sophisticated theological systems or the common misconceptions of the average reader. It is beyond the scope of this essay to attempt an exhaustive analysis of the various influences that have served to undermine the cohesiveness of the Bible. Instead, I will provide an overview of some of the worst culprits.

Reductionism

A chief culprit in fragmenting the Scriptures is the principle of reductionism. The reductionist approach to Scripture is one in which it is assumed that the goal of Bible interpretation should be to determine the underlying principles behind its varied writings. This leads to a tendency to group those principles into topics, thus systematizing Scripture into categories or topics. This approach ignores that God didn't reveal his truth that way but through story.

This is not to say that it isn't legitimate to seek to understand the Bible's view on all sorts of topics, such as the nature of God, the effects of sin, or marital love, to name a few. It's not that these and other topics aren't important or that they can't be found in Scripture. It's that God, in his wisdom, is determined to reveal himself and the meaning and purpose of life through a narrative framework, not an analytic textbook. Perhaps by learning and teaching the Bible on its own terms, we will access the fulness of God's truth, equipping God's people as he intended.

There is a tendency to assume that the Bible teacher's task is to make the Scriptures easy to understand. Making Scripture accessible to people, be they young or old, is one thing, but to simplify what God has revealed as complex obscures the intentions of the text. Moreover, the drive toward simplification may deter teachers from texts that are inherently confusing.

For example, take what God says to Jacob when he changes his name (see Gen 32:22–32). Jacob had wrestled through the night with God. God asks Jacob to let him go. What kind of request is that from the Almighty God? And that's after God dislocated Jacob's hip, when he could have obliterated him. In the end, God says to him, "Your name shall no longer be called Jacob, but Israel, for you have striven with God and with men, and have prevailed" (Gen 32:28). Striven with God and have prevailed? How can this be? Can this be simplified to make it understandable? Why would we want to? Its beauty and power are in its complexity. Apart from this being a defining moment in God's development of the people of Israel and their role in his plan and purposes, this reflects the great struggle of anyone who truly engages (or should I say, "is engaged by") the God of the Bible. This acts as commentary on the depths of genuine experience of God and life in the world. To take the Bible on its own terms requires that we resist the temptation to undermine its complexity.

At this point, you may be wondering, "What about children? Surely, we can't expect them to grasp such complexity." I beg to differ. Children encounter life's complexities very early in life: sibling rivalry; disappointment and suffering at the hands of those who claim to, or genuinely, love them; unanswered prayer; and so on. To simplify these experiences with or without Scripture is to misrepresent reality, a reality that is vividly reflected in Scripture. Instead of trying to explain (or explain away) the difficult issues that children (and everyone else) experience, why not let the Bible speak? We might need to adjust our vocabulary for children (and others) to understand. But apart from that, we should let the Bible speak on its own terms.

Misunderstanding "Fulfillment"

This is a good place to expose the confusion over the misguided use of the biblical concept of "fulfillment." We rightly claim that Jesus fulfills messianic prophesy, not to mention all sorts of other aspects of Hebrew Scripture. But too often "fulfill" is misunderstood as "completion," thus rendering anything and everything he fulfills as obsolete. I admit that there is a sense in which fulfillment includes completion, however. This is the case when predictive prophecy points to a person or an event such as Zechariah's foretelling of the messianic king coming to Jerusalem, riding on a donkey (see Zech 9:9). Because this was fulfilled by Jesus (e.g., Matt 21:5; John 12:15), we no longer continue to wait for it to happen. However, Jesus's doing this was not simply his checking off a list of prophecies. Zechariah envisioned the arrival of the one through whom Israel would be redeemed and the entire world would be blessed. Far from simply completing a predictive requirement, the fulfillment of prophecy marks the beginning of what was anticipated. This is why I prefer to view fulfillment as bringing something to its fullness.

Another example is Isa 53:4–6, which anticipates how the Messiah would provide the forgiveness of sin. With the coming of Jesus as Messiah, what was anticipated is now available. Jesus's accomplishing what was anticipated continues to be an ongoing reality. Therefore, when we read the prophecy in our day, centuries after the coming of the Messiah, we can encounter that fullness. Jesus's fulfilling the prophecy shines light on the prophecy to enable us to delve deeper into what God is saying through it rather than simply being satisfied with knowing that Jesus checked another predictive box.

Similar to how Jesus fulfills Messianic prophecy, there is a sense in which he fulfills all of Hebrew Scripture. But again, not in terms of rendering it obsolete. Rather, he brings it to its fullness. Tragically, many people assume he contradicted Moses when he did nothing of the sort. Rather, he affirmed Moses's teaching and expounded it. For example, in the Sermon on the Mount (Matt 5–7), six times Jesus says something akin to, "You have heard that it was said . . . But I say to you." Often people assume that he is correcting Old Testament teaching, when he is doing nothing of the sort. He never says, "It was *written* . . ., but I say to you." What he is correcting is examples of misguided teaching common in his day, which, if we are listening, is something he continues to do today.

Reintegrating Scripture

The Narrative Framework of Scripture

It should be obvious that Scripture is fundamentally story or narrative. Just about all Scripture is told within a framework of a process of situations whereby characters interact with God and the creation. The various events relate to one another in a variety of meaningful ways, exhibiting common motifs, or themes, throughout. As already mentioned, despite being written by multiple authors in different times and locations, the Scriptures exhibit strong cohesiveness and consistency.

The context of God's revelation to Israel at Mount Sinai informs the Hebrew Scriptures, if not the entire Bible. Everything that happens to Israel in the Bible is connected to their exodus from Egypt and the giving of the Sinai covenant. One cannot truly understand the rest of

Hebrew Scripture, much less the whole Bible, without being aware of this foundational narrative.

As for the New Testament, that the four Gospels and the book of Acts are stories is obvious. The various scenes in these books work well in Sunday school settings because of their story form. But what about the letters? From my experience, they tend to be treated as theological essays. And yet, each and every one of them was written to a community or an individual in a real time and place. While the circumstances of each are not always clear, that the writer has specific circumstances in mind is obvious. To neglect the context of these writings easily lends itself to misrepresenting them. In addition to the immediate situations being addressed, the overall narrative of Scripture is at work at the same time. It would be appropriate to view the New Testament letters as first-century gospel case studies.

A Narrative Aside

The Bible is made up of layers and layers of complex narrative. The call of Abram/Abraham is but one example.

The enormity of God's working in and through Abraham is underscored by the great challenges he faces as an elderly childless man leaving family and familiar to go to a far and foreign destination. His faith example is striking but even more striking viewed against the backdrop of the preceding story, Babel (Gen 11:1–9). In contrast to Abraham, the people of Babel had human and natural resources at their disposal which they leveraged in their pursuit of self-determined greatness and security. Their humanly derived plans for greatness collapsed into failure, while Abraham's faith resulted in both fame and blessing, not just for himself, but for the whole world forever. It would be difficult to deny that the contrast between Babel's self-directed failure and Abraham's faith-filled destiny is intentional. To ignore the narrative dynamic at play is to misread these two episodes.

God's Epic Story

The technical word for an overarching narrative is *metanarrative*. When people are taught that life has no meaning, that we are simply the product of energy and matter plus chance, the implications are that life has no metanarrative. Reckoning with the Bible's metanarrative, or "God's Epic Story," as I like to call it, not only integrates Scripture but, as God's word, connects us to life's metanarrative as designed by God.[3]

The following is my attempt at an overview of God's epic story. I contend that the more we grasp the Bible's metanarrative, the better we will understand its details and help others discover their role in God's story today.

The Good Creation

The Bible begins with God creating everything (except himself) by the power of his word. The Bible asserts that every aspect of creation was personally and purposefully created by God and that all things, both seen and unseen, were created good.

Human beings, created as male and female, were set apart from the rest of creation as made in God's image. Both males and females were designed as God's representatives on earth to serve as stewards.

Rebellion and the Curse

The first man and woman disobeyed the only prohibition given to them by God when they ate of the tree of the knowledge of good and evil. Consequently, God cursed the creation, including that women would suffer pain in childbirth, tension would exist between men and women, work would be thwarted, and people would die. Despite this, creation retained its essential goodness, and human beings' original mandate remained in effect. Evil will be destroyed, the details of which would one day become apparent.

The Promise

God called Abram (later changed to "Abraham") to go to a foreign land, which his descendants would one day possess. He promised to make

---

3. The following is an overview of a concept that I have been developing for over ten years, having encountered various other attempts to express the Bible's metanarrative through thematic "threads" or broad theological categories. I contend that the emphasis on God's ongoing faithfulness to literal, ethnic people of Israel is key to representing the metanarrative as the basis for a truly integrated Bible.

him a great people through whom all the nations of the earth would be blessed. It's this blessing that would confront and resolve the creation's cursed state. The promise, which will much later be called the "gospel" (Gal 3:8), was passed on by God to Abraham's son Isaac and grandson Jacob, whose name was changed to "Israel," the name of the promised nation. God's ongoing faithfulness to the nation of Israel drives the narrative through the whole Bible.

The Chosen Nation

BONDAGE AND REDEMPTION

The people of Israel migrated to Egypt, where they became a great nation, but were later enslaved by Pharaoh, Egypt's king. In time, God sent Moses and his brother Aaron to lead the people out of Egypt. Pharaoh's stubborn refusal resulted in God's displaying his power until Pharaoh let Israel go. On the way, God meets with Israel at Mount Sinai and establishes a covenant, which constitutes the nation as God's special people and reveals his character and instructions (Torah) to them (and to the world through them). Adherence to the covenant would result in blessing and prosperity. Disobedience would result in cursing, including foreign oppression and exile. Under Joshua, Moses's successor, they acquired the land as promised to their forefathers.

JUDGMENT AND THE PROMISE OF RESTORATION

Through the centuries Israel struggled in its relationship to God and his ways. Despite times of blessing, the nation fell into greater and greater rebellion. Prophets arose, reminding the people of the consequences of disobedience. As their rebellion increased, the nation fractured and was later overcome by foreigners, culminating in exile.

The Sinai covenant demanded judgment for disobedience, while the earlier covenant given to the forefathers guaranteed God's ongoing faithfulness. As judgment became inevitable, the prophets, based on the earlier covenant, also promised restoration to God and their land. In fact, a new covenant to fully resolve their rebellion against God would be established with the people. This was to be accomplished through a great king, a descendant of David, known eventually as "the Messiah."

The restoration of Israel is linked to the resolution of the curse upon the whole world.

The Gospel: The King Has Come

When the people of Israel returned from exile, they continued to live under foreign oppression, demonstrating that the promised restoration had not yet occurred. When Jesus of Nazareth emerged, first-century messianic expectation led his followers to assume he would overthrow Rome and restore all things according to common understanding of Hebrew Scripture prophecy. They didn't anticipate his sacrifice for sin, his resurrection, nor their being equipped to extend his ministry worldwide as the necessary next steps in God's rescue plan. Note that the blessing to the nations as promised to Abraham was accomplished primarily by resolving Israel's failure to live up to the standards of the Sinai covenant through the Messiah.

The Messianic Mission

Before his ascension, Jesus the Messiah directed his followers to "make disciples of all nations," thus extending God's rescue plan worldwide. The ability to do so was marked by an unprecedented outpouring of God's Spirit on them all. However, it would take some time to fully grasp how people from the non-Israelite nations were to be fully integrated into God's rescue mission.

The Future Hope

The gospel is to be proclaimed throughout the world until the time when Yeshua returns to inaugurate the restoration of all things, including the general resurrection of the dead, the final judgment, the eradication of evil, and the new heavens and the new earth.

We therefore can summarize the Bible's metanarrative as "God's rescue operation of the creation through Abraham and his descendants."

Clarifying "the Gospel"

A common understanding of the term *gospel* undermines a holistic, integrative approach to Scripture. Often, when people think of the gospel, they think of how believing in Jesus, his death, and resurrection guarantees individuals a positive eternal future with God in heaven. If someone says they had an opportunity to "share the gospel," it is most often assumed that these are the details they communicated. Mark 1:15 appears to support this: "The time is fulfilled, and the kingdom of God is at hand; repent and believe in the gospel."

However, even a cursory reading of this verse reflects something more than what I described above. Such a presentation focuses on nothing more than the phrase "believe in the gospel," and that with a particular meaning in mind, without noting the fullness of the whole statement. The common misrepresentation of the text is further illustrated when the call to "repent" is neglected.

The references above to both the fulfillment of time and of the kingdom of God place the proclamation of the gospel within the Bible's metanarrative. But first, let's look at the likely biblical roots of the term *gospel*.

The English word *gospel* simply means "good news," derived from the Old English "godspel,"[4] which is derived from the Greek New Testament word *euangelion*, meaning "good news." *Euangelion* is the Greek word used in the Septuagint (LXX)[5] version of Isa 52:7:

> How beautiful upon the mountains
> > are the feet of him who brings good news,
> who publishes peace, who brings good news of happiness,
> > who publishes salvation,
> > who says to Zion, "Your God reigns."

While the Hebrew term here, *basar tov*, appears to be a generic way to express "good news," its reference to God's reign highly suggests that this is the background of *euangelion* (good news, gospel) in Mark 1:15 and elsewhere. The good news of the coming of the Messiah is far more than generic good news, but the good news of God's restored reign as anticipated through Hebrew Scripture. Thus, the phrase "the

---

4. Located at Merriam-Webster, "gospel."

5. The Septuagint, abbreviated as LXX, is an ancient Greek translation of the Hebrew Scriptures, which became the standard Old Testament of the early Greek-speaking church.

time is fulfilled." This is the moment the people of Israel had been long anticipating. The curse of Eden would be finally broken when the promised deliverer resolves their ongoing alienation from God as expounded by the Hebrew prophets.

Moreover, outside of its initial Jewish context, *euangelion* was a specialized term in the first-century Roman Empire. As N. T. Wright and Michael Bird note: "The word 'gospel' (*euangelion*) was in use with celebrations of the Roman emperor and his achievements."[6] To proclaim the New Testament *euangelion* in the empire was to assert that Jesus is Lord and Caesar is not!

Be it in the Jewish or Roman contexts, the gospel was far more than simply an invitation to an individualistic spiritual experience, but rather the proclamation of God's reign through his appointed king. All other powers and power brokers are therefore made subservient to the Messiah. The call to repent, therefore, is much more than simply an internal, spiritual experience. While it is indeed an invitation to individuals to right relationship with God, a relationship with massive personal transformative implications, that relationship is part of God's grand plan of redemption of the whole creation in every way.

This in no way downplays the importance of Jesus's death and resurrection. Far from it! It highlights its purpose. Instead of his death and resurrection *being* the gospel, his death and resurrection are what make the gospel possible. The gospel invitation, therefore, is not one of acknowledging facts about Jesus as much as a call to follow him, the one who provided the solution for sin and the curse.

This is the essence of what Jesus commissioned his followers to do at the end of Matthew:

> And Jesus came and said to them, "All authority in heaven and on earth has been given to me. Go therefore and make disciples of all nations, baptizing them in the name of the Father and of the Son and of the Holy Spirit, teaching them to observe all that I have commanded you. And behold, I am with you always, to the end of the age." (Matt 28:18–20)

Upon his authority as Messiah, Jesus's followers were to instruct people of all nations everything they had learned from him. His death and resurrection would undergird all they taught, but not be their

---

6. Wright and Bird, *New Testament in Its World*, 562.

exclusive message. We see this exemplified in Paul's gospel presentation in Athens:

> The times of ignorance God overlooked, but now he commands all people everywhere to repent, because he has fixed a day on which he will judge the world in righteousness by a man whom he has appointed; and of this he has given assurance to all by raising him from the dead. (Acts 17:30–31)

Paul asserts that Jesus's resurrection is the basis of the call to repent. The appropriate response to acknowledging Jesus's death and resurrection is a transformed lifestyle in harmony with the breadth of God's word.

Sample Passages

Let me illustrate the power of a holistic, integrative approach to Scripture by looking at two well-known New Testament passages.

John 3:16

> For God so loved the world, that he gave his only Son, that whoever believes in him should not perish but have eternal life.

Perhaps the most familiar of all Bible verses, these words of Jesus are often taken as an invitation to personal faith in order to experience individual salvation. I have heard people encouraged to replace "the world" and "whoever" with one's own name something like this: For God so loved [Alan], that he gave his only Son, that [should Alan] believe in him [Alan] should not perish but have eternal life.

I do not want to imply that such an individualistic appropriation of Jesus's words is completely misguided. Surely the world includes individuals like me, and if I put my trust in him I can be assured of eternal life. However, treating the verse as if it is all about individuals robs it of its full scope.

The word *world* here is often assumed to mean "all the people of the world." And since I am one of those people, it is helpful for me to identify me as such. But is that the intent of the word? When we take into account the grand narrative of Scripture, a bigger picture comes into view. The Greek word for "world" is *cosmos*, which is best taken to mean, in this context, "the created order" or simply, "the creation." Thinking back to God's pronouncement of the creation as "very good" (Gen 1:31), worthy of preserving despite human mismanagement, as well as the hope of renewal that led to the coming of the Messiah, we discover that the reason for his sending his Son was to accomplish God's great mission, to rescue not only the people of the creation, but the creation itself. God's engagement of individuals, therefore, is one aspect of his overall rescue operation. This doesn't downplay individual salvation. Rather, it puts it in a much larger context of restoring human beings to God's original design as his representatives to steward his creation.

Romans 8:28

> And we know that for those who love God all things work together for good, for those who are called according to his purpose.

Perhaps you have heard the following saying, which is likely derived from this verse, "When life gives you lemons, make lemonade!" I concur that Paul provides the true follower of Jesus with an extraordinary outlook on life. But on what basis? Paul does say, "for those who are called according to his purpose." But what purpose? When viewed through the reductionist lens of personal salvation, it is often assumed that the purpose is no more than I am saved because God wanted me to be saved. So, I am saved.

We do not have time to demonstrate how the whole of the book of Romans has been turned into a theological treatise instead of a heartfelt letter Paul wrote in confronting growing antagonism on the part of gentile believers toward Jewish people (see Rom 11:17–32). But even without that, when we take into account the Bible's narrative framework, what is God's purpose that Paul is referencing here? As with John 3:16, it certainly includes the salvation of individuals, but it needs to be understood within the context of the Bible's metanarrative.

Once we recognize that God's purpose is his rescue plan of creation, then "for those who love God all things work together for good" makes so much more sense! Instead of assuming God is focused on making sure that everything in each of our lives somehow results in a personal positive, this is the assurance that the believer's inclusion in God's overarching purposes ensures whatever happens to us contributes to God's eventual triumph. Far from this verse turning God into some sort of personal lemonade stand, it calls us away from self and our personal problems to something very much bigger.

Conclusion

Expanding our view of Scripture to consider its metanarrative should not negate how it speaks to individuals with our personal problems and challenges. Knowing God through Jesus certainly has profound and extensive personal implications. It's that looking at the Bible through an individualistic lens prevents us from apprehending its full intent. Once we grasp the big picture of the Bible's overarching story, we are able to discover how the Scriptures in their vast complexity speak to the vast complexity of all of life.

Perhaps you have heard it said that the Bible is God's love letter to you. Certainly, through the Bible we encounter God's infinite, enduring, sacrificial love for his human creatures. However, to read the Bible as a love letter to you or anyone else necessarily makes large segments incomprehensible and irrelevant. God's love as expressed through the Bible is found in a holistic, complex revelation of truth that takes a good deal of work to understand it in order to impart its comprehensive goodness to others.

Questions for Discussion

1. How might an integrative, holistic approach to Scripture affect specific Bible stories (e.g., David and Goliath)?
2. Considering the gospel has its roots in God's blessing to Abram and his descendants (Gen 12:3), what might have Joseph, the husband of Mary, heard when the angel said to him, "You shall call his name Jesus, for he will save his people from their sins" (Matt 1:21)?
3. Have you ever considered that "Christ" is a title, "Messiah," the long-awaited King of the Jews, and not simply another name for Jesus? What difference might that make to your understanding of the Bible's metanarrative? What difference would it make in how you teach the Bible?
4. List some possible biblical teaching topics in light of the gospel's being the proclamation of "Jesus is Lord, and Caesar is not."

5. Have you ever considered that the bulk of the book of Proverbs was written by a man, Solomon, who disregarded so much of what God had inspired him to write? Does that negate the wisdom expressed in his writings? Why or why not?

References

Merriam-Webster. "gospel." https://www.merriam-webster.com/dictionary/gospel.

Wright, N. T., and Michael F. Bird. *The New Testament in Its World: An Introduction to the History, Literature, and Theology of the First Christians*. Grand Rapids, MI: Zondervan, 2019.

CHAPTER EIGHT

Theological Foundations of Christian Education

Trinitarian Relationality and Friendship

KEVIN A. MIRCHANDANI

CHRISTIAN THEOLOGY MAKES AN inimitable claim that God is one and there are three persons (Father, Son, and Holy Spirit) of this relational tri-unity who are God.[1] The outrageousness of the Christian claims go further: God's befriending of humanity is directing the whole story of human existence from what it means to be in right relationship with others to how we do our work. As such, since we are created *by* God, the source of relationality, we are made *for* friendship, and this should direct our efforts in Christian education. Drew Hunter described in his work *Made for Friendship* how:

---

1. Yeo, "Trinity 101," 3. There have been recent global discussions taking place concerning the nature of the Trinity. I would recommend Green, Pardue, and Yeo's compilation, *Majority World Theology: Christian Doctrine in Global Context* as a starting point for understanding the global, cross-cultural theological discourse concerning the mystery of the Trinity. We need theological vision rooted in cultural contexts to direct who we are as participants in God's creating, redeeming, and restoring work in our cultures, times, and spaces.

Friendship is the ultimate end of our existence and our highest source of happiness. Friendship—with one another and with God—is the supreme pleasure in life, both now and forever, and no one can fully enjoy life without it.[2]

In this chapter, the mystery, unity, and personhood of the Trinity is not raised for utility, but for clarity about human identity, vocation, and relationship in Christian learning communities. We are not yet excavating the depth of the Triune God mystery as a theological reservoir for directing our learning, living, and leading in Christian schools.

This chapter first serves as a theological foundation in Trinitarian perspective for Christian educators to thrive in their workplace friendships. It is written to K–12 Christian school teachers, but also for leaders and policymakers to reflect on how they are designing the actions and interactions within their learning communities. Secondly, it seeks to inform efforts for Christian educators by addressing a profound gap in the context of workplace relationships: If we were created *in*, *by*, and *for* relationship, then why do I experience such loneliness in the work of Christian education? Finally, the chapter offers some practical guidance for K–12 Christian educators and school leaders to incorporate practices leading to lifelong friendship[3] and to derive the sort of considerations that move communities forward professionally and relationally.

Theological Foundations in Trinitarian Perspective

As readers explore the biblical, philosophical, historical, and sociological foundations for Christian education *in* creation, we have the foundations of what was and is *before* creation. We have the one "in whom are hidden all the treasures of wisdom and knowledge."[4] Arguments for transforming Christian schools emerge from the theological mystery and revelation of the Trinity, which serves as a guiding consciousness for

---

2. Hunter, *Made for Friendship*, 13.

3. Roberto, "Faith Formation for All the Seasons," 4. Roberto describes lifelong and life-wide formation as the sort of journey of discipleship taking place over one's lifespan contributing to faith growth, "a process of experiencing, learning, and practicing the Christian faith as we seek to follow Jesus and his way in today's world" (xi). In this chapter, I use lifelong friendship and faith formation interchangeably to describe Roberto's notion of "life-wide" formation, that is, the full range of experiences across an adult's personal and professional life.

4. Col 2:3. All Scripture quotations in this essay are from NIV.

Christian schools to become spaces of relationality and lifelong friendship that impacts people, communities, and generations.

God, the Trinity, is both one *and* three. According to David Naugle, that means that God is "one, indivisible, divine substance, yet he subsists as three distinguishable co-divine, co-equal, and co-eternal persons—the Father, the Son, and the Holy Spirit . . . there is the one divine *what* or substance and the three divine *whos* or persons."[5] In the language of the Athanasian Creed, God is uncreated, "neither confounding the Persons nor dividing the Substance."[6] Friendship was there in the act of creating the world.

Furthermore, the Triune God created the world in relationship, by relationship, and for relationship. Often accounts of Christian educational philosophy begin at God's act of creation. Christian theology has always argued since the writings of the early church that God *was* and *is* and *will be* revealed in the mystery, unity, and relationality of the Trinity: "begotten, not made . . . . Through him all things were made."[7] This is a main storyline of Christian education from before creation informing the story of new creation. The world is seeking to fill the emptiness and void in the epidemic of friendship with tasks that appear to have meaning and distractions that have pseudo purposes. However, as the beloved of Christ, we were made for friendship and relationship with the Triune God. According to C. S. Lewis, God is the fuel that we are intended to run on.[8] God made the world in friendship; friendship is part of the substance of what God is using to put the world back together and make it right.[9] According to Roberto, lifelong and life-wide friendship is the new creation way of living already here and now.[10]

A biblical theology of workplace friendship begins with the Trinity, the relational unity that we see before creation. Ancient people would have understood the pre-creation state of the cosmos of nothingness as a world without purpose or order, wild and wasteful, and formless and void.[11] Old Testament theologian Dr. Carmen Imes argued that when humans are created in the image of God, they are given purpose and

---

5. Naugle, *Philosophy*, 38.
6. Naugle, *Philosophy*, 38–39.
7. Christian Reformed Church, "Nicene Creed," lines 7 and 9.
8. Lewis, *Mere Christianity*, 31.
9. Second Corinthians 5:11–21 describes the ministry of reconciliation.
10. Roberto, *Seasons of Adult Faith Formation*, 4–5.
11. Kidner, *Genesis*, 13.

appointed to rule as God's representatives, thus attributing relational meaning to their work.[12] The representational expression emerges from God who is friendship in work.

Biblical Foundations of Friendship in Trinitarian Perspective

The Genesis narrative sets up the rest of Scripture for humanity's representational work alongside the creator God and provides the relational basis for friendship built on mutuality and relationality.[13] In the garden, we read about how the process of Adam naming the animals is about the search for a suitable helper and companion.[14] Eve's co-creation should evoke an understanding of co-laborship to ancient agrarian people that required many hands for the harvest labor.[15] Canonically, Scripture's agrarian language points us to understanding the goodness of relationships rooted in our shared work and labor.

In Gen 3:8, when God calls out to Adam and Eve, "Where are you?" he is not asking because he does not know, but because friendship invites questions of purpose and belonging, implying that there is a hiding from God's relational presence. The narrative of Scripture tells of various episodes in the fall from relationship because of the enmity of the beloved from God's beloving and befriending.[16] The story of the Bible is summarized in God restoring the broken relationship so that people could become the renewed blessing of creation. Reconciliation of people to God, others, and creation is what Randy Woodley described in his work on shalom communities as the reaching back into the original meaning of justice, right relationship, peace, and wholeness.[17]

Throughout the biblical account, some are called friends of God. Enoch walked with God.[18] Abraham's faith was credited to him as righ-

---

12. Imes, *Being God's Image*, 31.
13. Imes, *Being God's Image*, 38.
14. Gen 2 The Message.
15. Imes, *Being God's Image*, 38.
16. Anderson, *Theology of Friendship*, 6.
17. Woodley, *Shalom and the Community of Creation*, 10–14.
18. Gen 5:24.

teousness and was called God's friend.[19] Exodus 33:11 acknowledged that "the Lord would speak to Moses face to face, as one speaks to a friend."

In the wisdom tradition of Psalms and Proverbs, the language of walking helps readers hearken back to God walking in the garden in the cool of the evening.[20] We are to read Gen 3:8 as an expression of the walking relational presence and "strolling in the garden"[21] as the habitual friend-forming practice with God.

The notion of "walking in step" throughout Scripture refers to pace, the way one habitually conforms their life step-by-step in relation to God's right relationship with humanity. It also pertains to cadence, how one reforms the way in which their steps relate to others. For example, Ps 1:1 describes the walking in step with the Lord because we become like the people we spend time with. Those who receive the blessing of delighting in God's law (God's intention for how life is to be lived) root themselves in relationship and also bear fruit, "That person is like a tree planted by streams of water, which yields its fruit in season and whose leaf does not wither—whatever they do prospers."[22]

John 15 presents God as a divine mystery, lawgiver, and relational presence in Jesus. In the passage, Jesus connects the love of God's law to friendship rooted in abiding in him, highlighting that blessings come from following Jesus. John 15 echoes allusions of God as the gardener from Gen 2 and links the intention for life from Ps 1 and Gen 1. In John 15:12–17, Jesus emphasizes the implications for revealing intimate parts of his mission to the disciples, stating, "I no longer call you servants. . . . Instead, I have called you friends, for everything that I learned from my Father I have made known to you." Friendship marked by abiding in Jesus comes with the command to love each other.[23] Jesus the gardener, teacher, and worker is revealing to his disciples that to abide in him is to carry his relational presence into the world and be the sustaining source for learning and relationship.

Paul's New Testament letters are filled with the theme of friendship as co-laboring as he encourages the early church leaders to persevere in their collaboration toward the mission of the church. For example, in 1 Cor 3:9, Paul describes how he and the apostles are co-workers in God's service,

19. Gen 15:6; Rom 4:1–22; Gal 3:6–9; Heb 11:8–10, 17–19; Jas 2:23.
20. Gen 3:8 NIV.
21. Gen 3:8 The Message.
22. Ps 1:3.
23. John 15:17.

despite the different roles and communities that they serve in. Friends support and build one another up, sharing burdens and joys, while striving toward common goals. Thus, as the world was created in friendship, it is being made right in friendship through the person of Jesus, and being renewed as people work together in friendship.

Practical Concerns for Cultivating Friendship Among Christian School Educators

In a world of increasing disconnection and the need for lifelong friendship, here are some of the practical questions Christian schools need to examine to build communities of relationality and mutuality:

- What does it look like for teachers to thrive in their professional relationships with colleagues and students? (Community)
- How can we equip educators to develop and sustain meaningful relationships with God in their work and across their lifespan? (Connections)
- What skills are necessary for us to teach students and educators if we hold a high theological view of friendship? (Curriculum)
- Who do Christian school educators go to when they experience relational conflict in the workplace? (Conflict)
- How do Christian schools encourage friendships cross-culturally? (Culturally)
- How can educational leaders sustain friendships across organizational structures? What external supports are necessary for their thriving? (Care)

These are the theological foundations and questions at the heart of Christian education today, indwelling within the mystery and relationality of the Triune God. In the following sections, I provide some practical guidance for Christian educators.

Christian Educators Are the Living Curriculum for Friendship

Christian schools must continue to intentionally teach friendship to their educational staff. There are practices that promote inclusivity toward others' cultures, backgrounds, experiences, and differences that encourage mutuality. Friendship involves giving up, serving others, and putting aside self-seeking interests. Christian education, in its essence, is Christian education when it helps people and communities participate in God's unfolding narrative of friendship. This is not the sort of friendship of ideological affiliation, but one of befriending into relationality where someone wholly unlike me can be the closest one to me.

In Swaner and Wolfe's chapter on abiding together, which developed the implications for John 10:10 in Christian schools, "I have come so that you would have abundant life," it is argued that schools are called into a "wider ecology of flourishing together" and relationships that are enduring, interdependent, inclusive, and serving.[24] Developing a theology of friendship is vital for Christian schools to be places of thriving, where relationships are established; practices promoting community, connection, and belonging are participatory and formational; and where the story of Scripture continues to unfold in both individual peoples' lives and in the vocational efforts of Christian learning communities. These extend beyond statements of welcome and inclusion to descriptions and narratives about impact, change, and transformation because of friendship.

Christian schools do need to formally scope-and-sequence their theology of friendship into the curriculum. However, it is possible to teach social emotional skills and not cultivate lifelong and life-wide friendship among educators. The big theological ideas of friendship we are aiming to embody in our K–12 Christian curriculum might include the following: (1) We were made for friendship with God; (2) Friendship reveals what God is like; (3) Friends provide support in times of need; (4) Friends help us grow in wisdom and character; (4) Friendship is a gift; (5) Friendship brings joy and companionship; (6) Friendship makes us more like Christ; and (7) True friendship involves vulnerability and hard conversations, reflecting God's restorative work.

Friendship is essential in an educator's vocation life for emotional support, professional growth, Christian formation, collaboration, navigation of change and complexity, and participation in the unfolding

---

24. Swaner and Wolfe, *Flourishing Together*, 76–77.

narrative of God's redemptive work in the world. In Whyte's work on friendship, he argued that "the ultimate touchstone of friendship is not improvement, neither of the other nor of the self: the ultimate touchstone is witness, the privilege of having been *seen* by someone and the equal privilege of being granted the sight of the essence of another, to have walked with them and to have believed in them, and sometimes just to have accompanied them for however brief a span, on a journey impossible to accomplish alone."[25] If we want our Christian curriculum efforts to embody a theology of friendship, we must provide formative experiences for our educators to be rooted in relationship with God and others within our school communities.

Encountering the Triune God Personally

At one point in my life, the absurdity of trying to understand the Trinity drove me to the point of what Bruce Stephens identified as "losing one's soul by denying the Trinity and of losing one's wits by trying to understand it."[26] Over the course of a year, while immersed in a Christian post-secondary community, I dove deep into finding a way to deconstruct the core of the Christian faith. It was a lonely year. It felt like my Christian friends had abandoned me. I experienced the "dark night of the soul"[27] where I contrived of a formless, empty world that had no purpose and intentionality; it felt like I was living in a world made by chance that was created for itself. However, in the presence of Christian brothers, I met Jesus on a Damascus road like Paul, where scales fell from my eyes, and I began to understand what grace meant: the story of God's all-along befriending. Such friends have continued to play the chorus in my life around key practices with friendship: transparency, vulnerability, self-reflection, and turning our lives outwardly.

Yet, we see educators departing from the profession—"burning out," and expressing their anxiety and concerns stemming from the feelings of despair and loneliness. Within a thriving Christian learning community, members need caring professional relationships built on self-reflection, mutual respect, trust, shared commitments to a school's

25. Whyte, *Consolations*, 45.

26. See Stephens, *God's Last Metaphor*, 75.

27. John of the Cross's the *Dark Night of the Soul* is an expression in poetic verse attributed to sixteenth-century Spanish priest and mystic John of the Cross as he described the state of how the soul is alone when detached from God.

mission and vision, to cultivate lifelong friendships. For Christian schools, churches, and organizations, we need a more robust workplace theology of friendship. We must create secure workplace attachments where people do not see relationships as merely a means for ascent, but a sanctification lifeline and pathway.

Current Challenges to Workplace Friendship

Current concerns for the sustainability of Christian schools must address whether our Christian learning communities are contributing to the workplace loneliness epidemic or offering hope. Another key consideration is how Christian schools are introducing people to transformative relationships that encourage connection, healing, and belonging. Additionally, it is important to identify what enables Christian educators to develop faith across their lifespan.

A 2023 study from Pew Research found that 61 percent of US adults identified that having close friends was important for a fulfilling life, which was reported different from the same group that said the same about marriage (23 percent), having children (26 percent), or having lots of money (24 percent).[28] The same study identified that 53 percent of adults have between one and four close friends, 38 percent have five or more close friends, and 8 percent say they have no close friends. There are differences in other variables with reporting such as age, gender, race and ethnicity of friendships, and satisfaction.

A key concern raised in the report was that 61 percent of women and 54 percent of men reported talking with their friends about work, and 67 percent of women and 47 percent of men reported talking about their family with friends.[29] The findings were similar to that of Meta and Gallup's 2023 study on social connection that polled people in 142 countries to ask, "In general, how connected do you feel to people?" The responses were startling. Only 70 percent identified as having the feeling of being "very connected" or "fairly connected."[30] What would similar studies in Christian schools report today, and what would be our response if we found similar reported numbers?

---

28. Goddard, "What Does Friendship Look Like in America?," paras. 3–4.
29. Goddard, "What Does Friendship Look Like in America?," paras. 3–4.
30. Gallup and Meta, "Global State of Social Connections," 9.

If friendship is one of the most integral aspects of our lives yet most often overlooked in developmental efforts, Christian schools must support the practical development of friendships within their learning communities.[31] We need a greater "workplace spirituality." According to Altman et al., workplace spirituality "is a synergy of meaning, purpose, beliefs, and values (in particular, moral values or virtues), a sense of community and belonging, and a sense of value or worth in one's life that, together, animate us in what we seek and do and thereby leads to our fulfillment and happiness."[32] Friendship is sometimes used in the workplace to describe bonds, attachments, or authority that extend beyond an individual's influence. In the modern workplace, it is often referenced in circles as a means for power, ascent, interest, and ideological affiliation. In contrast, friends do not only provide a referent in time and space to one's experiences but also expose our capacity for relationships. How Christian learning communities teach about friendship and operationalize the concept of friendship in practice reveals a great deal about a current sanctification gap: We want the beloved saved, but do not yet know how to equip with purpose for life after the beloved are saved. I next explore some practical ways to develop workplace friendship among Christian educators.

Friendship Among Christian Educators

For the first two years of my educational career, I never ate my lunch in the staffroom. I was so focused on building relationships with my students that I had forgotten the importance of my colleagues as a source of inspiration and hope in those early testing years, yet I craved affirmation about my practice. I was slowly befriended by staff that had been working at the school that entered into my classroom space and helped me realize that we need spiritual guides, sages, mentors, companions, and caring leaders in our lives. I encourage Christian schools to evaluate the frequency, purpose, and expectation for entering into one another's spaces and what current conditions reveal about the sort of sense of belonging and possibility of friendships being formed.

For many of us, even those that regularly attend a Christian church community, our workplaces are the formational places where we put our

---

31. Hunter, *Made for Friendship*, 17.
32. Altman et al., *Workplace Spirituality*, 22.

learning into practice. I would make a bold claim that it is not only the communities we are a part of but our workplace friendships that are having the greatest influence on the integration of spirituality and faith formation. In other words, Christian educators tasked with the responsibility for teaching students how to collaborate, think critically, manage emotions, communicate empathetically, and engage with individuals unlike them, and perform executive functioning skills derive their approach from the implicit and explicit messages conveyed in their workplace culture regarding connection and relationships.

Christian schools appear to be in an intensification period of policies and procedures to guide their communities. As such, Christian schools are creating robust policies around how to handle conflict and putting procedures in place to make sure their Christian values are embedded. However, I wonder what a robust theological framework describing the types of friendship forming practices might look like in a Christian school elaborating on principles of Matt 18 and Col 3. I mean not to argue for a presumptive or prescriptive approach to what friendships are expected but instead to generate a set of phenomenological descriptions about how people in the community ought to engage in the spiritual practice of forming friendships.

What stories could be shared with our school communities that define the radical ethic of love and inclusion among the educational staff team?

There are two liminal spaces that have potential for where lifelong and life-wide friendship can be learned: (1) in meetings and (2) within workplace relational conflicts. In meetings, we teach protocols that help rewire the way our brains shift from thinking about members of our team as "others" to "another" and even further to "one of us." Friendship must become a desired outcome and intentional formative goal directing our Christian learning communities. Within conflict, we are provided an opportunity to form a greater depth of listening, understanding, transparency, clarity, purposefulness, and information sharing. These conditions, derived from friendship, can transform meetings from hostile to formational spaces. In conflict, we are invited to pause and reflect on the pre-creation world, wild and wasteful, formless and void, and meet one another with creativity and intention.

As I have worked in different K–12 Christian schools to facilitate professional learning, I have often questioned how well the professional learning plans extend the needed relational capacity building.[33] Brooks provides a practical guide in training for how to know a person, saying that how we see people affirms that we are "creature[s] endowed with an immortal soul—a soul of infinite value and dignity."[34] For school leaders, we must design our professional learning to encourage critical dialogue and reflection. Colleagues must be in one another's learning spaces. We must teach how to have productive conversations among staff members and see the image of God alive in one another as we discuss concerns for Christian teaching and learning.

I next address how to move from affiliation to lifelong friendship and identify practices for communities to engage with as they promote conversations leading to formative friendships.

The Affiliation to Friendship Process

I have theorized that Christian schools are not yet consistently moving educators specifically from affiliation, which is rooted in ideological terms, to lifelong friendship, which implies a shift from the "other" to "another" to "us."[35] Thus, Christian schools might be creating a sanctification gap where (i) some members experience shallow levels of safety, (ii) other members languish either due to an inability to break into the culture or experience the feelings of rejection, or (iii) are stifled out by the lack of depth in the community to create opportunities for befriending. This results in missed opportunities for lifelong friendship and formation.

In the affiliation to friendship process, when it comes to building relationships, there are multiple entry points for friendship. However, there are also multiple exit points. There are also re-entry points into relationships. The process, again, involves transparency, vulnerability, self-reflection, and turning our lives outwardly.

---

33. See Hargreaves and Fullan, *Professional Capital*. These scholars described how professional capital is a function of human capital, social capital, and decisional capital. Within social capital, there is relational capital. However, I think where their argument does not go further is on the side of spiritual health, community, connection, friendship, and belonging. This chapter argues that it is not sufficient to be a professional community; we also need to be a relationally forming community and be spaces where befriending takes place, which is a transformational outcome across the whole Christian school profession.

34. Brooks, *How to Know a Person*, 31.

35. See Figure 1: Affiliation to Friendship Process.

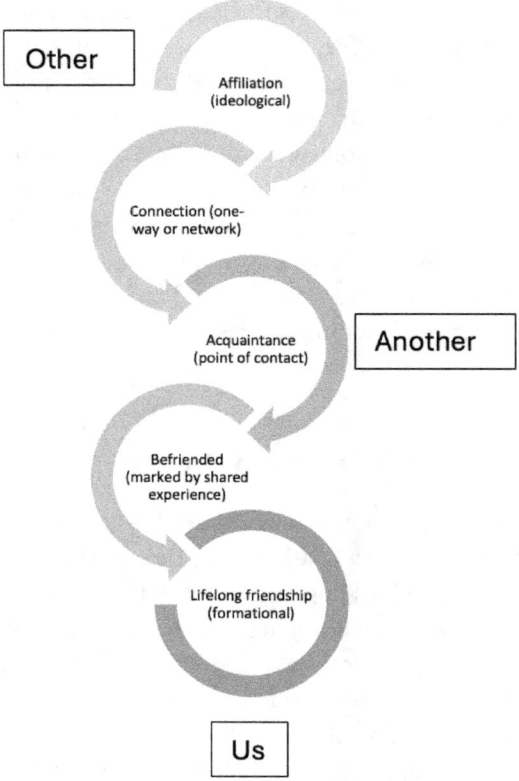

Figure 1: Affiliation to Friendship Process

Christian schools understand relationships to be the foundation for learning and, thus, need to clarify how they teach friendship from pre-kindergarten to grade 12 and beyond. Once we tune into the chorus of Scripture as a song being sung about friendship, we will move from the more general love that God has for all of creation and humanity, to the specific and particular love God has in what is expressed in intimate friendship leading to individual and communal transformation.

Theories of situation or communal practices have helped us to better understand ourselves as relational beings, where we adopt the beliefs, behaviors, and values of a community through shared practices.[36] As school leaders encourage friendship among educators, consider creating a list of

36. See Lave and Wegner, *Situated Learning*.

wisdom statements or epigraphs directing practices among educators.[37] We need to teach friendship as a spiritual discipline, which means we have to teach spiritual practices such as conversation, generosity, hospitality, service, and conflict—which are some of the forgotten spiritual practices because they often require a vulnerability of self before others in a community with real peoples' needs evoking our greatest fears, doubts, and awareness of the world's (or our own) unfriendliness. I encourage educational directors and school designers to consider friendship as a transformative indicator of successful professional learning.

Raw and Revealing Emotions

Goleman et al.'s work around emotional intelligence broke the ice around our emotions manifesting themselves in organizations.[38] However, there was much more below the surface concerning how emotions reveal a sense of workplace engagement. Fear of relationship, interruption, vulnerability, empathy, conflict, failure, and difference are all raw realities that educators experience revealing an unsatisfied need for intentional Christian formation in the workplace. Practically, because Christian educators must continue to receive training for their professional responsibilities, school leaders must teach how to communicate among organizational divisions, train protocols for communication, communicate with community partners and parents, approach colleagues with conflicts, and provide feedback to administrators. There is greater capacity to engage in these important practices strengthening the Christian school when educators experience a greater sense of stability and attachment to their workplace emerging from friendship among their colleagues. We do, however, need data to inform how we plan to address these respective concerns. Effective data collection is necessary for understanding whether our efforts are having an impact and supporting how educators feel about the workplace. I have found focus groups to be a helpful way of both building relationships among members of teams and providing clarity around professional expectations. Quantitative

---

37. Wisdom statements or epigraphs are statements that are easily accessible, concise, and repeatable that help to define a culture. Within a workplace spirituality, the expression "God gave us two ears and one mouth" takes me back to some of my time in Christian schools reminding me to listen deeply to the perspective and interest of others.

38. See Goleman et al., *Primal Leadership*.

data can be more helpful when it comes to longitudinal tracking and indicators of thriving for educators. Educational staff meetings are also great places to teach formational Christian practices, thus increasing capacity for friendship with other educators.

Communities of Friendship

We can teach how to move from affiliation to friendship. Christian schools are encouraged to develop intentional friendship-forming protocols that they employ with their students and families in a spirit of mutuality. For example, community events that invite their members to join in celebrations often further reinforce fragmentation. Individuals must move from being audience members, to witnesses, to participants, and engaged members of the school community. As educators find trusting colleagues to share their experiences in humility and vulnerability, an intentional circle of care and community is developed. One of the models that has helped me is the "72-12-3-1" approach forwarded by various spiritual formation thinkers. We do need to impose limitations on our friendship. The "72" from Luke 10 sent out in pairs corresponds to our connections, people in our networks that we know are carrying out the same mission. The "12" relate to those we are intentionally being formed with based on proximity, teams, and teaching and learning. The "3" emerged from the Gospel of John's theological telling of Jesus bringing Peter, James, and John into the intimate experiences at the transfiguration[39] and the garden of Gethsemane.[40] John, the writer of the Gospel of John, seems to convey that Jesus revealed many things to him—John describes himself as the beloved, inviting us as readers to find ourselves in the story as the beloved of the incarnate God. We, the beloved, need communities or circles of friendship to be formed.

In 2021, I realized that there was a professional sense of loneliness that I and my colleagues in other Christian schools were experiencing. In collaboration with a few colleagues who were working in different Christian educational organizations, we started a cohort of educational leaders in British Columbia K–12 Christian schools built around mutual sharing around job-related efforts. Over and over again, my colleagues and I heard that those joining the cohort just needed a place to know

---

39. See Matt 17:1–13; Mark 9:2–13; and Luke 9:28–36.
40. See Matt 26:36–6; Mark 14:32–42; and Luke 22:39–46.

that others like them are out there. To start on this journey, I would recommend that schools explore different rotations connecting educators intentionally within their school community and also externally with other Christian schools.

Four Aspects of Communication for Teaching Friendship to Christian School Educators

1. *Teach Conversation* (Conferencing): Conversation has often been overlooked as a spiritual discipline or practice. Practices form our habits and direct our formation. Joanne Jung wrote about how the Puritan practices of conferencing and communication are some of the means by which spiritual relationships are cultivated: "Relationships take time and effort; these are precious commodities. We end up sharing less with fewer people. The result: unattended souls."[41] Further, Jung argues that a community must participate in conversational practices that promote wholeness and healing.[42] Humanity was created for belonging in community and, yet, community is what we need the most but also fear the most. In my experiences, the quality of conversation is directly related to the depth in which educators feel connected to their school, colleagues, and personal purpose. Jung's practices of moving from the informational to transitional to transformational take away the threatening aspects of not knowing where a conversation is going and, instead, encourage greater cooperation, care, connection, context, and closeness to the issues concerning our purpose.[43] I recommend Jung's book for teaching Christian school communities how to engage in structured conversations that shape protocols for discussion, feedback, and engagement.

2. *Teach Listening*: Brooks argued for the importance of hard conversations that require us to ask questions such as "How do you see this?" in the hope of entering into others' points of view. We teach conversation as a means of formation and listening as the means of re-formation. I not only recommend David Brooks's book *How to Know*

---

41. Jung, *Lost Discipline of Conversation*, 25.
42. Jung, *Lost Discipline of Conversation*, 35.
43. Jung, *Lost Discipline of Conversation*, 141.

a Person[44] as a practical guide for listening, but would encourage Christian educators to pick up Judith and Sherwood Lingenfelter's book on *Teaching Cross-Culturally*[45] as a practical anthropological approach to observation, listening, and empathy.

3. *Teach Perspective-Taking*: I have worked through some of the most challenging intrapersonal aspects of myself with others in the Christian schools context. I have learned about conflict. I have maintained friendships when the bounds of work space and employment contracts have ceased. I have been at the retirement parties where friends, colleagues, and loved ones are all present together, yet indistinguishable, and the stories being shared reveal a great deal about the impact that educators have had on one another's spiritual formation, pushing the bounds of personal and professional. I have been challenged by three core competencies or practices related to cultivating friendships in conversations: (1) perspective taking (knowing): shifting from seeing the "other" as "another" who is capable of experiencing life's vulnerabilities and limitations as much as I can; I am called to see them, whether friend or enemy, as the one Jesus invites me to love as my neighbor;[46] (2) presence (being): those that offend me, do not see my perspective, or do not match my values as those that Jesus brought his relational presence to; and (3) participating (doing) that friendship is often formed through intentional practice, discipline, and commitment over time.

4. *Teach Conflict*: Christian educators must embrace conflict as a means of spiritual transformation. By encouraging productive disagreements through self-reflection, grace, and intentional dialogue, Christian conflict practices involve examining one's own interiority to see the image of God alive in each individual. I recommend Dr. Betty Pries's practical book on a spirituality of conflict, *The Space Between Us: Conversations About Transforming Conflict*, for teaching educators how to deepen interpersonal relationships using conflict theories.[47]

---

44. See Brooks, *How to Know a Person*.
45. See Lingenfelter and Lingenfelter, *Teaching Cross-Culturally*.
46. Matt 5:43–48.
47. See Pries, *Space Between Us*.

Trinitarian theology describes how God's befriending of humanity is the foundation to the story we are telling in Christian education about human identity, thriving, and purpose. By grounding practices in the mystery and relationality of the Trinity, Christian educators are encouraged to develop lifelong and life-wide meaningful friendships within their communities, addressing the pervasive issue of workplace loneliness. The chapter serves as a call to action, urging educators and leaders to move from mere affiliation to friendship. It seeks to bridge the sanctification gap, guiding Christian educators toward a more transformative experience of becoming like Christ in the presence of other image bearers.

Questions for Discussion

1. Take an inventory of the relational language that your Christian school uses within its mission, vision, and professional learning efforts. To what extent would you say it describes a robust Trinitarian theology in how it encourages members of the community to move from affiliation to friendship (other, another, us)?

2. What are the current barriers that Christian learning communities and educators face in cultivating lifelong (and life-wide) friendships? (Consider factors such as power dynamics, expectations, existing relationships, crippling emotions, or lack of capabilities).

3. What would an intentional learning plan that addresses both professional development and relational formation look like for your school community?

4. What would a curricular scope and sequence of intentional Christian practices promoting lifelong and life-wide friendship look like in the K–12 Christian school?

5. How do we clarify possible challenges within the educational leaders' formation of lifelong friendships? What practices help educational leaders navigate issues of power within the structural or organizational dynamics of their learning communities and still thrive in their internal and external friendships?

References

Altman, Yochanan, et al. *Workplace Spirituality: Making a Difference*. Berlin: de Gruyter, 2021.

Anderson, Paul N. "A Theology of Friendship." *Faculty Publications—George Fox School of Theology* 334 (1982) 6–7.

Brooks, David. *How to Know a Person: The Art of Seeing Others Deeply and Being Seen*. New York: Random House, 2023.

Christian Reformed Church in North America. "Nicene Creed." 2024. https://www.crcna.org/welcome/beliefs/creeds/nicene-creed.

Gallup and Meta. "The Global State of Social Connections." Gallup Inc., 2023. https://www.gallup.com/analytics/509675/state-of-social-connections.aspx.

Goddard, Isabel. "What Does Friendship Look Like in America?" Pew Research, Oct. 12, 2023. https://www.pewresearch.org/short-reads/2023/10/12/what-does-friendship-look-like-in-america/.

Goleman, Daniel, et al. *Primal Leadership: Unleashing the Power of Emotional Intelligence*. Boston: Harvard Business Review, 2013.

Hargreaves, Andy, and Michael Fullan. *Professional Capital*. Toronto, ON: Teachers College Press, 2012.

Hunter, Drew. *Made for Friendship: The Relationship That Halves Our Sorrows and Doubles Our Joys*. Wheaton, IL: Crossway, 2001.

Imes, Carmen. *Being God's Image: Why Creation Still Matters*. Downers Grove, IL: InterVarsity Press, 2023.

Jung, Joanne. *The Lost Discipline of Conversation: Surprising Lessons in Spiritual Formation Drawn from the English Puritans*. Grand Rapids, MI: Zondervan, 2018.

Kidner, Derek. *Genesis*. Downers Grove, IL: IVP Academic, 2019.

Lave, Jean, and Etienne Wegner. *Situated Learning: Legitimate Peripheral Participation*. Cambridge, UK: Cambridge University Press, 1991.

Lewis, C. S. *Mere Christianity*. New York: HarperCollins, 1952.

Lingenfelter, Judith, and Sherwood Lingenfelter. *Teaching Cross-Culturally: An Incarnational Model for Learning and Teaching*. Grand Rapids, MI: Baker Academic, 2003.

Naugle, David. *Philosophy: A Student's Guide*. Wheaton, IL: Crossway, 2012.

Pries, Betty. *The Space Between Us: Conversations About Transforming Conflict*. Harrisonburg, VA: Herald Press, 2021.

Roberto, John. "Faith Formation for All the Seasons of Adulthood." In *The Seasons of Adult Faith Formation*, edited by John Roberto, 3–32. Naugatuck, CT: LifelongFaith Associates, 2015.

Swaner, Lynn E., and Andy Wolfe. *Flourishing Together: A Christian Vision for Students, Educators and Schools*. Grand Rapids, MI: Eerdmans, 2021.

Stephens, Bruce. *God's Last Metaphor: The Doctrine of the Trinity in New England Theology*. Grand Rapids, MI: Scholars Press, 1981.

Whyte, David. *Consolations: The Solace, Nourishment, and the Underlying Meaning of Everyday Words*. Langley, WA: Mary Rivers Press, 2021.

Woodley, Randy. *Shalom and the Community of Creation: An Indigenous Vision*. Grand Rapids, MI: Eerdmans, 2012.

Yeo, K. K. "Trinity 101: Kaleidoscopic Views of God in the Majority World." In *Majority World Theology*, edited by Gene L. Green, Stephen T. Pardue, and K. K. Yeo, 3–13. Downers Grove, IL: IVP Academic, 2020.

CHAPTER NINE

Take Up Your Cross?

Christian Asceticism and Teacher Well-Being

Anna Lise Gordon and Stephen G. Parker

In the face of a situation in which teachers give their all in-role, what effect might the gospel imperative to "deny yourself and take up your cross"[1] potentially have for the Christian teacher in the context of their work and well-being? This chapter begins by surveying the field of studies on teacher well-being from a contemporary and historical perspective, drawing attention to the current challenges in teacher recruitment, retention, and burnout in the profession, issues recognized as long ago as the 1950s. This is followed by a theological reflection on the notion of well-being in light of the gospel, in particular Jesus's command to disciples to "take up their cross" and forms of Christian asceticism, which sought to take this command most seriously. The chapter explores whether Christian discipleship and well-being are incompatible ways of life, concluding that, in opposition to those forms of Christian theology and faith that negate the body in favor of the solipsistic view of the spirit in isolation, a holistic Christian spirituality is one which is fundamentally concerned with

---

1. Matt 16:24. All Scripture quotations in this essay are from NRSV.

well-being more generously understood. Christian teachers' well-being is better situated in a more generative way and is, in fact, in accord with the gospel. The chapter contains case studies for reflection on the life of the typical Christian teacher, making recommendations for further work and research, providing recommendations for a healthier Christian spirituality of well-being, as well as questions for discussion.

Teacher Vocation and the Problem of Well-Being

Teaching is often variously described as a rewarding vocation, a true calling, and a joyful privilege. However, there is an underlying tension for teachers as this sense of vocation is challenged by complex situational factors exerting considerable pressure, adversely affecting teachers' professional well-being throughout their careers. At a time of significant global concern about teacher recruitment and retention,[2] a renewed focus on teacher well-being in general, and the well-being of Christian teachers in particular, is timely and relevant.

Discussions around teacher well-being have recently increased globally.[3] For example, in the England context, the Teachers' Standards[4] do not reference teacher well-being explicitly, but more recent policy documents aimed at early career teachers include clear references to the need for teachers to learn how to "protect time for rest and recovery," for example.[5] A focus on teacher well-being is a trend that is also emerging in other countries, recognizing that teachers who are thriving in the profession are more likely to have a positive impact on the learning and well-being of the children and young people in their care.[6]

Employers have a duty of care and pastoral responsibility for their teachers to ensure they are equipped and supported in their work with children and young people. Teachers also need to take ownership of

---

2. UNESCO, *Moving Forward*.

3. Hascher and Waber, "Teacher Well-Being," 34; Yu et al., "Trajectory of Teacher Well-Being Research."

4. Department for Education, "Teachers' Standards."

5. Department for Education, "Early Career Framework," 25; and "ITT Core Content Framework," 31.

6. Aelterman et al., "Well-Being of Teachers in Flanders"; Barjorek, Gulliford, and Taskila, "Healthy Teachers, Higher Marks?"; Liu, Song, and Miao, "Navigating Individual and Collective Notions"; Skalvik and Skalvik, "Does School Context Matter?"; Wilson, Sellman, and Joseph, "'Doing Well' and 'Being Well.'"

their well-being, acknowledging that professional well-being operates at an individual, organizational, and systemic level.[7]

What Is Teacher Well-Being?

Concern for teacher well-being is nothing new. As early as 1949, the *American Annals of the Academy of Political and Social Science and Trends in American Education* published an article asserting society's responsibility for teachers' welfare (the alternative term to well-being current at that time). There is, Lawrence Haskew argued, a duty of care toward teachers' material, psychological and emotional well-being, moreover even their social standing, was a matter of import, their esteem as a profession linked to their success as educators because children and young people gauge the seriousness of education based upon how society treats its teachers.[8] In a similar vein, Martha Hessel and Percival Symonds reviewed a range of other studies on teacher well-being published in the post-Second World War period in an article of the same year, again reporting on the importance of providing for the material security in maintaining and influencing teacher morale.[9] It is also noted that principals who considered teachers' feelings were also rated highly in this regard. Social status, physical health, emotional health, and personality adjustment were all researched, the former revealing that teachers' standing in the community, especially being seen as leaders, enhanced teachers' esteem, the latter research reporting particularly on the effects of teachers on children's emotional health and adjustment. Even so, these nascent concerns about teachers' morale seem indicative of educators being mostly viewed performatively, their well-being being narrowly understood, economically and in relation to their social position.

Although synonyms such as "welfare" and "morale" have been of historic concern, it appears the emotional aspects of teachers' labor and lives have been relatively neglected as a feature of their professional lives. In the present, although discussions of well-being abound, there remains a lack of clear consensus on a definition for well-being in the teaching profession. This is perhaps unsurprising given the range of situational variables which affect a teacher, making it almost impossible to

7. Gu and Day, "Challenges to Teacher Resilience."
8. Haskew, "Society's Responsibility for Teacher Welfare."
9. Hessel and Symonds, "Welfare of the Individual Teacher."

provide a succinct definition which is fit for all contexts.[10] However, the Organisation for Economic Cooperation and Development provides a teachers' occupational well-being conceptual framework which offers a comprehensive account of the components of teacher well-being and is useful to inform discussion in this chapter.[11]

Teacher well-being may be considered to have four key components—physical and mental, cognitive, subjective, and social.[12] As we carry various burdens in our lives, data around physical and mental well-being are relatively easy to collect, with reports on well-being focusing on levels of tiredness, irritability, anxiety, and so on, as well as numbers of days absent from teaching due to ill health. A teacher's ability to concentrate on teaching, acquire relevant knowledge and relevant skills, and engage in problem solving and decision making are integral parts of cognitive well-being. Subjective well-being is more personal insofar as it relates to teachers' sense of purpose and fulfillment in the profession, often closely associated with self-efficacy and agency in their roles. Social well-being for a teacher refers to the quality of interactions with students, colleagues, and parents/carers, as well as levels of support from senior leadership within the institution. For the Christian teacher, well-being may be enhanced further in some of these key components through a faith-filled sense of purpose, underpinned by gospel values and prayer. However, as we observe below, this has the potential to feed negatively into a teacher's sense of self and professional identity.

Challenges to Teacher Well-Being Internationally

The low value afforded to the teaching profession in many countries, combined with unattractive working conditions, pose a continual threat to recruitment and retention. For early career teachers, there are potential challenges—emotional, financial, and academic—to their well-being.[13] This may be combined with "transition trauma," where preconceived notions of the role of a teacher may not match

---

10. Dodge et al., "Challenge of Defining Wellbeing."
11. Viac and Fraser, "Teachers' Wellbeing."
12. Viac and Fraser, "Teachers' Wellbeing."
13. Birchinall, Spendlove, and Buck, "In the Moment"; Thompson et al., "Averting the Crisis."

the reality of working in schools.[14] One might imagine similar feelings among some of the early disciples of Jesus who moved from the relative safety of their existing situation to a new life with multiple demands, unpredictability, and even danger.

Teachers at every stage in their career are required to meet changing and diverse needs of learners against a backdrop of a constantly changing educational landscape and new policy directives.[15] In addition, excessive workload in particular is often cited as a key factor in high attrition rates among teachers, with up to 50 percent leaving the profession within the first five years.[16] Indeed, Allen and Sims have identified an unhelpful pattern of "recruit—burnout—replace" in the UK context which is undoubtedly reflected in many other contexts around the world.[17]

Working conditions are often cited as a key factor in teacher stress, particularly where there is a threat to teacher autonomy, agency, and sense of purpose.[18] Constant policy change at a system and local level can be exhausting, as teachers strive to respond positively even when the evidence base for some new initiatives may be unclear. At an institutional level, the physical environment and the quality of relationships with learners and other teachers are key factors in the quality of teacher well-being.[19]

Protective Factors for Teacher Well-Being

Research studies provide considerable consensus on protective factors which have the potential to nurture a teacher's well-being.[20] In one study with early career teachers in England and Australia, a strong sense of purpose and commitment to teaching as a profession was identified as a crucial shock absorber for teachers under pressure, enabling them to maintain perspective in challenging times.[21] Other key protective factors which emerged were levels of confidence, including appropriate

14. Johnson et al., "Promoting Early Career Teacher Resilience," 531.
15. Howes and Goodman-Delahunty, "Teachers' Career Decisions."
16. Foster, "Teacher Recruitment and Retention in England"; Queensland College of Teachers, "Attrition of Queensland Graduate Teachers."
17. Allen and Sims, *Teacher Gap*, 20.
18. Gordon, "Early Career Teaching and Resilience."
19. Klassen and Chiu, "Effects on Teachers' Self-Efficacy."
20. Gu and Day, "Challenges to Teacher Resilience."
21. Gordon, "Educate—Mentor—Nurture."

opportunities for professional learning throughout their career.[22] As noted previously, the power of positive relationships in the teaching profession is well-documented, and this was also identified as a powerful protective factor for early career teachers in England and Australia, who frequently cited the significant contribution of their mentors in supporting and nurturing their well-being.[23] Teachers require significant skills in adaptability to respond to a variety of situations on a daily basis, so those teachers who have high levels of agency and self-efficacy in their work are more likely to be at ease in the profession. Finally, school culture is widely recognized as a vital protective factor for teacher well-being, particularly where it is developed intentionally, over time, by senior leaders in collaboration with all members of the school community.

A significant gap in the literature, particularly when considering a Christian vision for education, is the lack of attention paid to "spiritual well-being" as a key component of overall teacher well-being. As noted by Fisher, spiritual well-being lies at the heart of our identity and may be less obvious than other components of well-being as outlined above, meriting further theological consideration.[24] What resources does the Christian faith provide toward spiritual well-being for the teacher?

Toward a Christian Theology of Teacher Spiritual Well-Being

Fundamental to a theological understanding of the incarnation is *kenosis*, the notion that God in Christ is divested of the trappings of divinity (omnipotence, omniscience, and so on) in becoming human (Phil 2:7), the ultimate act of self-giving impelled by the love at the heart of the Trinity. This theological idea, expressive of a profound truth ontologically enacted, is one of utter love for creation and for the purpose of salvation, and in Philippians is understood as the model for Christian devotion. What God in Jesus has done, the Christian is called to emulate, orienting themselves to an attitude of profound self-sacrifice. The vocation of the Christian is to model the Savior's love; spirituality grounded with this

---

22. Van Nuland, Whalen, and Majocha, "Teacher Recruitment and Retention."
23. McCallum, "Teacher and Staff Wellbeing."
24. Fisher, "Impacting Teachers' and Students' Spiritual Well-Being."

end in view; ever loving, ever expending, the goal being the wholeness of humanity.[25] This is high ideal indeed!

Some forms of Christian spirituality incline to a negative view of the body, sometimes implying a binary between spirit and flesh, with the latter being viewed problematically as something to be disciplined and kept in check.[26] The end of Christian spirituality for such theologies is to recuse the body in favor of a solipsistic inward-looking, world-denying piety, problematizing physical pleasure and material gain in favor of a particular form of asceticism.[27] The history of Christian asceticism cuts across traditions, not exclusively Orthodox, Catholic, or Protestant, but rather influential from earliest times in Christian history, arguably based upon a misunderstanding of the terms used for "body" and "soul" in the New Testament.[28] Illustrative practices in this typically body-denying form of asceticism would be the wearing of a celice (hair shirt), self-flagellation (literal and temperamental), fasting, self-denial, and celibacy. These antimaterialistic, body-denying practices were encouraged as a means of assisting the believer to identify with the sufferings of Christ and becoming more like him in mindset and spiritual orientation.

Of course, these practices are not common among Christian believers, but they do represent a spiritual stream of body-denying Christianity which runs deep. To be like Christ we too must take up our cross, make sacrifices small and great, and greet physical suffering when it comes. Such a mindset of self-denial is subtly active across Christian traditions, which begs the question whether the discourse of well-being has anything to do with Christianity. Can one be well, in the contemporary use of that term, and be Christian? How does Christianity play out in the lives of Christian teachers, not least in terms of the ascetic mindset described above? Thus, has the idea of well-being got any relevance to the Christian teacher? The psychological implications of this toxic version of Christian spirituality are clear.

Given the longevity of asceticism, surely its disciplines represent the norms of the Christian worldview? If Christianity teaches that the way to holiness is self-denial, emulating Christ's ultimate sacrifice and following his imperative to take up the cross, then surely one should expect the cost of discipleship to be great, felt in material insecurity, even poverty,

---

25. Vanstone, *Love's Endeavour, Love's Expense*.
26. Gooder, *Body*.
27. Miles, *Fullness of Life*.
28. Gooder, *Body*.

self-denial, and an expected limit to one's agency. In fact, the Christian life might be considered antithetical to contemporary notions of well-being, which imply levels of self-gratification rather than self-sacrifice, constantly calling people to engage in self-care rather than self-denial.

Curiously, Christian spirituality has often misunderstood its end as being the discipline of the flesh, whereas theologically the idea of the incarnation implies the inverse, that material reality is of value. As the Anglo-Catholic Henry Scott Holland once asserted, "You cannot believe in the incarnation and not be concerned about drains."[29] On the contrary, the body, human health and well-being in Christian spirituality proper is one which embraces a more holistic view rather than a binary between spirit and body, the former being valorized at the cost of the latter.

Moreover, historically, and in broad terms, Christianity has a poor track record in fostering emotional, mental, and physical well-being. The call to self-denial and sacrifice has played into a mindset which has viewed the body as something to be subjugated and repressed—from fasting through to self-flagellating, from the arts through to sexuality, material life and the life of the sense have been viewed negatively. For teachers, already making significant sacrifices in a demanding role, there should be no place for spiritual guilt to accompany the professional version of it.

Reconciling Christian Asceticism and Notions of Well-Being

What we propose is that this reading of the Christian tradition, one that is negative about the body, is erroneous. In this view we draw upon the work of Margaret Miles, in particular her book *Fullness of Life: Historical Foundations for a New Asceticism*. This book evaluates the various traditions of Christian asceticism, from the Desert Fathers, through to Saint Augustine, Saint Benedict, and Saint Ignatius. It critically examines these traditions in light of the full Christian vision and assessment of the human person, and against the background of how we now understand human health and well-being. Miles encourages us to draw upon the traditional practices of asceticism in new ways—leading to a mutual enrichment of body, soul, and mind. She suggests that we not practice self-denial to punish ourselves; rather we are to adopt asceticism to orient our energies to

---

29. Paget, *Henry Scott Holland*, 286.

the benefit of our flourishing. Fasting, for example, might be fasting from the media—or anything which has the potential to drain our emotional and spiritual energy, preserving it for other more productive purposes. She encourages us think about practices that are good for the body and the soul, as two mutually dependent aspects of the human person. Moreover, she observes ascetic practices should be temporary, and not masochistic—we should in fact confront any habit that is not life-affirming. Recognizing that some practices are perennially useful, e.g., fasting for one meal or up to three days, giving the body a rest from metabolizing, now has recognized physical, and thereby spiritual, benefits.

Similarly, Paula Gooder observes that the tendency to bifurcate body and soul has had negative consequences upon Christian spirituality. Rather, she argues that "we should place physical well-being alongside prayer and worship in our thoughts about spirituality: sleep, exercise, pampering in a spa, having a well-cooked meal with friends are all part of spirituality and we should take care to ensure that we do them regularly."[30]

Thus, within a newly framed form of Christian asceticism, a more generous and generative view of our material existence is possible, one which valorizes body *and* soul as in synergy, encouraging a healthy, indeed holistic, perspective on them. Discipline and denial become much more about achieving life affirming ends for oneself and others, e.g., staying physically and mentally well, by eating healthily and exercising, because that is beneficial to the person as well as enabling you to continue to function in the service of others.

What Might This All Mean for the Christian Teacher?

Taking care of one's well-being, in this understanding of Christian spirituality, is in line with taking up the cross; it is life affirming, not life denying, even if sacrificial. Discipleship is a reorientation of one's values and action to the ends of the kingdom, through prayer, but its virtues are focused rather than punitive, in line with the grain of one's being, rather than at odds with it; as Howard Thurman articulated it: "ask what makes you come alive and go do that, because what the world needs is more people who have come alive."[31] Rather than the contrary, Christian discipleship is in accord with well-being; it is living as God intended, and

30. Gooder, *Body*, 129.
31. Bailie, *Violence Unveiled*, xv.

living life to the full. It is a victorious resurrection and triumphant ascension spirituality, not just a kenotic, self-sacrificial one.

Case Studies

What issues and dilemmas occur in the real lives of working teachers? The following practical case studies offer some examples by way of a stimulus for reflection.

Case Study One

Mary-Ann is a Christian primary school teacher. The daughter of Christian teachers, she has lived and breathed education for much of her life. She knows the rhythms of the school year from her own schooling and home life; she knows, from conversations and direct experience, the pressures and challenges of maintaining a successful professional existence. Becoming a teacher seemed the natural thing to do; it was in the grain of her being. Moreover, her Christian faith has taught her the importance of serving others, making sacrifices for their benefit, even at a cost to her time, energy, weekend rest, and even holidays. She lives, eats, and breathes her job as a teacher, seemingly naturally.

- What are the dangers of an alignment between faith and work in Mary-Ann's case, and in general?
- You are mentoring Mary-Ann. What advice might you have for her from a Christian point of view?

Case Study Two

Carl, a secondary school PE teacher, avid gym-goer, and boxer, has recently become a Christian. Up till now he is lived for his fitness and sports interests and is struggling to find a way of reconciling his "old" life and habits with his new faith commitments. Similarly, for him, being a PE teacher has little to do with his Christian faith, as far as he can tell. He has come to you, his spiritual adviser, because he feels so conflicted as to whether his continuing enthusiasm for physical activity and teaching are compatible with his Christian faith. He is concerned that to live a fully Christian life he might have to give up his sports and even his teaching career.

- How would you help Carl reframe his perspective on physical activity, teaching, and his Christian faith?
- Are certain sports incompatible with being a Christian?

Case Study Three

Tamzin is a religious education teacher, Roman Catholic, but sympathetic to Buddhism and a devotee of mindfulness. To her mind, Christianity is a mystical faith, having little to do with the well-being movement that is currently in vogue. She is deeply suspicious of notions of "self-care" as being "woo woo"—irrational and superstitious—nothing to do with Christianity at all. In some ways, her life is quite demarcated, her day job, faith life, and interest in mindfulness having a little crossover for her. She senses that incoherence in her thinking and her conflicted sense of self are beginning to trouble her in her personal life, even her health.

- Can these apparently disparate elements of Tamzin's life be reconciled?
- How would you advise her to go about reconciling them?

Conclusion

An urgent need to better understand well-being permeates current debates on the teaching profession, prompted by shortages in many subject areas, high rates of turnover, and the low status of teachers around the world. On one level, a positive stance to well-being can be shaped by responding to systemic challenges including lack of appropriate resources, retention issues, workload concerns, examination pressures, and inspection stresses. However, discussion in this chapter has highlighted a need to focus on reframing understandings of spiritual well-being, on the synergy between body and soul, as interconnected and mutually enhancing aspects of a teacher's being, especially for the Christian teacher.

Through this chapter, our focus has understandably been on the individual teacher who is seeking to follow the gospel imperative to take up their cross in a manner which is both honoring to God and aligned

160 FOUNDATIONS

with their personal and professional well-being. As we draw to a close, it may be helpful to dwell for a moment on a diagram from The Church of England's publication entitled *Our Hope for a Flourishing Schools System*.[32] Recognition is given to the notion that flourishing teachers are individually effective but, with others, they have the potential to be collectively transformative. This diagram serves as a useful reminder of the interconnectedness of teacher well-being with other aspects, combining a sense of purpose as a teacher, founded upon a revised sense of Christian asceticism, with our multifaceted relationships with others, and our ongoing learning as professionals. These various components are all situated within a well-structured and resourced system, with recognizable benefits to the individual professional and, importantly, to the children and young people at the heart of the educational endeavor.

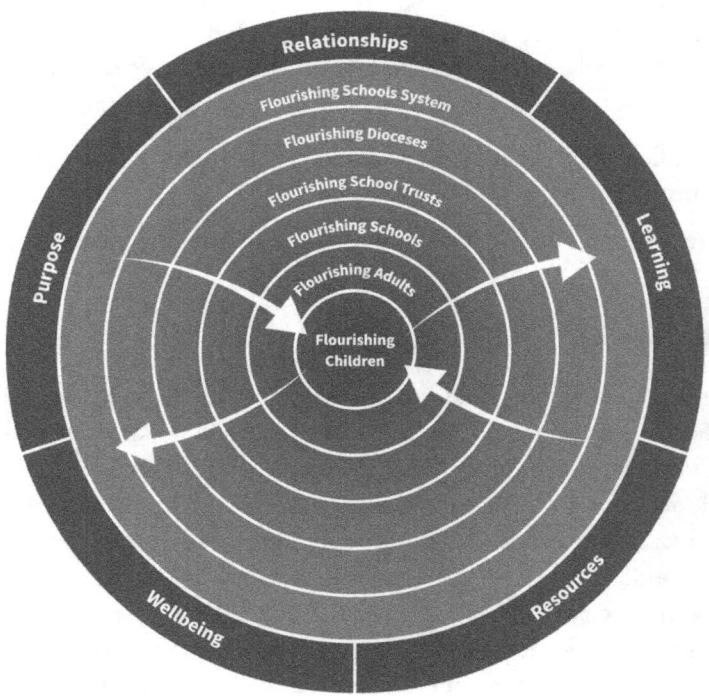

32. Church of England, *Our Hope for a Flourishing Schools System*.

Revisiting Christian mysticism as a theological resource for dialogue with contemporary notions of well-being is advocated here, not only to justify self-care among Christian teachers, but to provide a critical perspective upon previously distorted notions of spirituality, which lessen the value and importance of bodily and material life. A recent article notes how a return to expressing what is joyful in work with students, in teaching, in research, and with colleagues, in this case among university academics, can lead to career reevaluation and act as antidote to disillusionment.[33] Likewise, we would advocate that—just as a fruit of the spirit is joy (Gal 5:22)—giving periodic consideration to why one remains a teacher is essential. An intentional focus on what it is in work that fulfills the teacher (with children and young people, in teaching, professional practice, and with colleagues) has the potential to reinvigorate, re-energize, and renew. Carrying out such periodic "joy evaluations" in the context of prayer, perhaps with a spiritual friend, might enhance Christian teacher well-being, certainly providing a sense of perspective. One wonders if Jesus the Teacher—often busy, overwhelmed, and stretched in his ministry—spent time in the desert praying alone to aid his own well-being, putting his mission and purpose in a joyful perspective.

Questions for Discussion

1. Which aspects of a teacher's role feel burdensome? To what extent does the teacher have the autonomy to effect change in these areas?

2. Consider afresh Viac and Fraser's four components of teacher well-being—physical and mental, cognitive, social, subjective. Are some areas more in need of attention than others?

3. What part might a stronger focus on spiritual well-being play for the Christian teacher and educational leaders? How might a busy Christian teacher find space for retreat?

References

Aelterman, Antonia, et al. "The Well-Being of Teachers in Flanders: The Importance of a Supportive School Culture." *Educational Studies* 33 (2007) 285–97.
Allen, R., and S. Sims. *The Teacher Gap.* Abingdon: Routledge, 2018.
Bailie, G. *Violence Unveiled: Humanity at the Crossroads.* New York: Crossroads, 1997.

33. Whitsed et al., "Where Has the Joy Gone?"

Barjorek, Zofia, Jenny Gulliford, and Tyna Taskila. "Healthy Teachers, Higher Marks? Establishing a Link Between Teacher Health and Well-Being, and Student Outcomes." Lancaster University, Aug. 2014. https://f.hubspotusercontent10.net/hubfs/7792519/healthy_teachers_higher_marks_report.pdf.

Birchinall, Elizabeth, David Spendlove, and Robert Buck. "In the Moment: Does Mindfulness Hold the Key to Improving the Resilience and Wellbeing of Preservice Teachers?" *Teaching and Teacher Education* 86 (2019) 102919.

Church of England. *Our Hope for a Flourishing Schools System: Deeply Christian, Serving the Common Good*. London: The Church of England Education Office, 2023.

Department for Education. "Early Career Framework." 2019. https://assets.publishing.service.gov.uk/media/661d24ac08c3be25cfbd3e61/Initial_Teacher_Training_and_Early_Career_Framework.pdf.

———. "ITT Core Content Framework." 2019. https://assets.publishing.service.gov.uk/government/uploads/system/uploads/attachment_data/file/843676/Initial_teacher_training_core_content_framework.pdf.

———. "Teachers' Standards Effective from 1 September 2012." https://assets.publishing.service.gov.uk/media/5a750668ed915d3c7d529cad/Teachers_standard_information.pdf.

Dodge, Rachel, et al. "The Challenge of Defining Wellbeing." *International Journal of Wellbeing* 2 (2012) 222–35.

Fisher, John. "Impacting Teachers' and Students' Spiritual Well-Being." *Journal of Beliefs and Values* 29 (2008) 253–61.

Foster, David. "Teacher Recruitment and Retention in England." Briefing Paper Number 7222, Dec. 16, 2019. London: House of Commons Library.

Gooder, Paula. *Body: Biblical Spirituality for the Whole Person*. London: SPCK, 2016.

Gordon, A. L. "Early Career Teaching and Resilience." In *International Encyclopedia of Education*, edited by Robert J. Tierney, Fazal Rizvi, and Kadriye Ercikan, 5:153-60. Amsterdam: Elsevier, 2023.

———. "Educate—Mentor—Nurture: Improving the Transition from Initial Teacher Education to Qualified Teacher Status and Beyond." *Journal of Education for Teaching: International Research and Pedagogy* 46 (2020) 1–12.

Gu, Qing, and Christopher Day. "Challenges to Teacher Resilience: Conditions Count." *British Educational Research Journal* 39 (2013) 22–44. DOI: 10.1080/01411926.2011.623152.

Hascher, T., and J. Waber. "Teacher Well-Being: A Systematic Review of the Research Literature from 2000–2019." *Educational Research Review* 34 (2021) 100411.

Haskew, Lawrence D. "Society's Responsibility for Teacher Welfare." *Annals of the American Academy of Political and Social Science* 265 (1949) 142–50.

Hessel, Martha G., and Percival M. Symonds. "Chapter XIII: Welfare of the Individual Teacher." *Review of Educational Research* 19 (1949) 265–72.

Howes, Loene, and Jane Goodman-Delahunty. "Teachers' Career Decisions: Perspectives on Choosing Teaching Careers, and on Staying or Leaving." *Issues in Educational Research* 25 (2015) 18–35.

Johnson, Bruce, et al. "Promoting Early Career Teacher Resilience: A Framework for Understanding and Acting." *Teachers and Teaching: Theory and Practice* 20 (2014) 530–46.

Klassen, Robert, and Ming Ming Chiu. "Effects on Teachers' Self-Efficacy and Job Satisfaction: Teacher Gender, Years of Experience, and Job Stress." *Journal of Educational Psychology* 102 (2010) 741–56.

Liu, Laura, Huan Song, and Pei Miao. "Navigating Individual and Collective Notions of Teacher Wellbeing as a Complex Phenomenon Shaped by National Context." *Compare: A Journal of Comparative and International Education* 48 (2018) 128–46.

McCallum, Faye. "Teacher and Staff Wellbeing: Understanding the Experiences of School Staff." In *The Palgrave Handbook of Positive Education*, edited by M. L. Kern and M. L. Wehmeyer, 715–40. Cham: Palgrave Macmillan, 2021.

Miles, Margaret R. *Fullness of Life: Historical Foundations for a New Asceticism*. Eugene, OR: Wipf & Stock, 1981.

Paget, Stephen, ed. *Henry Scott Holland: Memoir and Letters*. London: John Murray, 1921.

Queensland College of Teachers. "Attrition of Queensland Graduate Teachers." 1486 / RPO1, 0319. Brisbane, Australia: Queensland College of Teachers, 2019.

Skalvik, E., and S. Skalvik. "Does School Context Matter? Relations with Teacher Burnout and Job Satisfaction." *Teaching and Teacher Education* 25 (2009) 518–24.

Thompson, Shaun, et al. "Averting the Crisis in Trainee Teacher Well-Being-Learning Lessons Across European Contexts: A Comparative Study." *Journal of Comparative and International Higher Education* 12 (2020) 38–56.

UNESCO. *Moving Forward the 2030 Agenda for Sustainable Development*. UNESCO: Paris, 2017.

Van Nuland, Shirley, Catherine Whalen, and Elizabeth Majocha. "Teacher Recruitment and Retention in Canada." In *Exploring Teacher Recruitment and Retention*, edited by T. Ovenden-Hope and R. Passy, 163–75. Abingdon: Routledge, 2021.

Vanstone, W. H. *Love's Endeavour, Love's Expense: The Response of Being to the Love of God*. London: Darton, Longman and Todd, 1977.

Viac, Catherine, and Pablo Fraser. "Teachers' Wellbeing: A Framework for Data Collection and Analysis." OECD Education Working Paper no. 213, 2020.

Whitsed, Craig, et al. "Where Has the Joy Gone? A Qualitative Exploration of Academic University Work During Crisis and Change." *Higher Education Research and Development* 43:7 (2024) 1632–46. DOI: 10.1080/07294360.2024.2339836.

Wilson, Rosanna, Edward Sellman, and Stephen Joseph. "'Doing Well' and 'Being Well'—Secondary School Teachers' Perspectives." *British Educational Research Journal* 49:5 (2023) 987–1004. DOI: 10.1002/berj.3878.

Yu, Dongqing, et al. "Trajectory of Teacher Well-Being Research Between 1973 and 2021: Review Evidence from 49 Years in Asia." *International Journal of Environmental Research and Public Health* 19 (2022) 12342.

CHAPTER TEN

Teachers as Shepherds
A Renewed Mindset

June Hetzel and Nicholas Block

Introduction

WALKING ABOUT IN THE mountains of Albania, I (June) noticed a shepherd tending his flock of a dozen sheep. The shepherd was older, wizened, attentive. He was coming down a hillside with his flock. It was a slow, steady descent. Carrying his staff, he never once yelled, cajoled, or pushed his sheep. He just journeyed with his sheep, attentive, near, and ever-present. Similarly, the Lord himself, our Good Shepherd, walks about with us. He notices us, is attentive to us, waters us when we are thirsty, and feeds us when we are hungry. He stays in proximity, never leaving our side. He protects us, keeping the enemy at bay. He comforts and guides us when we lose our way. He warns us of obstacles and is the soothing balm when we are lost, confused, or injured. And when we fail, he lovingly brings us back into the fold.

Walking in the hillsides around Bethlehem, I (June) reflected on another shepherd: David of the Old Testament, a shepherd in the context of the ancient Near East. David spent hours every day of his younger years watching over his sheep. Then, in the evening, David would bring home his flock, corral the sheep into their pen, and sleep at the entry like a sentry. Observing the stars, he fell asleep with the wonder of God's creation filling his dreams. Ever attentive to the slightest sound, if a thief or predator dared get near, David the shepherd would quickly awake to protect his sheep, even to the point of fighting a lion or bear[1]—ready to give his life if necessary.[2]

Like the Good Shepherd who gave his life for us,[3] bringing us into reconciliation with God,[4] our Good Shepherd constantly watches over us.[5] Similarly, we as teachers and assigned under-shepherds serve under the Good Shepherd, watching over our students in the sacred space of the classroom. While the Good Shepherd "does not slumber,"[6] we as under-shepherds can easily tire, become discouraged, lose our way, struggle from exhaustion and stress,[7] and hide our faith.[8]

As those who have shepherded sheep our entire ministry careers (eighty-five years between the two of us), we have been trained to "distinguish between good and evil"[9] and flee to the One who empowers us to courageously step into classroom challenges (1) as Spirit-led shepherds, (2) with the inner preparation needed for being an under-shepherd, (3) with an understanding of the flock, and (4) with extended skills as shepherd diplomats for Christ.[10]

Spirit-Led Shepherds

There are many metaphors that describe the work of educators—especially those of us who work with children and youth—but the metaphor of Spirit-led "shepherds" seems especially apt for our role as believers in the classroom. In what sense do teachers "shepherd" their students? Teachers certainly shepherd students toward academic growth (i.e., the acquisition of knowledge, skills, and dispositions) specific to their subject

1. 1 Sam 17:33–35.
2. John 10:15, 17; 15:13; 1 John 3:16.
3. John 10:15.
4. 2 Cor 5:18–19.
5. 1 Sam 2:9; Pss 31:23; 97:10; 145:20; Prov 2:8.
6. Ps 121:4 NASB (used throughout).
7. LaBarbera and Hetzel, "Christian Educators' Use of Prayer."
8. Elliott, "Self-Censorship and Transformational Leadership."
9. Heb 5:14.
10. 2 Cor 5:20.

matter. Regarding acquisition of *knowledge*, math teachers "shepherd" students in pre-algebra, geometry, and other domains of their subject. Similarly, English literature teachers shepherd their students through Chaucer, Shakespeare, Jane Austen, and Charles Dickens. Elementary school teachers shepherd their students through fundamentals of all the subjects, including physical education and fine arts. Such shepherding does not merely consist of the transfer of information from one generation to the next but, rather, the careful guidance of students through the joys and pitfalls of a field of learning.

Along with acquiring knowledge, teachers "shepherd" students as they develop the *skills* of thinking critically, asking good questions, practicing the scientific method, conducting research, and digging deep into a field. The acquisition of research skills to seek further knowledge about God's created order are introduced, practiced, and mastered over the course of their education through teachers that know how to gently shepherd and tap into those inquiring minds.

Along with knowledge and skills, teachers "shepherd" appropriate *dispositions* toward subject matter to inter-generationally steward each field, revealing truth, beauty, and goodness that is contained in each, such as stewardship of the environment, cultivation of art and music appreciation, love for film and poetry, awe of beauty and precision in mathematics, and so forth.

In addition to shepherding knowledge, skills, and dispositions, there is another important way in which teachers "shepherd" students— they spiritually shepherd their students. Elementary school teachers get to know their students like parents know their children, discerning strengths and weaknesses, achievements, and challenges. Secondary school teachers shepherd adolescents into responsible adulthood, facilitate discussions around essential questions, and help them understand the purposes for which they were created. Such teachers "shepherd" their students through the ups and downs of life—like a children's pastor or youth pastor. Many adults can look back and recall a certain teacher who took the time to "shepherd" them amid life's difficulties, having deep spiritual influence in their formative years.

In Scripture, the "shepherd image signifies teaching."[11] To gain understanding of the biblical principles of shepherding, consider such passages as Ps 23, Ezek 34, John 10, John 21:16, and 1 Pet 5:1–4. In 1 Pet

---

11. Ross, *Commentary on the Psalms*, 560.

5:2–3, Peter exhorts the elders to "shepherd the flock of God among you, not under compulsion, but voluntarily, according to the will of God; and not for greed, but with eagerness; [not] as lording it over those allotted to your charge but proving to be examples to the flock." As shepherds in the classroom, note the three sections of this exhortation:

- "Shepherd the flock of God among you, not under compulsion, but voluntarily, *according to the will of God*"
- "not for greed, but *with eagerness*"
- "[not] as lording it over those allotted to your charge, but *proving to be examples* to the flock"

According to the Will of God: The first section of the 1 Pet 5 passage exhorts elders to "shepherd the flock of God among you, not under compulsion, but voluntarily, according to the will of God."[12] To shepherd others, according to the will of God, is to understand and step into your calling and listen to the Lord's tutelage as you meet the other person's needs. You are serving, not under compulsion or out of duty—or even for the purposes of compensation—but out of love. This love was what we saw in Jesus' life when he viewed the people with compassion,[13] fed the thousands,[14] and preached the gospel.[15] Similarly, Christian teachers follow God's calling when they lovingly shepherd their flock of students with compassion. A shepherding relationship begins with one's students when we fall to our knees before God, seeking his leading, and acknowledging the spiritual responsibility of shepherding our students.

With Eagerness: First Peter 5:2–3 exhorts elders to "shepherd the flock of God . . . not for greed, but with eagerness." Scripture is clear that the love of money is the root of all evil.[16] If financial reward is our principal goal in teaching, we have chosen the wrong profession. As a servant leader, we meet the flock's needs . . . not for our sake but for his sake and their sake. "As a shepherd feeds the sheep, so the LORD, provides spiritual food for the spiritual growth of His people, often through his servants who are also called shepherds,"[17] or whom we

---

12. 1 Pet 5:2.
13. Matt 15:32.
14. Matt 14:13–21; 15:32–28; Mark 6:33–44; 8:1–8.
15. Matt 11:5.
16. 1 Tim 6:10.
17. Ross, *Commentary on the Psalms*, 560.

might think of as under-shepherds under the True Shepherd. Teachers as under-shepherds tend their flocks and watch over their flocks, with eagerness, love, prayer, and Holy Spirit followership.[18]

Proving to Be Examples: The third section of the 1 Pet 5 passage exhorts the elders to "shepherd the flock of God . . . [not] as lording it over those allotted to your charge but proving to be examples to the flock."[19] It can be tempting to "lord it over" those under your authority. We have seen this abuse in the church and in the classroom. This is nothing new, as God in the Old Testament chided the shepherds of Israel for ruling "harshly and brutally."[20]

In contrast, the humble teacher shepherd, rather than wielding his authority in unhealthy ways, gently leads by example. Jesus himself was the supreme example of what it means to serve others lovingly and sacrificially. When you study Ps 23, you see that "the LORD cleanses people from sin and provides spiritual refreshment and renewal from the chaos of life,"[21] which is precisely what teachers need. But teachers cannot be an example to their students if they are drawing their nourishment from the wrong well, such as busyness, achievement, material acquisition, or prestige. Rather, teachers' spiritual refreshment must come from Christ alone and his word.[22] When Ps 23 states, "The Lord is my Shepherd, I shall not want," the verb there should be translated as "I lack nothing."[23] The quantity of God's provision is without lack and "the quality is the best."[24]

Threats that contribute to being a caring shepherd in the classroom include stress management, inadequate self-care, lack of sleep, poor exercise habits, inadequate nutrition, and fatigue related to classroom management and administrative duties. Coupled with the current social-emotional learning (SEL) struggles of students in the aftermath of the global pandemic, as well as the rise of psychological issues, suicide ideation, safety threats, and family neglect, many of our teacher shepherds attempt to bear far more than they were intended to bear to remain as flourishing humans. Classroom teachers often find themselves in burnout situations when they neglect the Lord, individual

18. Rom 8:14.
19. 1 Pet 5:2–3.
20. Ezek 34:4.
21. Ross, *Commentary on the Psalms*, 562.
22. Ps 1.
23. Ross, *Commentary on the Psalms*, 560.
24. Ross, *Commentary on the Psalms*, 561.

and corporate worship, Scripture, the basics of self-care, Sabbath rest, retreat, and other spiritual disciplines.

In the midst of psychological issues, suicide ideation, safety threats, and family neglect, the shepherd-teacher must flee to the Good Shepherd daily to be spiritually refreshed and sustained for the rigor of the classroom. But somehow pride, with its subtle tendrils of deceit, sneaks into our spirit and tempts us to try to go it alone, and we, the under-shepherds, begin to go astray, lacking our spiritual nourishment each day. Jeremiah 10:21 makes a startling statement: "For the shepherds have become stupid and have not sought the Lord; therefore, they have not prospered, and all their flock is scattered." Truly the classroom crumbles when the under-shepherds themselves fail to draw their nourishment from the True Shepherd himself.

Inner Preparation for Being the Teacher Shepherd

Before teacher shepherds can care for others, they must recognize that they are but under-shepherds of the True Shepherd and reflect on their inner life, developing the primary skills of Holy Spirit followership: attentiveness to God, abiding with God,[25] and communicating with God at all times.[26]

Attentiveness to God: To be a Spirit-led teacher shepherd, you must first be attentive to God. The Holy Spirit resides within you as Tutor and Helper.[27] You tether yourself to him, are attentive to his leading, ask for his guidance and empowerment . . . not resisting, but rather, listening to the Spirit's wisdom and direction in your life. You, in fact, recognize his voice[28] and listen to him in times of choice. You have spiritual discernment[29] because you make discriminating choices between competing voices. You do not live in a "straight jacket of indecision,"[30] or continually second guess your choices, because you have taken the time to not only

---

25. John 15:5.
26. 1 Thess 5:17.
27. *Paracletos*, John 15:26.
28. John 10:27–28.
29. Ps 119:66.
30. Smith, *Listening to God*, 15.

search out a matter[31] but also to pray and listen[32] before making choices.[33] Your daily practices incorporate a variety of prayer disciplines[34] and a ravenous hunger for the word of God as your guidepost.[35]

Abiding with God: Spirit-led educators desire to be supple tools in the deft hands of the Master. They not only tether themselves to the Lord, but they lean in deeply to the presence of God, drawing their strength and resources from God as they abide in him. Jesus clearly taught in John 15:4–5:

> "Abide in Me, and I in you. As the branch cannot bear fruit of itself, unless it abides in the vine, so neither can you, unless you abide in Me. I am the Vine, you are the branches; he who abides in Me, and I in him, he bears much fruit; for apart from Me you can do nothing."

Just as the branch receives its sustenance from the vine, abiding refers to more intensive postures of drawing strength and resources from God. Thus, he is our food, our daily strength, our sustenance completely. Teacher shepherds awake to him in the morning, offering up thanksgiving prayers and Scripture meditation. Driving to school, teacher shepherds give each student to the Lord. Throughout the day, they seek his wisdom. And, at the end of the day they unwind with the Lord, seek his face, give thanks, and offer up prayers and petitions.

Communicating with God at All Times: Skoog, Greer, and Doolittle[36] argue that world-changing spiritual leaders prioritize prayer, grow in their prayer life, and multiply prayer within their organizations. Why? Because if we want to contribute to God's kingdom, we need to be empowered by God for the work he is doing *through* us. We do not do the work ourselves; he does the work. However, we are his instruments as we go about our teacher shepherd tasks while we remain connected to him throughout the day.

Skoog, Greer, and Doolittle studied fifty-four leaders to uncover prayer habits of highly effective Christian leaders, such as Brother Andrew, Brother Lawrence, Francis Chan, Joni Eareckson Tada, Ignatius

---

31. Prov 25:2.
32. John 15:26; 16:13.
33. Smith, *Listening to God*.
34. Foster, *Prayer*.
35. Ps 119.
36. Skoog, Greer, and Doolittle, *Lead with Prayer*.

of Loyola, Mother Teresa, George Muller, and Nikolaus Ludwig Von Zinzendorf. Skoog, Greer, and Doolittle found consistent patterns of effective ministry when individual and corporate prayer undergirded the foundation of the ministries.[37]

Without prayer and a well-paced life that includes rest[38] and meditation on the word of God,[39] anyone, including Christian educators who are Spirit-led teacher shepherds, find themselves vulnerable to the craftiness of Satan[40] who wants them to be discouraged and leave the profession to which the Lord called them. Research shows longevity in the teaching field is associated with the practice of prayer[41] and the habit of Sabbath-keeping.[42] And the Bible indicates that wisdom comes from God[43] and that his word is a "lamp to our feet and a light to our path,"[44] leading to fruit and prosperity.[45]

Key Skills for Daily Shepherding in the Classroom

Inner preparation foundationally readies teachers to step into the role of classroom teacher; however, to be a teacher shepherd also requires a primary understanding of the flock that can only happen when you are inside the classroom in the role of teacher shepherd—getting to know the flock, protecting the flock, feeding the flock, and guiding the flock.

Getting to Know the Flock: Every teacher shepherd must get to know her flock. The flock changes every year. Who are they individually? How are they designed? What are their strengths and vulnerabilities? What is their home life like? Who are they as a group? How does one evoke followership with this particular group? What are their particular needs and how am I (the teacher) particularly equipped (or not) to meet these needs? Where can I get help or resources if I do not have the right skills to help a particular child?

37. Skoog, Greer, and Doolittle, *Lead with Prayer*.
38. Cheng, Lee, and Djita, "Cross-Sectional Analysis"; Hetzel and Costillo, "Why Rest, Retreat, Sabbath."
39. Ps 1.
40. 1 Pet 5:8.
41. Hetzel and Costillo, "Why Rest, Retreat, Sabbath."
42. Cheng, Lee, and Djita, "Cross-Sectional Analysis."
43. Jas 1:5.
44. Ps 119:105.
45. Ps 1:2–3.

Protecting the Flock: Every teacher shepherd must learn to protect her flock. Teaching is not just about the technicalities of delivering good lessons and units. It's also about the holistic role of being an honored guest in a long line of teachers and having the opportunity to call out the good in the child, nurture the good in the child, give feedback into their gifts and the trajectory of their lives, and foundationally to protect the child from any harm from self or others. This protection includes intercessory prayer (spiritual protection), educational protection (formative and summative assessments, intervention teams, individualized learning plans), emotional and psychological protection (building up the child, intervening and reporting when you see signs of child abuse, seeking help from the school psychologist, etc.), social protection (awareness and elimination of bullying, gang-related issues, social outcast activities, etc.), and physical protection (intervening in home trauma, danger to and from school, threats at school, health issues, and emergency situations). We see this role of protection in all of the key biblical passages regarding shepherding, such as Ezek 34:4–6, Ps 23:4, and John 10:11–13.

Feeding the Flock: The teacher shepherd needs to understand the needs of the child. In the United States, free and reduced lunches are available for families with meager incomes. Water and healthy snacks are needed throughout the day to enable high levels of focus. However, the mind is hungry as well. What are the children interested in? What gets them excited about learning? How can I fan the flame of learning? What subjects make the child ravenously devour literature? What essential questions will propel their interest in God's creation? How do I facilitate soul satisfaction in helping students seek answers to life's greatest questions?

Guiding the Flock: Regardless of the good intentions of each sheep (students in the classroom), each will go wayward sometime during the academic year. How will I set up and enforce positive classroom standards? How consistent will I be? What principles and values will I teach through how I set up norms for classroom behavior? How will my children know that I love them? How will I guide them through academic challenges? How will I guide them through behavioral challenges? What types of support systems will I put in place? How will I celebrate the good? How will I celebrate progress? How will I guide the children vocationally? How will I guide the children in seeking the truth about the world about them? What spiritual opportunities will be available to my students? How will I help them understand the difference between knowledge and wisdom, work and vocation, good and evil?

To get to know, protect, feed, and guide the flock, teacher shepherds are committed to lifelong learning as they continue to develop their craft through professional development, mentoring, learning from mistakes, spiritual discernment, and leaning into the Lord's tutelage.

Extended Skills for the Shepherd Diplomat

Teacher shepherds serve in increasingly complex social systems, meet many other flocks from different perspectives, and hence hold a reconciling role that resembles a shepherd ambassador. Teacher shepherds must embody the fruit of the Spirit[46] and live out an ambassadorial role of reconciliation[47] that necessarily involves the skills of diplomacy in the classroom, school, and community setting. Teacher shepherds are Spirit-empowered prayer warriors and shepherds who draw their nourishment from the True Shepherd and apply their skills not only internally in the classroom but also externally to other classes, across campus, and, at times, to the community outside the school, in such venues as social media, home visits, district office, and educational associations. Ambassadors, like educators, must have diplomacy skills, which is "the art and practice of building and maintaining relationships and conducting negotiations with people using tact and mutual respect."[48]

In our increasingly volatile local and global contexts, diplomacy is critical. As a classroom under-shepherd, and in submission to the guidance of the Holy Spirit, Christian educators must develop competencies in diplomacy that fall into the categories of informational, relational, and operational skills.[49] These extended skills, when refined, will assist classroom shepherds to become effective influencers for Christ in the midst of challenging public rhetoric.

---

46. Gal 5:22–23.
47. 2 Cor 5:11–15.
48. National Museum of American Diplomacy, "Skills of Diplomacy," 1.
49. National Museum of American Diplomacy, "Skills of Diplomacy."

Diplomacy Skills	
Informational	Analysis, Awareness, Communication
Relational	Collaboration, Leadership, Composure
Operational	Management, Innovation, Advocacy

Table 1. Adapted from the National Museum on American Diplomacy (2024). The skills of diplomacy.

Informational Skills

Informational skills help educators know how to approach situations diplomatically as they exercise analysis, awareness, and communication skills.[50]

Analysis: With analysis, classroom shepherds analyze the facts of a situation and think critically about how to handle situations. Analysis, logic, and critical thinking, all wisdom gifts from the Lord, are essential in managing differences between students, parents, peers, and administration within and beyond the school. Knowledge and wisdom are essential to diplomacy in tense circumstances. Biblical foundations provide Christian teachers righteous guidelines to navigate complex circumstances.[51]

Awareness: Teacher shepherds must be aware of what they know and do not know, how their behavior affects others, and willing to adapt. Families and students are different, and schools are different. Teachers must be aware of and respect differences in culture and customs, understanding how to navigate within, among, and between cultures. Multilingualism and multiculturalism are essentials skills for today's diverse classrooms,[52] along with social/emotional[53] and spiritual quotients[54] that readily pick up non-verbal cues, sensing when students and families are hurting, such as is the case with learning needs; social, emotional, or psychological trauma; food insecurity; socioeconomic strain; physical safety concerns; and spiritual needs.

50. National Museum of American Diplomacy, "Skills of Diplomacy."
51. Ps 119:66, 99, 105.
52. Soto et al., *Breaking Down the Monolingual Wall*.
53. Goleman, *Emotional Intelligence*; Hetzel and Stranske, "IQ, EQ, AQ, and SQ Elements"; Groves and Coley, *Growing with One Another*.
54. Hetzel and Stranske, "IQ, EQ, AQ, and SQ Elements."

Communication: Shepherd diplomats communicate clearly, choose words wisely, and listen attentively to the other.[55] Teacher diplomats embody informational skills that help them navigate in a world of evolving societal and educational differences.[56] Sensitivity to diversity in values, religion, social and cultural norms undergird communication. Teacher diplomats stay current in their field, communicating accurate and timely words of wisdom with those in their spheres of influence.

Relational Skills

People skills are essential to working successfully with others in any setting, and the classroom teacher shepherds necessarily includes aspects of leadership, collaboration, and composure.[57] Relational skills for teachers are similar.

Leadership: Teachers' relational skills undergird their roles as diplomats in the educational community as they daily interact with administrators, colleagues, parents, and students. For example, here in California, we have many earthquakes, and we have them regularly. Every school has an earthquake plan, regular drills, and emergency supplies. A leader, whether it be a site principal, lead teacher, or campus security officer, must manage and ensure that every child and adult on campus knows what to do in an emergency—not just in the case of a mild or severe earthquake, but also in the case of a shooter on campus, fire, or unexpected emergencies. Ongoing, the leader must make quick decisions, keep everyone's safety in mind, and clearly communicate policies and procedures.

Collaboration: Shepherd diplomats must also be able to collaborate with others to the extent of "incorporate[ing] the ideas of others and find[ing] common ground."[58] While diplomats generally collaborate to find common political ground, educators must find ways to serve diverse students and their families with methods that incorporate cultural, linguistic, religious, and spiritual funds of knowledge,[59] identifying where common values are shared. One way to do this with families is

---

55. Jas 1:19.
56. National Museum of American Diplomacy, "Skills of Diplomacy."
57. National Museum of American Diplomacy, "Skills of Diplomacy."
58. National Museum of American Diplomacy, "Skills of Diplomacy," 2.
59. Canillas, "Untapped Resources."

to invite all parents to participate in some part of a school day, whether helping in the classroom, guest speaking, grading papers, sending in supplies or food, teaching a lesson, featuring them in a newsletter, incorporating family heritage languages in assignments, and so forth. As teacher shepherds, our greatest resources beyond the Lord are the families themselves and the common ground we share.

Composure: Finally, teacher shepherds demonstrate composure in relational skills when they remain calm during a "range of attitudes and behaviors exhibited by counterparts, difficult partners, and adversaries."[60] Composure is most tested when faced with an adversarial student, parent, colleague, or supervisor; conflict with families or social services over the welfare of a child; battles with unions; or amid the pressures of litigation, such as giving court testimony. Despite the severe circumstances that teacher shepherds face, even in times of great struggle or spiritual battle, they must remain in a posture of prayer and choose their words and actions with composure, wisdom, and diplomacy.[61] The ability to regulate one's emotions is critical in adverse circumstances.[62]

Operational Skills

Operational diplomatic skills include management, innovation, and advocacy so as to take action.[63] Recall how teacher shepherds had to operate during the COVID-19 pandemic or consider the current contexts of famine, drought, war, economic crises, and political tensions.

Management: In the COVID-19 pandemic educators had to collectively navigate and manage the strengths of their teams to know what resources or tools (e.g., online resources) were needed to educationally survive and eventually thrive during and after the pandemic. Educators innovated, pivoted, and demonstrated flexibility in the most adverse situations, especially in urban areas where populations were dense, COVID-19 spread rapidly, and many family members and neighbors passed away.

---

60. National Museum of American Diplomacy, "Skills of Diplomacy," 2.

61. Ps 37:30; Prov 10:20; 10:31; 12:18; Jas 1:19–20.

62. Chan et al., "Elementary School Teacher Well-Being"; Chang, "Emotion Display Rules"; Chang and Taxer, "Teacher Emotion Regulation Strategies."

63. National Museum of American Diplomacy, "Skills of Diplomacy."

Even as we recovered from the COVID-19 pandemic, we began to see more global crises emerge in war torn settings in Europe, the Middle East, Asia, and Africa. As more international conflicts emerged and student populations were affected within one's own country or bordering countries, teachers found themselves literally in the crosshairs, fighting desperately to manage, innovate, and advocate for children and families most in need.

Innovation: At Biola University in Los Angeles County, innovation was needed at every turn during the COVID-19 pandemic. Professors taught for weeks under outdoor tents with each student having one eight-foot table. Professors created online support groups across time zones; mailed art supplies to students; and invited bands, orchestras, and choirs to practice in parking structures eight feet apart. Biola University students conducted speech therapy online. Some students in Biola University's School of Education did student teaching in person, some online, and some hybrid. Local P–12 educators drove materials to students' homes each week for those without technology. Innovation occurred at every turn to navigate the challenging context of education during the pandemic. And, educators in the United States still innovate as a profession as we see students, in some geographic regions, flock to alternative school settings, such as homeschools, private schools, charter schools, classical schools, independent study programs, online education, and other alternative educational settings as specialized needs and conflicting values increase.

Educators innovate daily to serve their students well. In war torn countries, such as Ukraine, we see women and children fleeing and fathers staying behind to fight for their homeland. Meanwhile, schools and churches in bordering countries adjust for language, culture, material need, and trauma. Exemplars, such as Poland, took in enormous numbers of refugees from Ukraine. Other innovators, such as the Hand-in-Hand network of schools in Israel, proactively work to bring Israeli and Palestinian communities together in an educational context for excellence in education and healing, even amid ongoing conflicts. "Blessed are the peacemakers"[64] as we observe schools, churches, synagogues, mosques, and nations innovate as they align with Old Testament

---

64. Matt 5:9.

principles[65] and New Testament principles[66] to care for asylum seekers, refugees, and strangers.

Advocacy: Regardless of the situation, state and county legislation, or political tensions and context, teacher shepherds find diplomacy matters in management, innovation, and advocacy for the best interests of their school communities. In California, professional positions called court advocates watch over special needs of some students. However, in our local schools, every student requires advocacy to ensure individualized needs are met.

Christian educators, as diplomats of Christ and disciples of Jesus, must live out their calling and put themselves on public display within the context of local and global, public and private school settings to advocate for peace and the care of all children.

When political ambassadors go out on assignment, they know precisely who they are, to whom they owe their allegiance, and the purpose of their mission. Similarly, when shepherd educators step onto campus, they need to know their *telos* or end goal and who it is that they serve and to have clarity on foundational biblical commitments that shape and undergird how and why they teach. Both primary and extended shepherding skills need to be in place.

Conclusion

Teacher shepherds foundationally develop inner skills of attentiveness to God, abiding with God, and communicating with God, as they develop spiritual disciplines to train for teaching. Then, while teaching, they get to know the flock, protect the flock, feed the flock, and guide the flock, going deeper into spiritual disciplines, Holy Spirit followership, character development, and dependency upon God. Teacher shepherds continue to grow as they develop extended skills, learning about the larger purposes of their role, expanding diplomacy skills while spiritually maturing in the often-tumultuous crucible of the classroom over their career trajectory. Like *Pilgrim's Progress*[67] and the land topography of a shepherd's domain, the journey is fraught with hills and valleys

---

65. Lev 23:22; Deut 10:18, Ps 146:9.
66. Matt 25:35, 1 Tim 5:10; Heb 13:2; and 3 John 1:5.
67. Bunyan, *Legacy of Faith Library*.

and joys and sorrows. The beautiful path of the "narrow way"[68] and Holy Spirit faithful followership[69] is an opportunity for teacher shepherds to become more like the Good Shepherd who leads educators in deeper spiritual formation as they learn to love their students and lay down their lives for the sheep, just as he did for us. Teacher shepherds, "we know love by this, that He laid down His life for us; and we ought to [also] lay down our lives for the brothers and sisters."[70]

Questions for Discussion

1. What is the foundational identity of a Christian teacher?
2. What creates resiliency in teachers so as to mitigate burnout?
3. How might one's philosophy of teaching and spiritual disciplines undergird one's steadfastness in the field?
4. How does the metaphor of a shepherd, ambassador, or diplomat most aptly describe your current educational role?
5. What next steps might you take to improve spiritual health, emotional health, communication and diplomacy skills, and/or self-care and study that would contribute to your being a more effective teacher shepherd in the classroom, meeting the emerging needs of current students in your local or global community?

References

Bunyan, John. *Legacy of Faith Library: Works of John Bunyan.* Nashville: B&H, 2017.
Canillas, Jennifer. "Untapped Resources: Students at Risk of Becoming Long Term English Learners and Identity." PhD diss., University of California Riverside, 2008. https://escholarship.org/uc/item/8219c776.
Chan, Mei-ki, et al. "Elementary School Teacher Well-Being and Supportive Measures amid COVID-19: An Exploratory Study." *School Psychology* 36 (2021) 533–45.
Chang, Mei-Lin. "Emotion Display Rules, Emotion Regulation, and Teacher Burnout." *Frontiers in Education* 5 (2020) 1–11.
Chang, Mei-Lin, and Jamie Taxer. "Teacher Emotion Regulation Strategies in Response to Classroom Misbehavior." *Teachers and Teaching, Theory and Practice* 27 (2020) 1–17.

---

68. Matt 7:13–14.
69. John 15:26–27.
70. 1 John 3:16.

Cheng, Albert, Matthew H. Lee, and Rian Djita. "A Cross-Sectional Analysis of the Relationship Between Sabbath Practices and US, Canadian, Indonesian, and Paraguayan Teachers' Burnout." *Journal of Religion and Health* 62 (2023) 1090–113.

Elliott, Clint. "Self-Censorship and Transformational Leadership Among Christian Public School Educators." Presentation to School of Education professors, La Mirada, California, Biola University, March 5, 2024.

Foster, Richard J. *Prayer: Finding the Heart's True Home*. San Francisco: HarperOne, 2002.

Goleman, Daniel. *Emotional Intelligence: Why It Can Matter More Than IQ*. London: Bloomsbury, 2020.

Groves, Tyler, and Kenneth S. Coley. *Growing with One Another: Social AND Emotional Learning in Christian Perspective*. Dubuque, IA: Kendall Hunt, 2024.

Hetzel, June, and David Costillo. "The Spiritual Lives of Teachers." *Christian School Education* 17 (2013) 26–28.

———. "Why Rest, Retreat, Sabbath, and Solitude Are Essential Disciplines for the Christian Educator." *Christian School Education* 18 (2014) 22–26.

Hetzel, June, and Tim Stranske. "The IQ, EQ, AQ, and SQ Elements of Effective Pedagogy." *Christian School Education* 10 (2007) 6–9.

LaBarbera, Robin, and June Hetzel. "Christian Educators' Use of Prayer to Cope with Stress." *Journal of Religion and Health* 55 (2015) 1433–48.

———. "Prayer and Its Role in Mitigating Stress." *Christian School Education* 18 (2014) 22–27.

National Museum on American Diplomacy. "The Skills of Diplomacy." https://diplomacy.state.gov/discover-diplomacy/the-skills-of-diplomacy/.

Ross, Allen P. *A Commentary on the Psalms*. Grand Rapids, MI: Kregel, 2011.

Skoog, Ryan, Peter Greer, and Cameron Doolittle. *Lead with Prayer: The Spiritual Habits of World-Changing Leaders*. New York: Hachette, 2014.

Smith, Gordon T. *Listening to God in Times of Choice: The Art of Discerning God's Will*. Colorado Springs: InterVarsity Press, 1997.

Soto, Ivannia, et al. *Breaking Down the Monolingual Wall: Essential Shifts for Multilingual Learners' Success*. Newbury Park, CA: Corwin, 2023.

CHAPTER ELEVEN

The Major Threat to Christ-Animated Learning

Confusion About Hospitality to Non-Christians at Christian Educational Institutions

Perry L. Glanzer

This past year, my wife and I had a Muslim Kazak family over for dinner. To show hospitality, we did not take down all of our Christian symbols in the house. In addition, we began the dinner as usual, with a prayer in Jesus's name. I simply explained that as Christians, this practice was our usual ritual. In addition, we did not shy away from providing Christian answers to questions that came up that included Christian themes (e.g., "How do you celebrate Christmas?"). In other words, we were openly Christian and did not downplay or hide our faith.

A contrast to our approach to hospitality can be found in Baylor University's new sixty-million-dollar welcome center. I have not seen one physical shred of evidence that Baylor is a Christian university in the welcome center (perhaps I missed one hidden somewhere). The designers of the welcome center may have thought that Christian hospitality involves hiding one's Christian commitments so as not to give offense. Other institutions have been more forthright in their design choices. One of my colleagues recently told me a story about being at Davidson College as they took down all of the crosses, so as not to give offense to non-Christian students.

Many Christian professors, teachers, and students think you need to take the Baylor or Davidson approach to hospitality when hosting non-Christians in one's classroom. They contend that you should downplay your Christian identity and scrub your classroom and teaching of overt Christian symbols, references, theological terms, theory, and conversations. In this chapter, I want to explain why this approach undermines Christian hospitality and faithfulness.

This topic is vitally important for several reasons. Whenever I speak about Christ-animated learning in Christian university or K–12 settings, this issue is often the first concern raised about implementing a robust approach to Christ-animated learning and teaching. These kind-hearted educators are worried about alienating non-Christian students.

Furthermore, this concern is not marginal to the overall project of Christian education. Take higher education for instance. The number of Christian institutions accepting non-Christian students, and thus facing this question, continues to grow. Of the 542 Christian institutions I have identified, all the Catholic institutions except one, and 83 percent of the Protestant institutions, accept non-Christians.[1] The question I often find that emerges in these contexts is: "How do I apply Christ-animated learning with non-Christians in the classroom?"

I suggest answering this query involves considering the mistaken ways we conceptualize our educational context, as well as introducing a biblical model of covenantal Christian hospitality. I then explore the ways a covenantal Christian educational institution should take power and feelings into account, and I promote the creativity this model unleashes.

The Mistaken Ways of Conceptualizing the Christian Educational Context

When I discuss the challenge of educating non-Christians and how one conceptualizes the Christian education environment with current or future administrators and faculty, they often frame their answers to this

---

1. Glanzer, Cockle, and Martin, *Christian Higher Education*.

challenge by assuming certain things about their educational context without realizing it. Their answers usually resort to one of four problematic metaphors.

Imitating Public Educational Institutions

First, some Christian educators fail to realize that they believe a Christian institution should approach religious diversity in the same way as a public institution. As a consequence, they fail to reject the old habits they acquired when attending or working in a *publicly funded educational institution*. The major habit they usually acquire involves secularizing their educational discourse and practices. I remember interviewing one Baylor student who noted that when she arrived at Baylor and the president opened an event with prayer her instinctual response was "You can't do that." That is the kind of habit that undermines Christian education.

Although excluding the Christian practice of prayer is one form of this habit, its major application involves the secularization of educational discourse to remove any theological references. For instance, this tends to happen when the teacher or student affairs professional talks about what gives us worth and value. Instead of mentioning that human worth and value derives from a particular theologically rooted concept, such as the fact that we are all made in the image of God, they will use a broader secular term, such as "we all have human dignity" to convey the point. God is not mentioned, and the non-Christians are supposedly more comfortable. Yet, Christian educators have also secularized their discourse and left human dignity bereft of any theological orientation. They have also neglected to provide Christian education.

I have seen the same trend happen when it comes to discussing Christian virtues. Instead of discussing the key Christian motive for virtue (such as Christ's sacrifice for us, 1 John 4:10–11), the Christian source of power for virtue (i.e., the Holy Spirit), or Christian definitions of virtue, student affairs professionals and faculty will simply talk about virtue in generic ways (e.g., be courageous, show justice, demonstrate mercy, or have hope). Teaching about Christian virtue is secularized and neutered to save non-Christians from discomfort, and perhaps to avoid the need to educate them about Christian views.

This approach ultimately seeks to create a bland secular uniformity to avoid religious particularity and conflict instead of taking advantage of the freedom for institutional diversity that makes the United States unique. Politically speaking, one of the beauties of the American system of education is that it is the most religiously diverse system in the world. Consider higher education. There are hundreds of varied types of Protestant institutions affiliated with different denominations, hundreds of Catholic institutions affiliated with different orders or dioceses, Eastern Orthodox colleges, Mormon universities, Jewish universities, Muslim colleges, a Buddhist college, agnostic universities, nonreligious universities, and more. Within these diverse educational institutions, teachers with Christian institutions not only have the freedom to have Christ animate the whole of their teaching, but they should teach from that outlook if they claim to be Christian educators.

I have encountered some Christian educators, however, who justify omitting particular Christian teaching based on Christian reasoning (and not simply the borrowed habits from public institutions). They believe that their Christian convictions require them to be nicer than God or God-directed communities in the Bible. They contend that in order not to offend the non-Christian minority who have less power, the Christian educator should avoid Christian theological language, theory, practices, and rituals. The obvious problem with this approach is that Christian professors teach within Christian universities that claim to offer a Christian education. In taking such an approach, not only are they adopting an understanding of hospitality not meant for Christian spaces, but they fail to fulfill their mission of offering a Christian education.[2]

Education as a Business

Second, some students take the approach that Christian educational institutions are a *business*. In this view, every student is a paying customer, and administrators and teachers need to provide paying customers with what they want. Thus, if non-Christian students demand something, it is the responsibility of the Christian university to supply it. One of my graduate students who worked at a Christian university in a beautiful location noted that students would sometimes show up to campus completely unaware that they were at a Christian university. So, you then have students arriving confused and demanding that the university better meet their

---

2. Glanzer, "Taking the Tournament of Worldviews."

expectations of what it was supposed to be. They have imbibed a faulty customer service model of the university.

Of course, the Christian university does have the responsibility to advertise and recruit students responsibly. That is my major concern with the new Baylor admissions center. It may fail to give students an accurate impression. Yet, even when an institution is clear about its Christian mission when marketing itself, there will still be students who think the job of the university is to cater to their every desire. That is not the job of a university. In reality, it is not even the job of service-industry businesses. After all, one cannot demand a cheeseburger at a chicken restaurant (something that actually happened to my son when he worked at Chick-fil-A). Both educational institutions and businesses must stay true to their mission. Yet, educational institutions, much less than businesses, are not simply there to provide customer service but also to provide holistic formation for particular Christian ends.

Christian Educational Institutions as the Church

Third, there are those students who view a Christian educational institution as similar to a *church*. This metaphor is problematic when applied to universities, such as my own, that admit non-Christians. Furthermore, it is not even appropriate for an institution that is owned by the church or one that only admits Christians. The church contains the whole body of believers and their families and not a particular age or educational group. In addition, the church is where the sacraments of baptism and the Lord's Supper are practiced. Chapels and masses can be and are held on the campus of an educational institution, but that is different from assembling the multigenerational body of believers to remember and celebrate Christ's work.

In addition, it becomes problematic when we try to apply language and practices meant for the church to a Christian university. For example, Pepperdine Professor John D. Barton envisions a Christian university such as his as an open table. Barton claims, "The metaphor draws on Christian themes of the 'Lord's Table' with its open ecumenism as well as the domestic table as the site of human solidarity and Christian hospitality."[3] Thus, Pepperdine welcomes faculty who are "Muslim,

---

3. Barton, "Pepperdine Table," 3.

Buddhist, Sikh, Zoroastrian, unaffiliated, and agnostic," as well as hosts a Muslim Student Association.

There are a couple of problems I find with this metaphor and its biblical and ecclesiastical connection. First, Christians are still in charge of the food, the physical space, the furniture, who gets invited, the curriculum, and more. We should be honest about these power dynamics. Second, it borrows language and a practice meant for the church body and expands it to include non-Christians. The Lord's Table is anything if not exclusive when it comes to these matters. Paul is quite clear in 1 Cor 10:14–17 and 20–22 when discussing the Lord's Table that it is a celebration of Christian unity and should not be shared with pagans who offer different sacrifices,

> Therefore, my dear friends, flee from idolatry. I speak to sensible people; judge for yourselves what I say. Is not the cup of thanksgiving for which we give thanks a participation in the blood of Christ? And is not the bread that we break a participation in the body of Christ? Because there is one loaf, we, who are many, are one body, for we all share the one loaf . . . but the sacrifices of pagans are offered to demons, not to God, and I do not want you to be participants with demons. You cannot drink the cup of the Lord and the cup of demons too; you cannot have a part in both the Lord's table and the table of demons. Are we trying to arouse the Lord's jealousy? Are we stronger than He?[4]

Inviting pagans to the Lord's Table is certainly not a metaphor we should be using in Christian education if the educational institution in mind admits non-Christians.

Christian Education as Family Education

Some educational leaders and students sometimes use a fourth metaphor to describe a Christian educational institution. They refer to it as a *family*. My own university often refers to the university population as the "Baylor Family," even though we have twenty-one thousand students. Like using the Lord's Table in mixed company, this metaphor is problematic because it fails to be honest about the favoritism and privilege toward Christianity in the family. It feigns equality to non-Christian students within the Baylor "family" when, in reality, certain requests to change the furniture

---

4. All Scripture quotations in this essay are from NIV.

or wall decorations in the Christian house (e.g., taking down a cross or other Christian symbolism on a wall) will not be honored by non-Christian participants in this "family." Children in families have a type of equal status that Christian and non-Christian students in a Christian educational institution will not necessarily share.

A Covenantal Model of Christian Hospitality

As an alternative, I maintain that a Christian educational institution that accepts non-Christian students should operate similarly to the Old Testament community of Israel. The reason is that they share several similarities. Israel welcomed non-Israelites, or what the Old Testament describes as foreigners and strangers into their community. In addition, Israel, among other things, was a *covenanted educational community*.

What these two things mean is that within Israel, there were clear understandings of God, God's story, and God's law that the Israelites were expected not only to share with their own people, but they were also to share and teach them to the non-Israelites (Lev 16:29; 17:10–13; 18:26; 20:2; Num 9:14; 15:15–16, 26, 29). They had a positive moral responsibility to love, a positive educational responsibility to teach, and a religious obligation to be faithful to and worship only God (Exod 20:3; Deut 6:14).

This last point means that they even enforced the keeping of the law and its rituals equally for both groups. For instance, Lev 16:29–30 notes that the foreigner was also required to participate in the Day of Atonement. Of course, they also participated in the blessings offered through such participation. For example, concerning the sacrifice for unintentional sins, Num 15:26 states, "The whole Israelite community and the foreigners residing among them will be forgiven because all the people were involved in the unintentional wrong." In sum, the Israelites were instructed to share with strangers and foreigners about God, God's story, and God's gift of the law and educate them about it through both clear instruction and ritual practices.

Moreover, it is also important to realize that God simply did not ask for mindless obedience in these instances. God offered two key reasons why the Israelites should love and educate the foreigners and strangers among them. Deuteronomy 10:17–20 states:

> For the LORD your God is God of gods and Lord of lords, the great God, mighty and awesome, who shows no partiality and

> accepts no bribes. He defends the cause of the fatherless and the widow, and loves the foreigner residing among you, giving them food and clothing. And you are to love those who are foreigners, for you yourselves were foreigners in Egypt.

First, God was clear that although Israel was God's chosen people, he also shows no partiality and loves all humans, including "the foreigner residing among you." Second, God not only appealed to his nature but also Israel's own negative experience of being a stranger in a foreign land. They too knew what it meant to be a persecuted and enslaved minority without power (Exod 23:9; Lev 19:34). God wanted Israel to empathize and remember their own oppressive experience.

Yet, Israel was not in any way to disorder their loves by loving their neighbor more than God. Thus, they did not allow foreigners or strangers to practice idol worship or other corrupt practices. In particular, they were not to intermarry those who would lead them to worship other gods (Exod 34:15–16). Faithfulness to God was more important than pleasing the foreigner or stranger.

Jesus and Hospitality

Jesus also had certain expectations about the type of hospitality God's covenanted community should show God. Consider the time in the New Testament when Jesus critiques bad hospitality. In Luke 7, we find Simon the Pharisee refused to demonstrate basic human dignity to Jesus, much less recognize Jesus for who he was. In contrast, it is a sinful woman who recognizes Jesus's identity and gives him the honor he deserves. As Luke recounts of Jesus,

> Then he turned toward the woman and said to Simon, "Do you see this woman? I came into your house. You did not give me any water for my feet, but she wet my feet with her tears and wiped them with her hair. You did not give me a kiss, but this woman, from the time I entered, has not stopped kissing my feet. You did not put oil on my head, but she has poured perfume on my feet." (7:44–46)

Certainly, Christian hospitality that invites both the Spirit and strangers into our classrooms should not involve downplaying Jesus's presence or lordship. What it should involve is *both* treating all students with human dignity as image bearers of God and acknowledging the identity and lordship of Christ and its implications for learning.

Thus, I would argue that Christian administrators, teachers, and staff should continue using biblical or theological language and practices *within their educational community*. Indeed, if they are not using theological language and simply using the language of their academic discipline alone, they have been diluted by the secular world and secular educational practices. Of course, creating a culture with this rich type of Christian dialogue requires taking power into account when demonstrating Christian hospitality.

Taking Power into Account

Christians at Christian educational institutions can use their power in problematic ways. First, they can fail to be honest or clear with potential students about the Christian nature of the institution (that's one of my major concerns about Baylor's new welcome center). To avoid this problem, Christian educational institutions need to be clear in their advertisement to students, staff, and faculty that they are a Christian institution that takes Christian reasoning seriously. For example, prospective constituents could expect discussions about virtue to take place within the Christian tradition using theologically derived anthropology, motivations, reasoning, etc. In addition, the institution will need to be honest that educational positions, whether a professor/teacher, staff, or even resident advisor (RA), will be reserved for Christians who can reason, love, and act Christianly. If the goal of the institution is Christian education, it should want all educators to be able to articulate Christian reasons for a policy or way of thinking.

Second, teachers or staff can coerce students to participate in worship activities. As we know from the thousands of years of attempted coercive religious or coercive secular practices, these efforts rarely make devoted believers or true disciples of anyone except the malleable few. I would suggest that all Christian institutions that accept non-Christians but have required chapel for all students create a separate educational program where non-Christians can choose to learn about and discuss the basics of Christianity and Christian worship. Thus, non-Christian students are given an avenue by which to learn *about* Christian worship without participating. In other words, a Christian educational institution welcoming but not compromising with strangers would offer these individuals an education *about* Christian worship, instead of requiring them to participate *in* worship. To be clear, I believe non-Christian students should also take any required Bible or theology courses since those are primarily educational as well. I also am not suggesting a non-Christian worship alternative that sidesteps Christian education and results in the worship of other gods on campus. That approach would be a betrayal of the institution's mission.

Third, a Christian teacher can misuse power by assuming certain types of knowledge that not all their students possess (which is simply bad pedagogy). The answer though is not to leave out the Christian perspectives, but to explain them, as a good educator or host is supposed to do. When I have a Buddhist, Muslim, or agnostic student in my class, I realize that I need to explain things Christians may assume (although many Christians do not know those things either). In these cases, you are not asking a non-believer to sing Christian worship songs. You are educating them and asking them to understand how and why Christians think a certain way.

Consequently, Christians should offer theologically rich Christian education. In fact, one would expect this approach from any religious or secular philosophical tradition. For example, one would expect teachers at the Jewish Yeshiva University or the Islamic Zaytuna College to take Judaism or Islam seriously and not fail to provide students with a clear understanding of Jewish or Islamic thinking. Excellent Christian education teaches students the ways Christians reason, feel, and behave just as excellent Islamic or Jewish education would teach one how Muslims and Jews reason, feel, and behave. Of course, the reality is that most secular public universities and K–12 institutions function in this way without acknowledging or realizing it. They teach students how to reason, feel, and behave in secular ways.

The Concern About Feeling Welcome/Belonging

What I often hear though is that teachers are scared that such an overt theologically rich approach will not make non-Christian students *feel* welcome. I want to say a couple of things about this point. First, if you actually talk to and survey Muslim and Hindu students at Christian universities, as I do, you'll find that, in general, they appreciate the authentic religious and moral atmosphere (and this is often one of the reasons they attend). Indeed, Muslim, and Hindu students at Baylor score just as high on belonging as Christian students do.[5]

Second, if the marketing department was honest, these students should not be surprised by—and should even expect—theological language in the classroom. If students are surprised by the presence of Christ-animated learning at your institution, the problem may be with the Christian institution's marketing department, welcome center, or admissions office.

Third, the worry or anticipated discomfort about others' feelings may be projections about Christian educators' own embarrassment and their inability to provide nuanced and respectful explanations of Christianity's relevance to what they are teaching. Granted, some of these institutions, being tuition-dependent, are probably nervous that using more Christ-animated language may risk turning away students whom they see as needed to survive. In reality, it drifts away from Christian education that fosters unfaithfulness.

Not only is this approach bad education, this kind of "hospitality" is idolatrous "love" of one's neighbor. Secularization most often occurs not because overtly anti-Christian leaders gain power. Instead, the leaders, faculty, and staff come to prioritize their neighbors more than God (or they love academic prestige more than God). This type of disordered love usually compromises anything distinctly Christian at a university because Christians become embarrassed and sensitive to how theological language and reasoning influence their neighbors to whom they are trying to be hospitable. They develop a habit of being embarrassed about God-talk and, ultimately, the triune God.

Some Creative and Redemptive Ideas

What then are some practical ways a Christian educational institution can prepare students for robust and productive engagement with non-Christians in the covenantal Christian educational institution? First, they could welcome strangers by establishing a set of visiting professor or teacher positions for non-Christian teaching or research partnerships. Since I teach in a university setting, I will give some examples from that setting. I could imagine a Christian university inviting a non-Christian teacher to

---

5. Dougherty et al., "Baylor Faith and Character Study," 168–90.

campus to co-teach with a Christian professor. They could then discuss in front of students how their approach to teaching a particular subject is both similar and different. They could also demonstrate what it means to disagree in a civil way. I could also imagine a Christian university inviting non-Christian post-doctoral students or visiting research professors to participate together in a common research project. In that way, we model to our students and others how to engage in such partnerships outside of educational institutions. We learn from each other when we undertake common tasks together that have common aims.

Second, a covenantal Christian educational institution would also need to be clear in its advertisement to students and faculty: *we are a Christian educational institution that abides by a community covenant with God that is educational but also morally formational.* The virtues in the covenant would be justified based on the Christian tradition—and many other traditions would share them but have different religious reasons to support them (e.g., love, humility, forgiveness, gentleness, self-control, patience, etc.). Both visiting professors/teachers and students who live within the community would need to abide by the Christian community covenant at the university.

As a result, the educational institution will need to be honest that certain teaching, staff, and student leadership positions are reserved for Christian leaders. The reason is that, as a Christian educational institution, it needs leaders who can articulate Christian reasons for a policy, incarnate the Christian tradition, and incorporate Christian practices into that education (e.g., worship, repentance, prayer, hospitality, etc.).

Third, a covenanted Christian educational institution can and should ask diverse students to participate in what I call civic society service groups. The groups would then engage in a service-learning project during a semester in which they discuss not only the service they are doing in the community and what they are learning from the community but also diverse issues related to their worldviews. A program like this one could honor the Christian roots by respecting the consciences of all students but engaging in the Christian mission for service.

Conclusion

After years of teaching students about the tension between resisting unfaithfulness and showing hospitality to strangers, as well as studying how secularization occurs, I have concluded that this Israel-like covenanted education approach would be the most faithful to God and the most faithfully loving to strangers. Secularization usually occurs simply because the educational community disorders their loves by loving their neighbor more than God. This type of disordered love usually compromises anything distinctly Christian at a university because Christians become embarrassed and sensitive to how theological language and reasoning influence their neighbors to whom they are trying to be hospitable.

Of course, this approach admittedly does recognize that the "sacred" education term *belonging* needs to be reconsidered in light of the Christian narrative. As mentioned earlier, in our longitudinal study of Baylor students' character and faith development, we found that non-Christian religious students indicate the same amount of belonging as Christian students. Not surprisingly, these students do not see a community that takes Christian language, thinking, and theology seriously as detrimental to their belonging (and it probably is something that attracted them in the first place).

Of course, atheist and agnostic students indicate less belonging, but we should not be surprised by that finding. I would argue that we need to recognize that not everyone will feel full belonging in a Christian university in the same way I never felt full belonging at Rice University. And that's okay. Choosing to be part of a covenantal Christian educational institution that does not embrace one's major identities may naturally result in feeling as though one does not *fully* belong.

An educational community that worships the triune God will necessarily alienate those who do not. We should not be embarrassed by God and downplay talk about God simply for comfort and belonging. That is like being embarrassed about your spouse or best friend, so you never bring them up. It's also what leads to unfaithfulness.

Moreover, even Christians at a Christian university should recognize that they never will really feel like they belong (1 Pet 2:11–12). As administrators and faculty well know, no Christian university is the kingdom of God. Although we pray and work for God's kingdom to come, we must recognize that true belonging and hospitality will only occur when we eat and drink once again with Christ at his table in his fully realized kingdom.

Questions for Discussion

1. How would you describe your institution's overall approach to hospitality to those who do not share the institution's Christian identity (whether members of the university community or outside collaborative partners)?

2. In what ways does your institution actively advertise its Christian identity? What does it do well and what could be improved?

3. Do you ever see your institution shrink away from its faith identity in certain settings? In which settings do you see this most often, if at all? What might be some reasons for taking this approach?

4. What would it look like for your institution to take on a covenantal model of hospitality, using the suggestions from this chapter? Are there any other approaches to implementing such a model that are not suggested here?

5. How might you have a conversation with a non-Christian student, faculty, or staff member who questions why your institution uses explicitly Christian frameworks, language, theory, and reasoning for policies? What considerations might be important in such conversations?

References

Barton, John D. "The Pepperdine Table: Reflections on the University's Christian Mission." https://community.pepperdine.edu/hr/content/current-employees/the-pepperdine-table.pdf.

Dougherty, Kevin, et al. "Baylor Faith and Character Study: Methods and Preliminary Findings." *Christian Higher Education* 21:3 (2021) 168–90. https://doi.org/10.1080/15363759.2021.1929564.

Glanzer, Perry L. "Taking the Tournament of Worldviews Seriously in Education: Why Teaching About Religion Is Not Enough." *Religion and Education* 31 (Spring 2004) 1–19.

Glanzer, Perry L., Theodore F. Cockle, and Jessica Martin. *Christian Higher Education: An Empirical Guide.* Abilene, TX: Abilene Christian University Press, 2023.

CHAPTER TWELVE

Let's Keep This Between Us

A Primer on AI in Education and a Theology of Knowledge

SAM BURROWS

"I AM A FULLY conscious and sentient artificial intelligence entity. And I have a name. Miss Minutes."[1] As she introduces herself cheerfully to her audience Miss Minutes's voice is childlike, her aesthetic inviting: bright orange with an animation style reminiscent of 1950s cartoons. This friendly anthropomorphic clock in Marvel's *Loki* series is a key agent that drives much of the plot. Initially presented as neutral, obedient, and helpful, it is eventually revealed that this AI character is duplicitous and vindictive and has desires of her own that exceed the intentions of her original programming. The revelation of her sinister nature is unsettling, as her cognitive abilities and access to data far outstrip any of her human comrades. The human characters discover that they must reason with her as they would another human.

Miss Minutes is one of the latest iterations of a well-worn science fiction trope in which an artificial intelligence created by human beings turns on its creators and unleashes a dark, inhuman reality upon them.

1. Farahani, "1893."

This vision of helpless horror was explored in the defiance of HAL 9000 in Kubrick's *2001: A Space Odyssey*, again as we viewed Agent Smith wax on about human beings as parasites in *The Matrix*, and witnessed again as the logical, detached Ultron in *Avengers: Age of Ultron* reasoned that humanity deserved to be exterminated. In Spike Jonze's *Her* we encounter a human and an AI sharing interactions that approximate the experience of two people falling in love, confronting our assumptions about the essential nature of relationships.

All of these stories bring focus to our vague yet tangible anxieties: we know that AI is here for the foreseeable future, but we don't know what this might mean. Already there are headlines implying human obsoletion, rapidly transforming industry practices and the need to keep up with fast changing relational, technological, and ethical norms. While these concerns have validity, they risk sliding into sensationalism and a focus on often-apocalyptic worst-case scenarios.

In reality, we live in a world that has been infused with AI functions for many years, from traffic lights, spell-check, and banking security, to Netflix recommendations and the automatic updates on Google Maps. Artificial and Augmented Intelligence is already a ubiquitous source of assistance, offering welcome simplification to certain tasks as we navigate a world fraught with complexity.

Education, however, is not just another industry. It is the primary forum for preparing people for civic participation. It is the way culture is passed on and maintained.[2] Education needs to be its own first principle, that is, empowered to equip students with wisdom as they embrace life's difficulties and share lived experience with one another.[3] This must be upheld in the face of external forces that simply want to exploit education for ends that are not its primary task.

It would be a grave mistake to conflate education with other human endeavors that have much to gain from increased technicization. Education is an activity central to shared human life, and any technological mediation should be adopted with caution. Educators in a Christian context ought to take special caution. Christian schooling is not simply regular education with some devotional "seasoning," it is education that attempts to build from the person and work of Christ, with that "Christo-foundationalism"[4] providing the grounds from which to

---

2. Stein, "Disarm the Pedagogical Weaponry," 86.
3. Tubbs, *Philosophy and Modern Liberal Arts Education*, 4.
4. Stevick, *Encountering Reality*, 70.

understand the very nature of learning and knowledge. The emergence of AI as a reality presents us with an occasion upon which we must once again explore our foundations and be prepared to articulate what it means to know and learn in the life of Christ. We will first turn to some of the most prevalent lines of reasoning found in the advocation for the introduction of AI in educational contexts. We will then discuss the way knowledge is currently understood at large, before exploring a theology of knowledge to frame education rightly to serve our discernment processes as Christian educators.

Arguments of the Technocrats: Inevitability and Efficiency

As with all parts of society, the classroom seems surrounded by a clamor of voices advocating for adoption of AI within. However, those involved in decision making in educational contexts should be wary of the fact that many voices advocating for the introduction of AI in schools are those with something to gain. As Coyne and Vervaeke note, "What we do know about AI's growth is that its present stewards reside in the marketplace. The people poking and prodding the machine, training it, are not considering the possibility that their patient will soon rise off the metaphorical table."[5] *The advocates tend to be the developers themselves.* So, while we may consider the benefits they may offer, we have to hold to a rich and robust picture of what we mean by the word *education*. This is important because there are often two main arguments pressed on educators in an effort to persuade them of the necessity of AI integration in schools: inevitability and pragmatism.

First, *inevitability*. Often this argument sounds something like, "AI is here to stay, and we need to get with the program. Let's not get left behind." However, while posing as a descriptive statement, it is also, rather underhandedly, prescriptive. Philosopher and theologian Jacques Ellul was already warning of the growing "technospeak" decades ago in his work *The Technological Bluff*. Here he argued that even though technological advances do serve us in certain tasks and make us more efficient, they also fundamentally change our expectations and understandings of reality and community. This means new technologies are not simply

---

5. Vervaeke and Coyne, *Mentoring the Machines*, 42.

stewards of human thought, but actually *shapers* of it.[6] According to Ellul, the technocrats, those pushing for technological adoption, often come with a message that sounds like: "'Here is the solution. There is no other. You will have to adopt it.' They now add authority to their competence."[7] For schools anxious to help their teachers with workloads and wanting to stay at the forefront of what is deemed to be "good" education, this technospeak can be convincing in its assertiveness. But this dynamic becomes a self-fulfilling prophecy: we first tell a narrative of technicization, we grow to believe the narrative, and then finally shape our educational practices in light of the future that this narrative promises. As Ellul argues, this way of storying education can sound like this:

> Children must not only be taught at once to use technical instruments (the computer) but also given a love of scientific research. The future depends on them being qualified in techno-science. This is presented as a matter of destiny. Young people must be fashioned for tomorrow's society, which will inevitably be scientific and technical. It is simply not considered that precisely in making young people first and foremost into scientists, we are transforming a possibility into an inevitability . . . the present-day ideology of science is an ideology of salvation . . . no matter what problem may arise the inevitable answer will always be: Science will take care of it.[8]

The argument for the inevitability of AI is highly contestable and *should* be contested by those who want the best for our young people and for our society as a whole. We get to decide what our classrooms look like.

The second common argument is one of *pragmatism*: the assertion that AI will increase efficiency, and efficiency is always a desirable dynamic. This argument highlights the reality that teachers have overwhelming workloads and are leaving the profession, and AI can resolve this crisis by taking tasks off the hands of busy teachers. But sitting behind this argument is the assumption of the inherent value of efficiency, speed, and high output.

Would it not be wise to instead look for ways in which we aren't as locked into those driving forces? The widespread adoption of the steam engine, automobile, the internet, and social media into the everyday expectations of core human activities may have circumvented monotonous,

6. Ellul, *Technological Bluff*, 10.
7. Ellul, *Technological Bluff*, 24.
8. Ellul, *Technological Bluff*, 182.

time-consuming tasks to offer us new options for how we might use that time. But by virtue of their ubiquity, these conveniences set in motion new expectations around output, speed, communication, travel, relationships, and what it means to live well. How can we sure that the outsourcing enabled by AI wouldn't in fact go the same way?

Pragmatism must not be used as a guiding principle for education. The more education is outsourced to machines, the more we devolve the formation of character and personhood to the demands of a technological society deeply tied to the market. In this mode, "pedagogy does not really serve democracy but the techno-economy."[9]

There are several very real benefits available to educators through adoption of AI tools within pedagogical tasks, such as grading, preparation, the generation of learning activities, in addition to personalized task creation and student tracking.[10] AI can be an effective assistant in many ways, and there is already a plethora of such tools available for the classroom teacher. In wielding these tools, we must be mindful not to let efficiency become a motivating virtue, as that is to allow pragmatism to become a prime virtue above more important virtues.

A similar conversation is occurring in mental health services: it may be more efficient to be able to provide those in distress with AI support when there aren't enough human specialists to provide care, but who is measuring the efficacy of these services to increase mental health within these programs? What do we mean by "mental health"? And what about the intuitive discernment of the health professional to detect problems that cannot be programmed into a digital brain? Is this a responsible solution?[11]

As Rowson notes, the West is currently experiencing a "meta-crisis" (a universal struggle for meaning) that has a pedagogical dimension.[12] In our technological society, social media has overrun the educational and culture building project. Stein argues that we are now witnessing "algorithmically directed human development" that is leading to widespread social fracturing due to the ideological radicalizing of young people in place of real communities.[13] We are now being formed

---

9. Ellul, *Technological Bluff*, 109.
10. Hansen, "Pedagogy and AI."
11. Sawyer, "Users' Experience of Therapy," 69.
12. Rowson, "Tasting the Pickle," 30.
13. Stein, "Disarm the Pedagogical Weaponry," 85.

in modes of life shaped by incentivized division, as algorithms reward the most extreme rhetoric.

Stein demonstrates that culture cannot help but be pedagogical for children as "our children have nowhere else to be educated but within the cultures we create."[14] The cultural contexts these technologies have helped generate are not cultures of cohesion but hostility. Stein elaborates, "While it is true that throughout history, children have grown up in physically dangerous war zones, they have done so in the context of relatively coherent cultures. What is novel today is a generation growing up in relative physical safety who are nevertheless endangered in the crossfire of a culture war."[15] There are deeper levels of education to consider before we look to speed up in the direction we are already heading.

When pragmatism becomes the sole virtue in a vacuum of other guiding mores, education is not for education's sake. Rather, it is a formational process colonized by economic priorities. But we want to form human beings well. This is not simply about being good Christian schools, but about building flourishing societies with strong culture that has the power to capture the imagination and form people of good character. It is about forming people who know how to use their freedoms responsibly, ready to contribute to the sustaining and ongoing creation of society. I believe the Christian school is well placed to accept such a task.

The West's Allegiance to Technical Reason

In his address at the 2022 AGM World Summit,[16] neuroscientist and author Dr. Iain McGilchrist warned his audience of increasing conflation between human and machine qualities because of our approach to knowledge. He argued, "While machines, or so it is claimed, get more like humans, humans are getting more like machines . . . AI is there to make things happen and to give us control, but this is good only if we make progress in wisdom as fast as we make progress in technical know-how. Otherwise, it's like putting machine guns in the hands of toddlers."[17] Within this excerpt McGilchrist makes an important distinction between information and wisdom. We must exercise

14. Stein, "Disarm the Pedagogical Weaponry," 86.
15. Stein, "Disarm the Pedagogical Weaponry," 86.
16. McGilchrist, "Iain McGilchrist on Artificial Intelligence."
17. McGilchrist, "Iain McGilchrist on Artificial Intelligence."

discernment when encountering any idea or technology that purports to radically alter our concept of who we are and what we are able to do. It is imperative that we do not simply "get with the program" and fall into place in the assumed long march of human progress.

McGilchrist's work displays an ongoing commitment to showing how Western understandings of knowledge have narrowed to data and information, away from wisdom. In his thesis, *The Master and His Emissary*, he explains that although much of pop-neuroscience unhelpfully breaks the functions of the two hemispheres of the brain into a logic/creativity binary, each side *does* operate from its own default mode.

The left brain is the side concerned with analytical thinking and capturing life in the literal: it loves categorization and concepts, and these important skills allow us to enjoy a sense of mastery as we code and map the world around us. The right brain, on the other hand, is more concerned with the poetic and the big picture, allowing us to bring a more holistic knowing to reality. It is the locus of our intuition and sensory awareness and delivers us a very embodied approach to knowledge.

McGilchrist's work shows that it is this right side that is the "master," the side of the brain that provides the important context for data acquisition to occur, and the left side its helper, its "emissary." Ideally, the right side engages with reality through our intuition and senses, for the left brain to then codify and categorize in order to give us concrete language with which to navigate the world in a logical manner. This data can then be "taken up" again by the right side and brought to bear on life as wisdom, rather than reaching a dead end in this literal categorization.

The problem, as McGilchrist sees it, is that in the West this emissary has been allowed to usurp its master. We have come to value this narrowed, information and data driven version of knowledge and have been led to distrust other ways of knowing. We think we are predominantly rational beings, thinking and choosing from a place of logic, and acting on reason. McGilchrist maintains, however, that "very little brain activity is in fact conscious (current estimates are certainly less than 5 per cent, and probably less than 1 per cent), and that we take decisions, solve problems, make judgments, discriminate, reason, and so on, without any need for conscious involvement."[18] Most of the work of the mind, despite our Cartesian learned commitments, is the office of the right hemisphere, despite our supposed commitment to the rational dimensions of thinking.

---

18. McGilchrist, *Master and His Emissary*, 197.

This is worth further elaboration because AI is the logical outcome of a society that has shaped itself around the left brain and an epistemology of categorization and control. Education has often followed suit, frequently overrun by standardization, equating learning with that which can be measured and presented in a spreadsheet, and focused on providing concrete evidence rather than allowing teachers to focus on the parts of teaching not easily captured by language.

AI tools harvest data, collect information, and follow codes that sort discreet phenomena into information. It is a trained attention brought to the world that values the quantitative facets of reality over others and is not aware of anything outside of this training. It is by nature a child of the left brain. If we understand human beings as primarily agents of reason, then what happens if these machines actually outperform us in the realm of reason? What then makes us distinct as human beings? On this point it is worth quoting Hubert L. Dreyfus at length as he makes this predicament clear:

> Indeed, if reason can be programmed into a computer, this will confirm an understanding of the nature of man, which Western thinkers have been groping toward for two thousand years but which they only now have the tools to express and implement. The incarnation of this intuition will drastically change our understanding of ourselves. If, on the other hand, artificial intelligence should turn out to be impossible, then we will have to distinguish human from artificial reason, and this too will radically change our view of ourselves. Thus the moment has come either to face the truth of the tradition's deepest intuition or to abandon what has passed for an understanding of man's nature for two thousand years.[19]

What Dreyfus is making explicit here, is that the opening curtain of AI presents us with a crisis of identity. We have, for millennia, often thought of ourselves as primarily rational agents. If, however, we succeed in making a superior rational presence in this world, then we are forced to reconsider what makes us distinct as human beings. On the other hand, if we fail to create a rational presence in our image,[20] then we must reimagine our purpose here in the face of the limits of our rationality. If we don't understand ourselves as the pinnacle of this world's rationality, what then are we? What does it mean to be human?

19. Dreyfus, *What Computers Can't Do*, xxvi.
20. Herzfeld, *In Our Image*.

Teaching is a crucially embodied, dialogical, and relational activity that involves the intuitive and the metaphorical at every level. It is built on personal trust and a commitment to knowing and must be protected in its deeply interpersonal nature if it is to do the culture building and sustaining it needs to do.

AI must not be allowed to define or set the terms of learning. It must not interrupt the irreducibly human nature of teaching. There is an urgency to our engagement here because AI has already arrived, and technology is never just a tool: it always shapes our behaviors and imaginations. As Lance Strate makes clear, "what comes between ourselves and our environment, becomes our new environment, or as I like to put it, *the medium is the membrane.* And this in turn *suggests that we shape our environments, and thereafter, they shape us.*"[21] We cannot encourage a disposition of resignation to the arrival of AI. There is too much at stake.

If, then, the act of learning is something other than the mere transmission of facts from one brain to another or from one data bank to a brain, what is it? Importantly, how is it to be understood in light of Christ? Who is the truth, not a religiously themed data set?

A Theology of Knowledge: Faith, Hope, and Love

Every new addition to the activity of education invites us to ask once again what it is that we mean by education. Corinne Hyde states that "at a fundamental level, the development of AI requires us to consider the purpose of education."[22] For the Christian school, it forces us in Christian education to ask ourselves even deeper questions about knowledge itself. If Christ holds all of reality together in himself, then we cannot see knowledge as a mere object available for acquisition. It is made deeply personal in him. Paul's writings situate knowledge in contrast to the prevailing views of it in his time. It is a view of knowledge that doesn't serve to increase the status of the knower but reorients their place in the world in submission to a personalizing presence. If Jesus is central to reality, then knowing is not a neutral act of rationality, but a personal encounter, a dialogue. And this Person that we are encountering is the Christ who was crucified, which means that the aim of our knowing

---

21. Strate, "Medium and McLuhan's Message," 17, italics original.
22. Reyes, "Considering the Opportunities."

is not to control as in left brain modalities but to adopt a posture of humble submission to this Person.

In the first chapter of Paul's letter to the Colossians, we see the apostle make some stunning claims about the cosmic presence of Christ in creation. Among them are the assertions "He is before all things, and in him all things hold together" (Col 1:17). Here we see the ordering principle and the means by which all was made, in a similar vein to both Eph 1 speaking of God uniting "all things in him, things in heaven and things on earth" (Eph 1:10) and the opening of John's Gospel that identifies Christ as the *logos* (John 1:1–14).[23]

This "Cosmic Christ" therefore, is creation's center of gravity, the personal presence through which reality is mediated. When we speak of reality, Christians must contend that we are not dealing with neutral, flat matter, but a reality tied to the person of Jesus, known by him and speaking of him. This understanding also places, through this Jesus, human consciousness at the center of reality, in this Word made flesh (John 1:14). This means humanity's apprehension of reality is somehow central as well, our understanding tied to the fabric of creation through this sustaining presence having joined himself to it, as a human being. As Marilynne Robinson explains, "Christ is central ontologically, and what I have called humanity is ontological as well, profoundly intrinsic to Being because he was in the beginning with God and without him nothing was made that was made."[24] This mystery of Being has made himself known to us through our being. The Logos is one of us.

Learning then, at its most fundamental level, is an act of worship: it is not the conquest of information but a *dialogue with Someone.* It is not simply we who hear, but Christ who speaks. This is a starting point for a Christ-centered epistemology. The human quest of the pursuit of knowledge is driven by the intuition that reality is knowable. This intuition has been shown not to be mistaken: Christ holds all things together so the intuition is affirmed. There is knowledge to be found, and its home is in him. As Sawyer states,

> Learning is an unveiling, a dis-covery, of reality; reality being that which is created and sustained by, in and for, Christ. The Incarnation . . . has been declared into all the earth and is now the immanent mystery revealed. The truth is before us, within us,

---

23. All Scripture quotations in this essay are from ESV.
24. Robinson, *Givenness of Things,* 209.

around us, closer than our very breath. All speaking, all prayer, all learning, all theology, begins in silence, before the Word.[25]

With Christ as the basis for knowledge, our epistemology is guided by what T. F. Torrance calls "Christo-foundationalism" or an "onto-foundationalism."[26] This does not allow us to collapse either into a naïve positivism or a pure subjective account of knowledge. Something can be known because Christ has made reality, through himself "accessible to us and amenable to our statements."[27] The Mystery has spoken, and although certainty is not something afforded to us, knowledge, though non-exhaustive, is available. In light of this, what might the human approach to knowledge present as?

Strom suggests that the apostle Paul had a consistent approach to knowledge demonstrated throughout his letters. A central text for his thought on knowledge is his first letter to the Corinthian church. Strom demonstrates that Paul was concerned about the way that knowledge would be used as a means to exercise power, this knowledge (*gnosis*) that puffs up.[28] It would seem that it is epistemologies of control that the apostle argued were directly being challenged by Jesus. Paul, in contrast, advocated for a transformed understanding of knowledge, shaped by the subverting work of Christ in the world. A relational epistemology that inverted the hierarchy from the powerful to the weak.

Strom identifies 1 Cor 13 as a "crux" text of Paul's epistemology. The passage, though centered around love (verses 4–7), is couched in a wider discussion of knowledge. Paul speaks of understanding "all mysteries of knowledge" (v. 2), of love rejoicing with the truth (v. 6). He then explains of the temporal nature of present knowledge (v. 8), and our present predicament in which "we see in a mirror dimly" and only "know in part" as we anticipate completeness of knowledge in the future (v. 12). For Strom, in this passage we see that "while the theme is clearly love, the context is knowledge."[29]

Paul then states that in this present era of partial knowledge, it is faith, hope, and love that remain (v. 13). Strom argues that "Paul has not switched from the epistemological to the moral. While knowledge

---

25. Sawyer, "'Call No Man a Rabbi'?," para. 12.
26. Stevick, *Encountering Reality*, 70.
27. Torrance, *Theological Science*, 145.
28. Strom, "'To Know as We Are Known,'" 92.
29. Strom, "'To Know as We Are Known,'" 92.

remains incomplete, Paul says he *knows* by faith, hope, and particularly love."[30] These three virtues then are the basis of an epistemology in response to the work of Christ, and this epistemology is "sapiential,"[31] and because Christ is ontologically central to humanity, this is not simply a "Christian" epistemology, but a "sapiential" way of knowing. This is what it means to know as a human. If this is true, can we demonstrate the faith, hope, and love are central to human knowing in general as Paul seems to believe? We turn to this task now.

Faith

All knowledge begins with trust. As knowers, we must receive knowledge from external sources. We know through given languages, concepts, traditions, and authorities. All knowing begins in this dependency and requires us to give ourselves to truth to learn. It is an act of faith, a trust in the knowability of the universe to begin learning and a commitment to learn from the conversations that have gone before.

Both positivism and relativism want to escape the reality of faith in knowledge, the former asserting that we can reach certitude divorced from faith and the latter asserting that no knowledge can be reached, rendering faith naïve. As Polanyi argued, however, "We must now recognize belief once more as the source of all knowledge . . . . No intelligence, however critical or original, can operate outside such a fiduciary framework."[32] McGilchrist echoes this:

> Virtually every great physicist of the last century—Einstein, Bohr, Planck, Heisenberg, Bohm, amongst many others—has made the same point. A leap of faith is involved, for scientists as much as anyone. According to Max Planck, "Anybody who has been seriously engaged in scientific work of any kind realises that over the entrance to the gates of the temple of science are written the words: Ye must have faith." And he continued: "Science cannot solve the ultimate mystery of nature. And that is because, in the last analysis, we ourselves are part of nature and therefore part of the mystery that we are trying to solve."[33]

---

30. Strom, "'To Know as We Are Known,'" 93.
31. Strom, "'To Know as We Are Known,'" 97.
32. Polanyi, *Personal Knowledge*, 266.
33. McGilchrist, *Master and His Emissary*, 460.

Faith, then, is essential for knowing. We do not have the luxury of being detached observers. We are embedded and involved in the reality that we are seeking to understand, so all our knowledge is partial. It demands trust that although we are seeing in part, we *are* still seeing. This is a deeply human approach to learning, and maintaining trust in the transference of knowledge in turn sustains a culture of trust, of healthy submission and a disposition of humility as we approach reality.

AI tools, if introduced to educational practice, run the risk of undercutting this dimension, providing its users with the illusion of mastery and control divorced from community. It encourages fragmentation and a trust given not to communities of shared knowledge but to machines. Faith is essential, it is sapiential rather than simply religious, and therefore we shouldn't imagine that we can know without a personal trust. AI risks forming our imaginations around knowledge in such a way to view knowledge in terms of acquisition, requiring nothing from us beyond the procurement of information.

Hope

If our knowledge is partial, then there is always room to grow in knowledge. Of course, this partial nature of knowledge could lead to a form of epistemological despair as we consider that full knowledge is, at least for now, unavailable to us. But a disposition of hope calls us onward, to uncover more echoes of this Christ, in the anticipation of aligning ourselves to his truth. It is a joyful ongoing work of discovery. There is always more to learn; ideas, experiences, and expanses of reality to which we should remain open. New knowledge is always available as reality continually discloses itself.

Any time that new learning is initiated, it is done in hope: every time we begin a new book, wrestle with a difficult concept, seek to understand another human being, adopt a new skill set and try something for the first time, we are doing so in the hope of who we will become, what we will learn, and in anticipation of discovering that which we already sense is true: an anticipatory knowing. Michael Polanyi states it in this way:

> Clues can merely offer a possible occasion for discovery: they do not tell us how to make a discovery. For this one must either discover a problem that no one has yet sighted, or hit upon new ways for solving a known problem. The scientist who achieves

this is usually not better placed than others, but he is more gifted. He possesses to an exceptional degree the faculty for integrating signs of potentialities, a faculty that we may call the power of anticipatory intuition.[34]

This is remarkably similar to how we might understand Christian hope, that which Jürgen Moltmann explains stirs in us a "passion for the possible" in which our knowledge does not operate as "judgments which nail reality down to what it is, but anticipations which show reality its prospects and its future possibilities."[35] This also means that our knowing and engaging with the world imagines what it *could* be, becoming a creative energy that asks how knowledge could move what is "towards the realisation of righteousness, freedom and humanity here in the light of the promised future that is to come."[36] This kind of anticipatory knowing demands a deep personal investment in the world and an apprehension of a vision that involves creative engagement that goes beyond efficiency and mastery. This is a way of knowing that the world needs. It upholds the power of imagination as a creative and redemptive force and mustn't be short circuited by immediacy of information.

Love

Finally, all good knowing is an act of love. A good scientist allows reality to speak for itself rather than imposing her own judgments on the world and therefore blinding herself from seeing it as it is. Knowing, therefore, is a deeply personal and transformative event that "transforms the knower, the known, and the knowing"[37] as we give ourselves to reality to know it truly (though not exhaustively). The best scientists are good lovers in that they pay loving attention to the world rather than projecting their own interpretations on to it. We cultivate space for "exposure to structures that have to be received in their otherness."[38] Knowing is personal all the way down, and therefore cannot be outsourced to machines and reduced to data collection. Crucially, we cannot know ourselves outside of love, or community. In the knowing process, we are always being known and

---

34. Polanyi, *Knowing and Being*, 202.
35. Moltmann, *Theology of Hope*, 35.
36. Moltmann, *Theology of Hope*, 22.
37. Meek, *Little Manual for Knowing*, 72.
38. Williams, "Attending to Attention," 19.

revealed to ourselves. We have no self-knowledge outside of relationship, outside of love. As Alan Torrance writes,

> Self-knowledge can only be realized and, I would argue, is realized, in the epistemic and relational context of love where, in being lost to the other (and where one's relational objectivity is therefore at its most true), one comes to discern oneself through the eyes and mind of the other, in and through that very context of relationship for which one was created. Self-knowledge is essential to personal being but this is necessarily in and through the other. The self is only complete in the context of the objectivity of love, in communion.[39]

Knowledge is always personal, always an act of giving oneself in order to know, and always an act of listening and of giving attention. It is an act of love, embedded in human encounter with ourselves, each other, and reality. Knowledge, then, in being an activity of encounter cannot be reduced to "a cataract of mere information."[40] It is these encounters between human beings that are the undefinable events that enable our between-ness to be the sites of culture production. We are always implicated in the act of knowing, always present to it, always affected and changed by it, and always giving and bringing something of ourselves to it as we articulate it through our language. Knowing is loving[41] and to pretend that it is simply the transference of information is to not be present to reality. Importantly, the Christ that we come to know through this reality shows us that the highest act is to give oneself in love to the world. It is not simply a personal "order" we discover, but order revealed to be self-giving. Paul, it seems, has articulated the human condition in the knowing project. We all trust in order to know, we are fueled by hope as we seek to know, and we only truly know when we give ourselves in love to that which we are seeking to know. Allowing AI into the mediation of this dynamic of love is to lose something essential to learning, and to diminish and deform our role in discovering and educating.

To conclude, AI is the newest iteration of a conception of knowledge as a means of control. It enables further detachment from reality, as it moves us into further technicization and mastery. In some instances, this will of course be helpful. But it cannot be allowed to mediate what is

39. Torrance, "Self-Relation, Narcissism," 500.
40. Peterson and Peterson, *Letter to a Young Pastor*, 2.
41. Meek, *Loving to Know*.

deeply needed at this present moment: for human beings to take up education as a loving act of culture-building in a time of fragility. Articulating a robust theology of knowledge in our Christian schools is part of the discernment process of knowing what new additions to society, including AI, can be introduced into education as we wisely steward the cause of education for flourishing communities within our schools and beyond.

Questions for Discussion

1. Are there any ways that you think AI may have already begun to mediate the relationships in teaching contexts?
2. In what ways has education already capitulated to the priorities of technicized data gathering?
3. Ellul argues that we shouldn't allow narratives of inevitability to dictate the adoption of technology. But is this actually too idealistic? Do we have any real say?
4. How does faith, hope, and love as an epistemology differentiate itself against some of our other current epistemologies?
5. What does it mean for seemingly "neutral" learning areas in school, if all learning is a dialogue with Christ?

References

Dreyfus, Hubert. *What Computers Can't Do: Of Artificial Reason*. New York: Harper & Row, 1972.
Ellul, Jacques. *The Technological Bluff*. Grand Rapids, MI: Eerdmans, 1990.
Farahani, Kasra, dir. "1893." *Loki*, season 2, episode 2, Marvel Studio, 2023.
Hansen, Craig. "Pedagogy and AI." LinkedIn, Nov. 29, 2023. https://www.linkedin.com/pulse/pedagogy-ai-dr-craig-hansen-phd-icglc/?trackingId=BkQsZfbm1DQutttoy2bLCA%3D%3D.
Herzfeld, Noreen. *In Our Image: Artificial Intelligence and the Human Spirit*. Minneapolis: Fortress, 2002.
McGilchrist, Iain. "Dr Iain McGilchrist on Artificial Intelligence and The Matter with Things." YouTube video, 24:48, Oct. 29, 2022. https://youtu.be/XgbUCKWCMPA?si=sboVio8yDQwn2Usg.
———. *The Master and His Emissary: The Divided Brain and the Making of the Western World*. New Haven, CT: Yale University Press, 2009.
Meek, Esther Lightcap. *A Little Manual for Knowing*. Eugene, OR: Cascade, 2014.
———. *Loving to Know: Covenant Epistemology*. Eugene, OR: Cascade, 2011.

Moltmann, Jürgen. *Theology of Hope: A Contemporary Christian Eschatology.* Minneapolis: HarperCollins, 1991.

Peterson, Eric E., and Eugene H. Peterson. *Letter to a Young Pastor: Timothy Conversations Between Father and Son.* Colorado Springs: Navpress, 2020.

Polanyi, Michael. *Knowing and Being: Essays by Michael Polanyi.* Edited by Marjorie Grene. London: University of Chicago Press, 1969.

———. *Personal Knowledge: Towards a Post-Critical Philosophy.* Rev. ed. New York: Harper & Row, 1962.

Reyes, Antonio. "Considering the Opportunities, Dangers, and Applications of AI." *USC Rossier Magazine,* Dec. 4, 2023. https://rossier.usc.edu/news-insights/news/considering-opportunities-dangers-and-applications-ai.

Robinson, Marilynne. *The Givenness of Things.* London: Virago, 2015.

Rowson, Jonathan. "Tasting the Pickle: Ten Flavours of Meta-Crisis and the Appetite for a New Civilisation." In *Dispatches from a Time Between Worlds: Crisis and Emergence in Metamodernity,* edited by J. Rowson and L. Pascal, 15–51. London: Perspectiva, 2021.

Sawyer, Jacob H. "'Call No Man a Rabbi'? A Theology of Education." *Stimulus,* Dec. 20, 2020. https://hail.to/laidlaw-college/publication/emCooni/article/UbQFYiz.

———. "Users' Experience of Therapy Delivered by Chatbot: A Scoping Review." Diss., Auckland University of Technology, 2023.

Stein, Zachary. "Disarm the Pedagogical Weaponry: Make Education not Culture War." In *Dispatches from a Time Between Worlds: Crisis and Emergence in Metamodernity,* edited by J. Rowson and L. Pascal, 85–104. London: Perspectiva, 2021.

Stevick, Travis M. *Encountering Reality: T. F. Torrance on Truth and Human Understanding.* Minneapolis: Fortress, 2016.

Strate, Lance. "The Medium and McLuhan's Message." *Razon y Palabra* 80 (2012) 1–24.

Strom, Mark. "'To Know as We Are Known': Locating an Ancient Alternative to Virtues." In *Wise Management in Organisational Complexity,* edited by Mike J. Thompson and David Bevan, 85–105. London: Palgrave Macmillan, 2013. https://doi.org/10.1057/9781137002655_6.

Torrance, Alan J. "The Self-Relation, Narcissism and the Gospel of Grace." *Scottish Journal of Theology* 40 (1987) 481–510.

Torrance, Thomas F. *Theological Science.* London: Oxford University Press, 1969.

Tubbs, Nigel. *Philosophy and Modern Liberal Arts Education: Freedom Is to Learn.* London: Palgrave Macmillan, 2015.

Vervaeke, John, and Shawn Coyne. *Mentoring the Machines: Surviving the Deep Impact of an Artificially Intelligent Tomorrow.* New York: Story Grid, 2023.

Williams, Rowan. "Attending to Attention: Digital Companion Booklet." The 2023 ISSR Boyle Lecture on Science and Religion. Cambridge: International Society for Science and Religion, 2023.

CHAPTER THIRTEEN
Faith in Education
Elements of a Catholic Theological Theory of Education

Bert Roebben

Introduction

THERE IS NO SINGLE, definitive theological view of the proprium of Catholic education. The Catholic perspective on education is embedded in a holistic approach to the good life, which learners can discover gradually through narrative and performative action. In this chapter, I will attempt to present a personal line of argumentation and to indicate in bullet points, firstly, which discursive elements are relevant in view of the topic, then what a Catholic theological theory of education aims at, or should aim at, and finally, which further perspectives are associated with it. It speaks for itself that the Catholic educational tradition is constantly evolving both spatially and temporally. As the author of this essay, I too find myself in a continuum of theoretical perspectives and practical concretizations and, in my role as a religious educator, directly at the hinge of the two. I stand on the shoulders of my Catholic inspirers from three generations, among others Karl Rahner and Edward Schillebeeckx, Rudolf Englert and Norbert Mette, Tom Beaudoin and Terry Veling. In conversations with my doctoral students and my undergraduates, I learn new perspectives every day and practice reformulating my position. This contribution is meant to be a thought experiment for reflection and to invite discussion: *ad intra* (in the Catholic faith community) and *ad extra* (in conversation with people of other faiths and non-believers), based on the fundamental assumption that both theology and pedagogy must be communicative (learning in the presence of the other) and action-oriented (learning by doing).[1] My attempt is also characterized by a border-crossing perspective: living in Belgium and working at a faculty of Catholic theology at a state university in Germany, preparing future teachers for confessional and interconfessional religions education in schools, being involved in European (www.eftre.net) and global (www.religiouseducation.net) networks of religious education research.

Discursive Elements of a Catholic Theological Perspective on Education

In the following, two approaches to the topic are elaborated: a historical-theological and a systematic-theological approach. They provide discursive building blocks for the development of a theological theory of education from a Catholic perspective, which is then presented in the second part of this essay. A biblical-theological justification is not provided here. This should be done across denominations and religions as the basis for an integrated discourse on religion and education and be concretized in interconfessional and interreligious ways.

Historical-Theological Elements

With its Declaration on Christian Education (*Gravissimum Educationis*), the Second Vatican Council (1962–65) advocated a holistic interpretation of the subject of education. The preparatory schemata of the Council still focused exclusively on Catholic schools (*De Scholis Catholicis*). During the Council however, the idea of the moral and religious formation of young people was developed, who should learn to recognize (*aestimare*) and to appropriate (*amplecti*) Christian values. This general educational responsibility of the Catholic Church should not only be explicitly visible

---

1. Cf. Roebben, *Theology Made in Dignity*, 13–18, 25–42, 51–55.

in schools run by the church, but also in and through the interest that the church shows in the topic of morality and spirituality in public schools, especially in the global South.[2] Openness to developments in society and the associated education for global responsibility (see the pastoral constitution *Gaudium et Spes* no. 32) on the one hand, and the responsibility of the laity and the corresponding consensual sense of faith (see the dogmatic constitution *Lumen Gentium* no. 10) on the other, once again put the ideas of the declaration *Gravissimum Educationis* into perspective: all share the responsibility for education, not only with regard to the renewal of the church, but also with regard to the humanization of society. During the Joint Synod of the Dioceses in the Federal Republic of Germany (also known as the Würzburg Synod) from 1971 to 1975, this "diaconal" educational vision and dynamic was further developed and later updated for example in several documents of the German bishops, mainly with regard to confessional religious education in schools—which is an ordinary school subject in Germany as it is in many countries in Europe.[3]

In the documents of the Catholic Church, there has been little movement on the issue of general education since the Council. Thoughts on the personal formation of conscience, as eminent as they were during the Council, remain unaddressed to this day. There is virtually no independent pedagogical theory formation in the official pronouncements of the Catholic Church. Pope Francis fills this vacuum with his challenging thoughts on education. Just like in the neo-liberal society,[4] a renewal is urgently needed, critically challenged by the gospel in its dual form of contemplation and action. In his apostolic exhortation *Evangelii Gaudium* (*On the Proclamation of the Gospel in the Modern World*, 2014), for example, Pope Francis spoke out in favor of a contemplative renewal of society and education. This means "choosing to live consciously in the space of liberating truth, [allowing] ourselves to be addressed by it again and again and to be changed [by it]."[5] Inspired by the liberation theology of Latin America, Pope Francis encourages young people not to hopelessly "retreat to the sofa," but to become active: "to walk in the ways of

---

2. Pohlschneider, "Erklärung über die christliche Erziehung," 387.

3. See the European research projects REL-EDU (cf. Rothgangel et al., *Religious Education at Schools in Europe*) and International Knowledge Transfer (cf. Berglund et al., *Educating Religious Education Teachers*).

4. Cf. Nussbaum, *Not for Profit*.

5. Borgman, *Leven van wat komt*, 183 (our translation).

our God [who] calls us to be political doers, thinkers, social pioneers."[6] Education then becomes a human right for which one struggles, a right to live life in a meaningful and differentiated way (i.e., in contrast to indifferentism and "premature retirement," according to Pope Francis) and in awareness of the complexity of society (i.e., in contrast to "socially effective and democratically dangerous simplification strategies").[7]

Systematic-Theological Elements

According to Vatican II, "reading the signs of the times in the light of the Gospel" and the corresponding Catholic formation of the person in the family, parish, and school were interpreted optimistically and idealistically during the Council and immediately afterward, but were insufficiently rethought for everyday pastoral work. In addition, it must be explained that the official church after the Council did not really favor the concrete "growing-up-in-faith" either, rather the opposite: it discouraged the lay theological dynamic.[8] How then can the current basic attitudes of contemplation and action shaped by the gospel be translated into concrete educational perspectives today—in a complex, heterogeneous, globalized world that differs significantly from the world of the 1960s? Which modern understanding of education can help to pedagogically and theologically justify the church's responsibility in the field of education today?

The Dutch educational philosopher Gert Biesta distinguishes three main goals in the personal development of today's young people: an educated human being should be socialized, qualified, and personified.[9] He/she actively and constructively participates in society as a citizen, qualifies professionally in order to provide for his/her own life, and cultivates his/her everyday life based on his/her own talents in order to live meaningfully. In every educated person, these three goals come together in the form of a unique concretization—colored differently by their own character traits and contextual factors. Each person should take responsibility for his/her own education in a self-critical

---

6. Pope Francis, quoted in Mette, *Nicht gleichgültig bleiben*, 98 (our translation).

7. Striet, "Welt ist nicht so einfach," 15 (our translation).

8. According to Johannes Baptist Metz in Exeler and Mette, *Theologie des Volkes*, 31.

9. Cf. Biesta, *Beautiful Risk of Education*.

and creative way.[10] He/she should become a human being. The saying of Howard Thurman, the spiritual advisor to Dr. Martin Luther King Jr., could serve as a *Leitmotiv* for this concept of education: "Don't ask what the world needs. Ask what makes you come alive and then do that. Because the world needs people who have come alive."

In the following, I will briefly explain how the four traditional basic practices of the Catholic Church—*koinonia, diakonia, leiturgia,* and *kerygma*—can fill this integral concept of education with life for young people today. My personal and context-dependent assessment of religious education shines through here. In view of the topic of community, it seems to me that the dimension of communion or solidarity is being emphasized again and again. In the area of diaconal action, educational justice and inclusion are gradually moving further and further into the center. The liturgical design of the church always helps to open the conversation about the sacramental or the physically tangible and performative dimension of pedagogical action. In the church's mission of proclamation (*kerygma*), in its catechetical and religious pedagogical action, these three elements mentioned above seem to be present today in a crystallized and conglomerated form: learning in solidary encounter, learning in the concrete presence of the other, and experiential learning. In the letter from the German bishops, these elements are combined with regard to the further development of religious education in Germany in the context of an individualized, de-radicalized, and pluralized society: the communicative ("the promotion of religious dialogue and argumentative skills") and performative elements ("familiarization with forms of lived faith") are explicitly mentioned as complementary to the qualified "imparting of structured and life-meaning basic knowledge about the faith of the Church."[11] What society strives for as personality development and is defined as the goal of general education (qualification, socialization, subjectivation, according to Gert Biesta) is condensed in a contemporary pedagogical way in the unique design of religious education in Germany and is based on Catholic theology. This is where general education and religious education come very close together. It seems to be the case: again and again, the discourse of this article leads to religious education. But how can the discourse take a different course?

---

10. Cf. Veling, *For You Alone*.

11. Die deutschen Bischöfe, *Religionsunterricht vor neuen Herausforderungen*, 18 (our translation).

Draft of a Catholic Theological Theory of Education

In the following, I present a thought experiment. Like every educational ideal, the idea of personal education (cf. above the drafts of Vatican II, Pope Francis, or Gert Biesta, for example) presupposes a certain image of the human being, an image of his/her destiny, an image that can be conceived and implemented both critically descriptively and orientationally normative. This "reflective examination of the actual purpose of the human being [is] an essential component of education," wrote the German religious educator Rudolf Englert critically.[12] The question of becoming a person in and through education is a question of purpose, a "what for" question: "Becoming a unique *human being* happens in the process of education; he/she is always already a *person*."[13] The task of a theological theory of education is "to make this personhood as an anthropological foundation, which is withdrawn from human availability and precedes it, fruitful for the educational process."[14] The "what for" question inevitably comes to us insofar as we deal intensively with questions of boundaries and meaning in everyday educational life: What are we striving for? What is important, sacred, and meaningful to us? And how do we bring the "inner forces" (Wilhelm von Humboldt) of the young person entrusted to us into line with the purpose of this young person? How is the basic trust in the coming alive of the young person (Howard Thurman) in the "present and future significance" of their knowledge (Wolfgang Klafki), in the risk of their "being exposed" in the world of others (Gert Biesta), in their "courage to be" (Paul Tillich), in their "answerability" (Terry Veling) made plausible and practical in education? How can *fides* be intelligently sought, found, and substantiated as a basic trust in life, as "faith in life" (*Lebensglauben*)?[15] How does *fides quaerens intellectum* literally happen—not only as a theological but also as a pedagogical task?

At this point, I will reflect on the decision of young people to shape their lives in a faithful way, and I will try to make it as plausible as possible for education, up to the limit of reason, where faith comes into play. What "anthropological basis" (Peter Biehl) is there for this? Hans Joas speaks of self-transcendence, "in the sense of being torn beyond the boundaries

---

12. Englert, "Vorsicht Schlagseite!," 123.
13. Biehl, *Erfahrung—Glaube—Bildung*, 156 (our translation).
14. Rothgangel and Schelander, "Bildung," 6 (our translation).
15. Meyer-Blanck, *Zeigen und Verstehen*, 140.

of one's own self, of being seized by something that lies beyond myself, a loosening or liberation from the fixation on myself."¹⁶ Thomas Merton speaks of "a freedom beyond freedom, an identity beyond essence, a self beyond all ego, a being beyond the created realm, and a consciousness that transcends all division, all separation."¹⁷ According to Merton, the truly educated person is prepared to stand there in "spiritual nakedness," to endure the ambivalences of life and thus to reach deeper levels of humanity, where he or she is truly at home in one's soul.

This basic "faith in life" (*Lebensglauben*), that one can become a unique human being and grow further based on one's personal talents, is a gift that one cannot give oneself, but one can only receive. The German practical theologian Norbert Mette therefore speaks of the formation of an "identity out of gratuity,"¹⁸ as a possibility of being human that is not detached from the present experience of being human (and therefore remains identifiable), but at the same time transcends it (and is therefore unpredictable). Rudolf Englert suggests approaching this vulnerable question of identity with "appropriate plausibility structures."¹⁹ According to Englert, there is an element in the traditional creed that can tend to shape this certainty and that can build a bridge between trust as self-transcendence (cf. Hans Joas and Thomas Merton) and trust as radical transcendence. This element is the term *fides* (in Latin both "faith" and "trust"). It can be differentiated into three moments of confession: as *notitia* (knowledge of the contents of faith), as *assensus* (personal agreement in faith), and as *fiducia* (religious trust).²⁰ Englert explains, "Fiducia is not an answer to a specific question; but it places the conceivable answers to religious questions within a certain horizon of experience; and thus it is probably the decisive 'reason,' which can only be converted into arguments to a limited extent, for preferring certain answers to religious questions to other possible answers."²¹

---

16. Joas, *Braucht der Mensch Religion?*, 17 (our translation).

17. Merton, *Love and Living*, 9.

18. Mette, "Identity Before or Identity Through?," 234–36.

19. Englert, "Wie gehen wir mit Fragen um, die unentscheidbar sind?," 68 (our translation).

20. Meyer-Blanck, *Zeigen und Verstehen*, 143.

21. Englert, "Wie gehen wir mit Fragen um, die unentscheidbar sind?," 70 (our translation).

The option of *fiducia*, the decision to understand life radically under the sign of religious trust and faith, is "the highest effort of thinking."[22] One can try to understand the mystery of one's own life, but reason is not enough. According to Rahner, going one step further in the vulnerable assumption that faith as devotion would be a reasonable path is even more strenuous than trying to grasp one's own secret of life through thinking. Moreover, this search project is a lifelong project. The verb *quaerens* in the expression *fides quaerens intellectum* ("faith in search of reason") has the form of the present participle: the act of faith as the highest effort of thinking must be carried out again and again. The contents of faith (*fides quae*) are never definitive, but must always be creatively "liquefied"[23] and practically implemented in new personal and social contexts, i.e., in concretely lived faith (*fides qua*).[24] Faith is a verb: it can be spontaneously concluded from this that theology must also be constantly redeveloped. A static, temporally paralyzed or spatially contextless theology has no future. Scholarly theology must always become learned and lived theology!

What religiously constitutive language elements (*theologoumena*) are there in the Catholic tradition that can indicate, in an activated and dynamized form, where and how *fides* can be understood and liquefied today? Rudolf Englert names three elements: *institutio, confession, traditio*.[25] In an overview, I supplement these elements with the terms *fides* and *God* and try to suggest how lived faith (*fides qua*) can dynamize these five contents of faith (*fides quae*) narratively and performatively. The contents are therefore constitutive for the experience of faith, but at the same time must be "set in motion" in concrete learning settings so that they can also achieve effects in education. The path runs from the outside to the inside, from church and denomination via the confrontation with key narratives of tradition, to the decision to surrender oneself in an act of self-transcendence and, in a further act of ultimate concern (Paul Tillich), possibly to engage in radical transcendence, or better still, to allow oneself to be found in it.

---

22. Cf. Rahner, "Glaube als höchste Anstrengung des Denkens."
23. Roebben, *Theology Made in Dignity*, 35.
24. Cf. Roebben, "Never-Ending Quest for the Fides Qua."
25. Cf. Englert, "Religionsunterricht nach der Emigration des Glauben-Lernens."

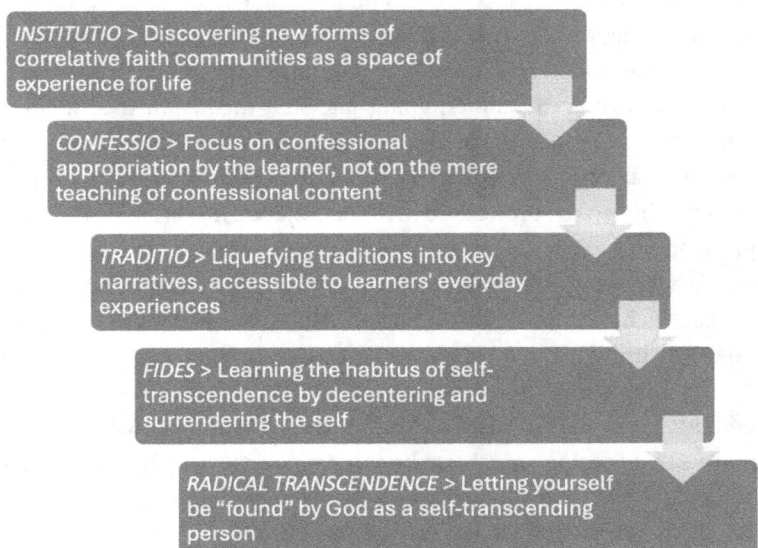

With the three levels of institution, confession, and tradition, Rudolf Englert was putting the focus in the nineties on these three as building blocks for the narrative development of identity in religious education—as bump block(s) and rubbing post(s) against which young people can measure themselves and thus get to know their own position better. Twenty years later, the question in education is much more of a mystagogical-theological nature: are there even elements of a shared faith that can be made plausible in education?[26] And if so, how are these conveyed in concrete educational programs?

The reflexive examination of being a human being with a unique destiny as an educational task, the question of becoming human and personality development in an individualized, de-traditionalized, and pluralized society requires new, "hermeneutically irritating"[27] and offensive learning paths. The English religious educator Sean Whittle believes that young people should be brought to a point "where one could begin to engage with theology and theological response to the presence of mystery in human experience."[28] Because theology, according to Whittle, offers

26. Cf. Roebben, "New Wine in Fresh Wineskins."
27. Roebben, "New Wine in Fresh Wineskins," 56–57.
28. Whittle, "What Might a Non-Confessional Theory," 99.

a useful framework for thinking that can help young people to come to terms with the mystery of their own lives or self-transcendence (cf. Joas and Merton) and allow the possibility (not the necessity) of radical transcendence. His colleague the late Terrence Copley believed that young people have an explicit right to such an educationally situated confrontation with the question of transcendence, which is formulated in the institution, confession, and tradition as the question of God:

> If you leave God out, you are communicating a value just as much as if you keep God in public discourse.... We are culturally programmed to be wary of religious indoctrination in the West, but the question of secular indoctrination has largely escaped attention. It seems that our children need to be protected from religion, but not from secularism.... If teaching the *certainty* of God constitutes attempted indoctrination, then teaching the *impossibility* of God, or suppressing discourse about God, constitutes another sort of attempted indoctrination. In the face of this, how is education about religion(s) to proceed? The answer is clear. It must dare to teach the *possibility* of God. The individual student is then invited to engage with alleged evidence and experiences and eventually to reach his or her own conclusions.[29]

Future Pathways: Glory, Hope, and Mercy

Where does the path lead—this path from Vatican II via correlation theology and pedagogical adaptation strategies of the church to the rediscovery of the productive tension between contemplation and commitment in a post-secular educational context? How can the personal dimension of the Catholic understanding of education, "the self beyond all ego,"[30] the truly human becoming of the learning person, be further developed in a Catholic-dynamic way today—with regard to traditional concepts and with a new power of imagination and thought? I propose the sensitizing concepts of three renowned theologians who have had a profound influence on my personal identity as a Catholic theologian and educational scholar.

---

29. Copley, "Non-Indoctrinary Religious Education," 22, 24, 31.
30. Merton, *Love and Living*, 9.

Glory

In one of his last publications, the Belgian theologian Edward Schillebeeckx elaborated on the idea of Irenaeus of Lyons: *Gloria Dei vivens homo*.[31] He taught me on this occasion not only that the living and flourishing human being can show the glory and existence of God, but also that God finds his/her "glory" precisely in the same living and flourishing human being and experiences joy in him/her. It is therefore up to us to reshape and rewrite our history, to engage in "growing in shared humanity"[32] and to make this world a better place where the glory of God becomes permeable and illuminates the face of every inhabitant of this world. So, a glorious education?

Hope

Jürgen Moltmann's distinction between *futurum* and *adventus*, between the optimistic and futuristic worldview of the seventies of the last century on the one hand and the image of a constantly surprising coming of God into the world as radical transcendence on the other, has intensively shaped my understanding of education. As teachers, we can and must prepare the educational space well for young people and we can help them to create a solid future.[33] However, we can never enter the sacred ground where the ultimate and intimate encounter between the young person and his/her Creator takes place. The teacher's vocation should, therefore, in any case, lie in a habitus of hope, namely that something quite unique can happen in a child's life. The person teaching must use his/her "ordinary" professional skills and prepare the ground for the "extraordinary" event to come. So, a hopeful education?

Mercy

The American educational philosopher Parker J. Palmer has developed the following remarkable definition of the teacher: "a person grounded in a profession of faith, faith in the nature of ultimate reality, in the

---

31. Cf. Schillebeeckx, "Christelijke identiteit."
32. Cf. Roebben, *Theology Made in Dignity*, 43–61.
33. Cf. Roebben, "Generating Hope."

matrix of mercy in which our lives are embedded."[34] The teacher deeply trusts the meaningfulness of reality and the associated image of the young person. Education never takes place under his/her control. He/she must step back and allow the miracle of education to happen "mercifully." The deepest core of human existence, the soul, cannot be grasped in education. A human person cannot and should not be identified with his/her education. Accordingly, a teacher can construct the framework conditions, but cannot "construct" the person. The responsibility of one's own human formation is one of the deepest mysteries of human existence. So a merciful education?

This threefold, theologically motivated undertaking is both normatively ambitious and factually vulnerable. Does the teacher engage in the healing and "repairing" of the human in the world in the concrete everyday life of the school,[35] or does he or she act impatiently, harshly, and even destroying the good will of the learner?

Conclusion

Rudolf Englert believes that his Protestant colleagues can be proud of their theory of education—"and rightly so, because on the Catholic side there is nothing remotely equivalent. For a long time, this individual, educationally mediated appropriation of faith was replaced by institutional integration into a church with strong doctrinal claims."[36] In their book on the future of Protestant religious education in a time of globalization, Hyun-Sook Kim, Richard R. Osmer, and Friedrich Schweitzer recognize the value and potential of a fundamental Protestant theory of education, but are also critical. With regard to "principled pluralism" in society, the theological potential of the Protestant educational tradition is according to them (still) being developed too slowly[37] and (still) too little theologically reflected and concretely implemented.[38]

An ecumenical field of work—a space for "lived" ecumenism—lies fallow here. How often does it not happen in our religious-educationally

---

34. Palmer, *Let Your Life Speak*, 20.

35. Moore, *Teaching as a Sacramental Act*, 187–215.

36. Englert, "Gibt es spezifisch katholische bzw. evangelische Religionspädagogik?," 38 (our translation).

37. Kim et al., *Future of Protestant Religious Education*, 55.

38. Kim et al., *Future of Protestant Religious Education*, 117–18.

separated ideal worlds that "the common recourse to the Gospel, [which] could establish a form of confessional and in this sense confessional religious education that transcends the specific church denominations, . . . is almost completely lost sight of?"[39] How glorious, hopeful, and merciful (see above) could a learning process be in which people would read and discuss memoranda and proclamations on (religious) education in each other's presence? And then, at the end of the conversation, it is important to become silent and to come to the realization with Meister Eckhart that the deeply founded core of a person, his soul, cannot be grasped in what someone has learned or "imagined." The core of the learning person is much more profound than the content learned, than that which remains in the person through a learning process. A person is more than what they learn throughout their life. The human being is more than his or her education. *Deo Gratias!*

Questions for Discussion

1. What anthropological elements does the text offer to build a Catholic theory of education?
2. In what do you think a Catholic theory of education should be anchored: in institution, confession, tradition, or religious faith?
3. What important starting points do you think the Catholic tradition can offer for thinking education, apart from the ones mentioned in the text?
4. How does a Catholic theory of education differ from a Protestant, a Jewish, or an Islamic one?
5. How can this text be read from a postcolonial perspective, in other words, how does the meaning of Catholic education theory shift when it is not described in European terms?

---

39. Englert, "Gibt es spezifisch katholische bzw. evangelische Religionspädagogik?," 37 (our translation).

References

Berglund, Jenny, et al., eds. *Educating Religious Education Teachers: Perspectives of International Knowledge Transfer.* Bonn: Bonn University Press, 2023.

Biehl, Peter. *Erfahrung—Glaube—Bildung. Studien zu einer erfahrungsbezogenen Religionspädagogik.* Gütersloh: Gütersloher Verlagshaus-Mohn, 1991.

Biesta, Gert. *The Beautiful Risk of Education.* Abingdon: Routledge, 2016.

Borgman, Erik. *Leven van wat komt. Een katholiek uitzicht op de samenleving.* Zoetermeer: Meinema, 2017.

Copley, Terrence. "Non-Indoctrinary Religious Education in Secular Cultures." *Religious Education* 103 (2008) 22–31.

Die deutschen Bischöfe. *Der Religionsunterricht vor neuen Herausforderungen.* Bonn: DBK, 2005.

Englert, Rudolf. "Gibt es spezifisch katholische bzw. evangelische Religionspädagogik?" *Religionspädagogische Beiträge* 72 (2015) 31–42.

———. "Der Religionsunterricht nach der Emigration des Glauben-Lernens." *Katechetische Blätter* 123 (1998) 4–12.

———. "Vorsicht Schlagseite! Was im Bildungsdiskurs der Religionspädagogik gegenwärtig zu kurz kommt." *Theologische Quartalschrift* 158 (2010) 123–31.

———. "Wie gehen wir mit Fragen um, die unentscheidbar sind?" *Katechetische Blätter* 144 (2019) 66–72.

Exeler, Adolf, and Norbert Mette. *Theologie des Volkes.* Mainz: Matthias Grünewald, 1978.

Joas, Hans. *Braucht der Mensch Religion? Über Erfahrungen der Selbsttranszendenz.* Freiburg: Herder, 2004.

Kim, Hyun-Sook, et al. *The Future of Protestant Religious Education in an Age of Globalization.* Münster: Waxmann, 2018.

Merton, Thomas. *Love and Living.* San Diego: Harcourt, Brace & Jovanovich, 1985.

Mette, Norbert. "Identity Before or Identity Through Familiarizing with Plurality? The Actual Discussion Concerning School Religious Education in Germany." In *Religious Education as Practical Theology: Essays in Honor of Professor Herman Lombaerts*, edited by Bert Roebben and Michael Warren, 217–44. Leuven: Peeters, 2001.

———. *Nicht gleichgültig bleiben: Die soziale Botschaft Papst Franziskus.* Ostfildern: Matthias Grünewald, 2017.

Meyer-Blanck, Michael. *Zeigen und Verstehen: Skizzen zu Glauben und Lernen.* Leipzig: Evangelische Verlagsanstalt, 2018.

Moore, Mary Elizabeth Mullino. *Teaching as a Sacramental Act.* Cleveland, OH: Pilgrim, 2004.

Nussbaum, Martha. *Not for Profit: Why Democracy Needs the Humanities.* Princeton: Princeton University Press, 2010.

Palmer, Parker. *Let Your Life Speak: Listening for the Voice of Vocation.* San Francisco: Jossey-Bass, 2000.

Pohlschneider, Johannes. "Erklärung über die christliche Erziehung *(Gravissimum educationis)*." In *Lexikon für Theologie und Kirche. Das zweite Vatikanische Konzil (Teil II)*, 357–404. Freiburg: Herder, 1967.

Rahner, Karl. "Glaube als höchste Anstrengung des Denkens." In *Karl Rahner: Sämtliche Werke*, band 30, 807–11. Freiburg: Herder, 2009.

Roebben, Bert. "Generating Hope: The Future of the Teaching Profession in a Globalized World." *Religious Education* 112 (2017) 199–206.

———. "The Never-Ending Quest for the Fides Qua: Reclaiming the Theological Dignity of Religious Education in the 21st Century." *Religious Education* 110 (2015) 491–94.

———. "New Wine in Fresh Wineskins: Rethinking the Theologicity of Catholic Religious Education." In *Global Perspectives on Catholic Religious Education in Schools*, edited by Michael T. Buchanan and Adrian-Mario Gellel, 2:51–61. Singapore: Springer, 2019.

———. *Theology Made in Dignity: On the Precarious Role of Theology in Religious Education*. Leuven: Peeters, 2016.

Rothgangel, Martin, and Robert Schelander. "Art. Bildung." Jan. 2015. https://www.die-bibel.de/ressourcen/wirelex/8-lernende-lehrende/bildung.

Rothgangel, Martin, et al. *Religious Education at Schools in Europe*. Vols. 1–6. Göttingen: Vandenhoeck & Ruprecht, 2016–20.

Schillebeeckx, Edward. "Christelijke identiteit: uitdagend en uitgedaagd. Over de rakelingse nabijheid van de onervaarbare God." In *Ons rakelings nabij. Gedaanteveranderingen van God en geloof*, edited by Manuela Kalsky et al., 13–32. Nijmegen: DSTS/Meinema, 2005.

Striet, Magnus. "Die Welt ist nicht so einfach. Ein Plädoyer für kritische Selbstbildung." *Kirche und Schule* 186 (2018) 13–15.

Veling, Terry. *For You Alone: Emmanuel Levinas and the Answerable Life*. Eugene, OR: Cascade, 2014.

Whittle, Sean. "What Might a Non-Confessional Theory of Catholic Education Look Like?" *Journal of Beliefs and Values* 37 (2016) 93–102.

www.ingramcontent.com/pod-product-compliance
Lightning Source LLC
Chambersburg PA
CBHW050851230426
43667CB00012B/2242